Pamela Logan

AMONG WARRIORS

Pamela Logan holds a third-degree black belt in Shotokan karate under Tsutomu Ohshima, whose direct student she has been for twenty years. Born in Chicago in 1959, she earned a doctorate in aerospace science from Stanford University. In 1992 she assumed the post of Director of Research for the China Exploration and Research Society in Hong Kong. At present, she is managing a project to restore two Tibetan monasteries she visited in the course of her 1991 *Among Warriors* adventures. With well-known explorer How Man Wong, she is also working with radar images obtained by NASA's space shuttle, looking for signs of lost cities on China's Silk Road. As a freelance writer and photojournalist, her work has appeared in numerous publications, including *The Los Angeles Times, The Christian Science Monitor, Far Eastern Economic Review,* and *Asia Magazine.* Now based in Southern California, she spends much of her time in the Far East.

AMONG WARRIORS

A WOMAN MARTIAL ARTIST IN TIBET

PAMELA LOGAN

Best wishes,
Pamela Logan

VINTAGE DEPARTURES

VINTAGE BOOKS

A DIVISION OF RANDOM HOUSE, INC.

NEW YORK

To pilgrims everywhere

FIRST VINTAGE DEPARTURES EDITION, MARCH 1998

Copyright © 1996 by Pamela Logan

Library of Congress Cataloging-in-Publication Data
Logan, Pamela
Among Warriors: A Woman Martial Artist in Tibet / Pamela Logan—
1st Vintage Departures Edition
p. cm.
ISBN 0-375-70076-5
1. Tibet (China)—Description and travel. 2. Logan, Pamela—Journeys—
China—Tibet.
3. Buddhism—China—Tibet. I. Title. II. Title: Woman martial
artist in Tibet
DS786.L59 1998
915.1'50459—dc21 97-43978
CIP

Book design by Jo Anne Metsch
Author photograph © Martin Sage

www.randomhouse.com

First Edition

10 9 8 7 6 5 4 3 2 1

CONTENTS

MAP I: ASIA

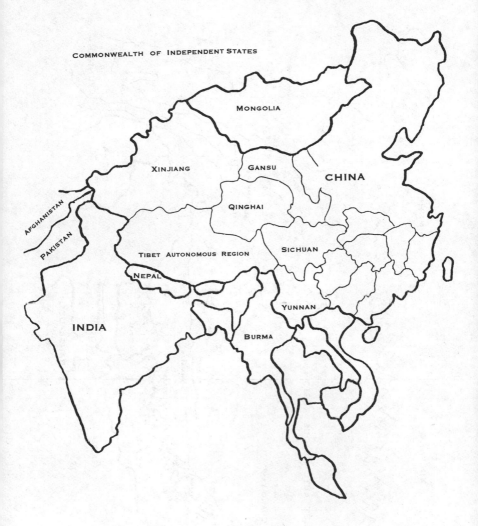

COMMONWEALTH OF INDEPENDENT STATES

MONGOLIA

XINJIANG

GANSU

CHINA

AFGHANISTAN

QINGHAI

PAKISTAN

TIBET AUTONOMOUS REGION

SICHUAN

NEPAL

INDIA

YUNNAN

BURMA

MAP 2: THE TIBETAN PLATEAU

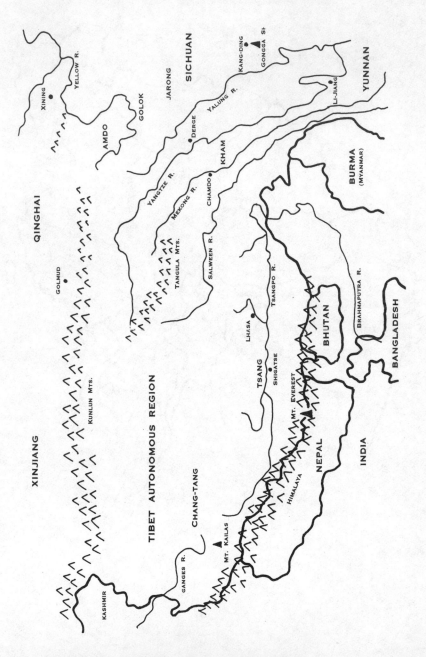

MAP 3: AMDO, GOLOK, AND KHAM

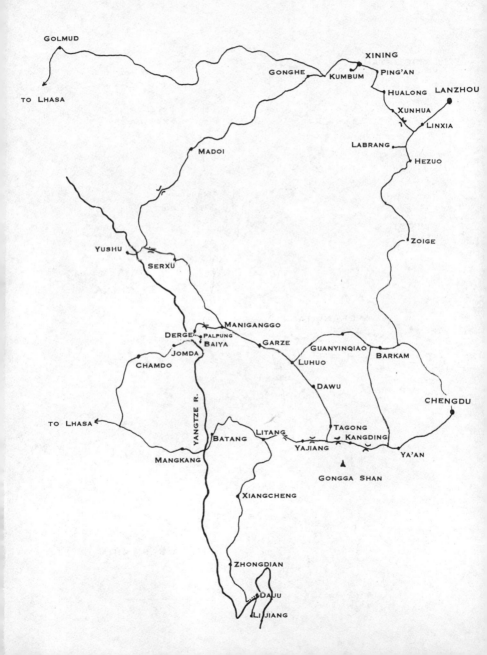

MAP 4: THE KARAKORAM HIGHWAY

KIRGIZSTAN

→ TO URUMQI

● KASHGAR

UPAL

TAJIKISTAN

GHEZ

▲ KONGUR

○ KARAKUL LAKE

▲

MUSTAGHATA

TASHKURGAN

CHINA

AFGHANISTAN

PIRALI

KHUNJERAB PASS

SUST

BALTIT

PASSU

▲ RAKAPOSHI

PAKISTAN

GILGIT

▲ K2

▲ NANGA PARBAT

KASHMIR

● ISLAMABAD
● RAWALPINDI

⊢————⊣ 100 KM.

MAP 5: NEPAL TREKKING ROUTES

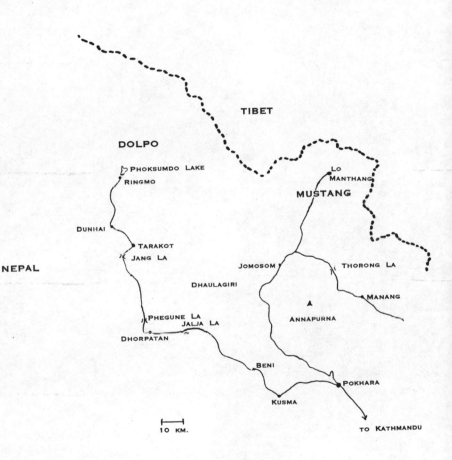

PREFACE

I ALWAYS WONDERED how books like this—tales of real-life experience—get written. Now I know. It has been a journey not so different from the one you will shortly read about, and has taken me more than twice as long. A stack of journals was the raw data; my scientific training begged me to simply copy and concatenate them, altering nothing. But writing, I discovered, is not science—or at any rate not all science. To put this story in readable form I had to reconstruct, simplify, prune, and interpret. I found this process difficult but illuminating; it drew me into a wholly different kind of exploration.

As a person with as-yet imperfect realization of the Buddhist virtue of compassion, I am deeply concerned that I may have unwittingly distorted the people described in this book. Their personalities, words, and ideals have all passed through the highly fallible filter of my own mind, which is no doubt riddled with misremembering, mistranslating, misinterpretation. In particular, much of what I was told about Tibetan Buddhism in Chapters 4, 6, and 7 I certainly didn't understand on first hearing. To re-create this dialogue I have had to integrate real-life memories with knowledge gleaned from books (see the references on page 291). This was not easy, and if errors have crept in, the fault rests with me, not with those quoted. And although I have drawn heavily from a fund of wisdom acquired over the years from my many karate instructors, the interpretations presented here (which my teachers may find inappropriate or even heretical) are my responsibility alone.

Now for the acknowledgments. My greatest debt is divided into three parts. First, I thank the Durfee Foundation for funding my adventure and thereby making a wildly improbable dream come true. Second, I thank my friend and mentor How Man Wong, explorer extraordinaire, whose advice and assistance pushed me off the beaten path and into the unknown—the place where travel becomes adventure. Third (but definitely not last) I thank my karate instructor Tsutomu Ohshima, whose influence has so shaped my life and the lives of others I regard as my teachers that this book would be impossible without him.

No back-roads journey can happen without the generosity and kindness of people on the traveler's path. Most who helped me are mentioned within the book itself; to their names I would like to add the following: Paul Tabe, Peter Klimenko, Lobsang Drakpa, His Eminence the Baiya Rinpoche, Wang Xingao, Shankar Adkihari, and Deepak Roka. Gratitude is also due the monks of Palpung and Baiya, and especially to the many truck drivers (most of whose names I either do not know or cannot mention) who picked me up during my sojourns around Tibet. I would like to thank those who read and commented on the early drafts: Tom Blaschko, Tracy Carns, Alaa Morsi, Julian Bach, David Holmstrom, Joseph Planer, and Lee Muhl.

Finally, I am grateful to my father for planting a seed of curiosity that did not reach full flower until after he was gone; and to my mother, who nourished the seedling and then, in the purest expression of enlightened nonattachment, released me into the wilds of Asia to find my own way.

AMONG
WARRIORS

1

THE BEGINNING

A kata begins in a state of quiet readiness: motionless, calm but mentally poised, a fuse awaiting a flame. We will start with *Heian Shodan*, fundamental to Shotokan karate. *Heian* means Peaceful Mind, symbolic perhaps of the silence that precedes new knowledge taking shape.

I WAS PEDALING my bike over a bleak, frozen, achingly monotonous land. Everything, everywhere, in every direction, was the same merciless color of brown. For limitless miles the dun-colored earth had been dug, combed, piled, and compacted with that peasant ferocity that is ubiquitous in China, and now it was all frozen solid. Mud-brick dwellings squatted sullenly on frozen ground. In the lanes footprints had ossified in the mud. Wheat fields, plowed up and dormant for the winter, were graveyards of hard-edged dirt. Leafless willows brushed their skeletal fingers across an icicle-blue sky. Apart from a dusting of snow on distant ridges, there was nothing but dirt-brown and steely blue as far as my eyes could see.

I had come here looking for Tibetans, not all these Chinese farms; but along this highway there was no sign of Tibet whatsoever. People walking along the road were faceless bundles of winter clothes; their white skullcaps and black lace head covering were discouraging evidence that I hadn't reached Tibet, but was still in a Muslim region. After three hours of slow ascent, I came to a steep incline. Then the pavement gave way to mud, rutted and icy, that at length ended in a plaza.

Suddenly I was standing before a row of eight Buddhist *chörten*[1]—square plinths of dazzling white, their gold-banded crowns flowing up into graceful spires. Across the plaza, Tibetans walked to and fro, their faces dark under the noonday glare. From somewhere nearby a loudspeaker broadcast a deep, melodic male voice crooning a gentle song, almost a chant.

Wintry air, merciless sun, dark Tibetan faces, blazing *chörten,* and chanting—they all struck a sudden forceful chord. Tears came to my eyes. At last I was in Tibet!

"Heian Shodan!" Out of the quiet comes a voice strongly announcing the kata's name. Now the fuse is lit. Outwardly nothing has changed, yet from this moment there is no going back.

FOR SOME MINUTES I stood before the *chörten* wondering what to do. Meanwhile, a crowd slowly collected. Young and old, monk and lay, they gathered around my bike: squeezing the tires, fondling the gearshift levers, and admiring the many-compartmented luggage. Now, at last, was the chance to use the Tibetan I had learned so laboriously back home in Los Angeles. Of course, this was the Amdo region—not central Tibet—so the dialect would be different from what I had studied. But surely in this important monastery someone would understand Lhasa speech, the *lingua franca* of Buddhist discourse in this part of the world. Timidly, I began.

"Tashi Delek!" Hello! The phrase seemed to register—at

---

1. For an explanation of foreign terms, see the Pronunciation Guide and Glossary.

least they looked up at me, but no one answered. I went on: *"Drun-khang kaba yo-re?"* Where is a hotel?

I knew there was a hostel in Kumbum Monastery—the guidebook *said* so—but I could see no sign of it. The *gonpa* was bound to be a sprawling campus of many buildings, and I needed directions. But I might as well have been speaking pig latin for all they cared. Next I tried *"Nga America-ne yin"*—I come from America. Still nothing. I said it all again, and even while they stared at me and ogled my bike, they utterly ignored my words. I was afraid that if I spoke Chinese they would be offended, but at last there seemed no other way. "Please, where is the hotel?"

At this, they perked right up. "I know! Come with me!" replied a boy in piping Mandarin. I followed him past the *chörten* to a two-story square building with a pair of heavy double doors opening into a central courtyard. Over the entryway was a sign in Chinese, English, and Tibetan: the GOLDEN PAGODA HOTEL.

The boy deposited me at the office, where a gray-haired Tibetan man in baggy Chinese blues registered me, then led me out into the courtyard and upstairs. From the second-floor balcony a thin plywood door opened into my room. The chamber had the usual Chinese fixtures: a thinly padded bed and heavy quilt, a rickety stand bearing an enamel washbasin, a plain wooden chair and table, and a thermos of boiled water for washing and drinking. The electricity, the man told me, worked only at night; and the nearest running water was in the boiler room of an adjacent building. Presently someone came to fill my stove with coal and to light it.

Here I was, in a real Tibetan monastery—cold, austere, and primitive, just the way it was supposed to be. I was thrilled.

KUMBUM MONASTERY IS located in what Tibetans call Amdo— that is, the northeastern part of the Tibetan plateau. But Amdo was not my real objective; it was just another phase of my ongoing research into Tibet travel. My real goal was Kham, or eastern Tibet, several hundred kilometers to the south. Few Westerners have visited Kham since China's occupation of the Tibetan plateau, not only because the journey is long and hard, but also because the Chinese government considers it an unfit place to entertain foreign tourists. Those few who manage to sidestep the restrictions almost invariably have their sights set on Lhasa, Tibet's capital, and view Kham as an obstacle in their path, not a place to be explored in its own right. Lhasa, legendary for its isolation and crowded with centers of Buddhist learning, has a mystery and romance that easily eclipses Tibet's outer provinces of Amdo and Kham.

But Kham is exactly where I wanted to go. It is the homeland of the people I was seeking: Khampas—Tibet's infamous race of warriors.

LET'S BE PERFECTLY clear: in the field of Tibet exploration I was a complete amateur. At this point in my life—thirty-two years old, holding advanced degrees in aerospace from Stanford and Caltech, and on the threshold of an illustrious academic career—riding a bicycle on the Tibetan plateau in search of warriors was definitely a radical departure from my life's intended path. How did it come about?

It all started with a few casual words by an Australian woman I had met in Nepal four years earlier. The Nepal trip had been a post-Ph.D. present to myself, my last fling before surrendering to a life of ivory-tower imprisonment—the trip that was supposed to "get it out of my system." Judy was the leader of our group of twelve in a three-week walk around the Annapurnas. She was a Himalayan veteran, and had so many stories about the mountains and their people that I never tired of hearing her. But one night, as we were gathered around our tiny fold-up table for the evening meal, she told a story that surpassed all the others.

"We were in a teahouse," she began in a low voice, "and three Khampas[2] came in. It was obvious who they were, with their long dirty hair and huge daggers stuck in their belts, wearing filthy old Tibetan coats and boots full of holes. They were really big guys compared to the little Nepalese, really tough and dangerous-looking. Everyone in the place was pretty intimidated, but some of my group started to lift up their cameras for a shot. But before the cameras were even six inches in the air, the Khampas turned their heads and gave us a really *cold* look—just one look, but it was enough: the cameras went right back down! Everyone talked really quietly until they left."

"Who are these people?" someone asked.

"The Khampas are from a place called Kham—that is, eastern Tibet," she replied. "They are famous all over the Himalayas for being tough, fearless warriors. They've been fighting the Chinese occupation of Tibet ever since the Chinese invaded in 1950. For a long time the Khampas had a guerrilla base in Mustang—that's a piece of Nepal that sticks up into Tibet. They hid out there for years, riding horses into Tibet to harass the Chinese and then riding back out again, until finally the Chinese government leaned on the Nepalese government to do something about them. So in 1974 the Nepalese government sent troops over to Mustang to kick them out. They're all scattered now—gone to India, gone into hiding, or dead. You hardly ever see them anymore."

Warriors on horseback! Her words conjured images I thought had long vanished from the face of the earth. Can it be true that such people still exist? I was captivated, although at that moment the idea of meeting these fabulous Tibetan knights seemed little more than fantasy. Nevertheless Judy's story together with the images of courageous heroes wielding long

2. KHAM-pas, where KH is an aspirated K, the A is like a in father, and the P is almost like a B.

knives from the backs of their faithful steeds was filed away in the back of my mind.

Judy and I and the others were in the valley of Manang, about a week into our journey, two days before crossing the formidable Thorong La (pass). Here, in late November and not far from the Tibetan border, it was high, dry, windy, and bitterly cold. Everything in the valley—from the stones in the fields, to the mud walls of the houses, to the rags of the inhabitants—cowered under the icy eyes of the Annapurnas.

In this wintry valley I had my first encounter with Tibetan Buddhism. I knew nothing about the philosophy of that creed, I saw only its outward manifestations: glowering, fortresslike monasteries built of stone and clay planted on the high slopes, piled slabs carved with the sacred mantra *om mani padme hum,* crude stone *chörten* marking the high passes, and prayer-imprinted flags waving from every house. I was moved by the ferocity of the Manangis' faith—that in spite of the harsh circumstances of their lives, they built these primitive but compelling testaments. Prayer flags flapping in the bitter winter wind made a stirring, defiant sound that, together with dream-images of Khampa horsemen, stayed in my head long after I had left the Himalayas.

SO THAT'S HOW I first heard of Khampas. My Nepal trekking companions went home, I suppose, put their suits and ties back on, and quickly forgot Judy's story. I went home, but I didn't forget, for in me her words had struck a powerful chord. To explain why, I must jump from stark, windblown Tibet to sunny southern California, and turn the clock back another eight years. Picture a gawky teenager arriving to begin her freshman year at Caltech, eager to plunge into its insular atmosphere of scientific ferment—inexperienced, idealistic, and heady with naive excitement.

One does not go to a world-renowned institute of science and technology expecting to find a world-renowned master of martial arts; but once I was at Caltech I soon heard about Tsutomu Ohshima. In his youth he had been a star pupil of Master Gichin Funakoshi, founder of the Shotokan school of karate, a weaponless Japanese art. I had always been hopeless in sports; nevertheless I knew that Ohshima-Sensei's notoriously difficult class was something I needed—not because I wanted to learn self-defense, but because the sheer challenge of it would satisfy some inexpressible longing. I went, and from the first day I was hooked.

Why karate? And what do martial arts have to do with Tibet?

In many ways a martial artist is like other athletes: he or she seeks to build strength and endurance, to polish technical skills, to conquer aching muscles, and to overcome fear of failure and injury. What is special about the martial arts is the reasoning that lies at its root: that our purpose for training is not to prepare for a contest or show, but *for a fight to the death*. In a fight to the death there can be no excuses and there is no time-out; you live or you die—that's all. To hold the idea of mortal combat unceasingly in your mind—to mentally face death during every exercise, every technique—this is the highest standard of karate practice. What could be more challenging? More intense?

In the Khampas perhaps I would find people who *lived* this death-facing ideal, a mentality that for so many years I was trying to instill in my karate. True warriors! Men and women who not only had faced death many times in the course of the guerrilla war against the Chinese, but who had been raised from childhood to destroy their enemies instantly, unwaveringly, completely.

And there was another reason to go looking for Khampas: the challenge of the journey itself. The search would take me to a completely alien land, where I would need two foreign lan-

guages and much practical know-how to get around. I would
have to make my way to the rugged Tibetan plateau, crossing
high passes and dodging unsympathetic authorities as I went.
And the trip's culmination would bring me face to face with
men notorious not only for fierceness, but for banditry and
mayhem all over the Himalayas. And, somehow, I would have to
befriend them, learn from them.

The challenge of this quest would go far beyond anything
I had ever dreamed; the obstacles ahead would surpass the
toughest of sparring opponents. And there was something else:
in Shotokan karate at regular intervals my seniors create for
their students something called "special training." It's a period of
intense practice, far from home and isolated from all that is safe
and familiar. At special training the student is called upon to
push past physical and mental barriers, to train harder than he
ever thought possible. My first special training, made when I was
still a white belt, taught me that my limits are much further than
I imagine, and that exploring those limits is gloriously liberating. It was an unforgettable experience, and it brought a quan-
tum leap in my abilities as a martial artist.

By now, after twelve years of practice, I had finished more
than thirty special trainings. Those subsequent special trainings,
though true in form to the original, had waned in the intensity
of their effect until lately they had become—no, certainly not
easy, for I still had doors yet unopened, subtleties yet unmas-
tered. Perhaps karate special training had become just a little too
familiar. The fear of the unknown was gone, and with it a big
share of the challenge.

This was my second reason for coming to Asia. I had come
to create for myself a special training of another sort: a solitary
pilgrimage into the wilderness of Tibet, where I would con-
front my own weaknesses and fears. And as I had learned in
karate special training, to face oneself, strictly and seriously, is
the hardest—and most enlightening—practice of all.

*   *   *

BUT WHILE I was in Nepal this crazy plan to look for Khampas was not even dreamed of. After I returned home my memories of the Himalayas slowly faded—like a mouthful of butterscotch candy—to faint sweetness. I was too busy starting my career as a research scientist to dwell on the past. Yet something about the Nepal adventure had shifted, ever so slightly, the continental plates of my mind, and I always knew that someday I would return to Asia. A few years later and not long after I was promoted to *sandan* (third-degree black belt), the chance came. In the Caltech alumni newsletter I spotted a brief announcement saying that something called the Durfee Foundation was funding trips to China for Caltech alumni.

China? Hmm. What I knew of China was bleak and unappealing; did I really want to go there?

Just a minute! Isn't Tibet considered, at least officially, a part of China? Ah . . .! But the place I wanted to go—Kham—must be the most rebellious, most intransigent region in the whole People's Republic. How could I ever get permission? The whole thing seemed quite impossible. I put down the announcement, for surely it would be a waste of time even to write for information. But I didn't throw the article away. Three weeks later, scarcely knowing why, I wrote the letter.

Soon a glossy brochure came in the mail with the words "ORIGINAL AND DARING IDEAS ARE WELCOME" emblazoned on the cover. Inside it said, "We are interested in the way your project specifically relates to your interests, history, abilities, and/or aspirations." My notion of a karate student traveling to the remote plateau to look for warriors seemed to fit well enough. The brochure went on to describe past projects, and the application procedure. Then came the words that dispelled all doubt: "We expect to take risks."

I wrote a proposal and mailed it in.

"Yo–i!" At this command, mental readiness flows to physical readiness. Fists close. Belly sucks a rock of air inside. Eyes become glittery, intent. Without moving, feet awaken, as if the floor is suddenly hot. Interior muscles gather the body's power. All is ready now, waiting for explosive release. . . .

AFTER THAT FATEFUL step, there was no turning back. My proposal was approved, and funds awarded for seven months of travel. However, the Durfee Foundation could offer no help whatsoever in getting me permission to go to Kham. That was my job. I tracked down several experts and learned that obtaining a permit to go rambling around Kham on my own was completely impossible, especially if I applied at the Chinese embassy at home. There was a chance, however, that once I was already inside China I might be able to sneak into Kham clandestinely. And if that failed, I could go to Amdo instead, parts of which were freely open to independent travelers. Amdo had no warriors, so it was a feeble substitute. But I had no choice: I would have to go to China and try my luck.

It took two more years to finish my research work before I could leave for Tibet. Meanwhile all my spare time was crammed with preparation. I combed bookstores and libraries, and read feverishly. I enrolled in Mandarin Chinese, and found a refugee to tutor me in Tibetan. I decided that a bicycle would give me the independence I would need to penetrate Kham, so I spent hours honing my cycling equipment list.

At first friends reacted to the lunatic project with polite silence, as if by ignoring this impossible obsession of mine they could make it go away. But I didn't care, for spread over my kitchen table was a rapturous secret universe: musty history books, Tibetan grammar texts, equipment catalogs, and navigation charts ordered from Washington. As time went by and the trip came closer to reality, even the most skeptical had to admit that I was serious.

My family supported me from the start; but although

everyone knew, in a vague sort of way, that I was going to eastern Tibet, I kept the Khampas' fearsome reputation to myself.
No point in worrying them; and besides, I might not even get
into Kham.

Through a chain of acquaintances I found someone who
had lived among Amdo nomads and had traveled to the edge of
Kham. Ahrin was in his early twenties, tall, bearded, and mag-
netic. His eyes threw out a compelling magical radiance when
he talked of Tibet; and he was full of useful information.

"Watch out for Tibetan dogs," he told me sagely over a
plate of Chinese food in a booth of a West Los Angeles restaurant. "They are vicious and attack without warning. You should
always carry one of these—" He took out an iron bar that had
mysterious figures engraved into it and a leather thong tied at
one end. He gave it to me to examine. "You hang onto the end
of the thong and twirl it over your head," he explained. "The
dogs hear the sound and they know what it means, so they back
off. You can buy one in Tibet."

I wordlessly handed it back to him. He put it in his knapsack.

"Even if you have one of those," Ahrin continued, "you
should never approach a nomad camp without being escorted
by a member of the family. The dogs will attack. And you
shouldn't go to a camp without being invited—"

How can I get invited? I wondered despairingly. I don't
know *anyone* in Tibet.

"—But you will really like the Khampas," he was saying.
"They are very direct and always speak their minds—kind of
like Americans. Khampas say that Lhasa Tibetans are two-faced
because Lhasa people are so polite, and because Lhasa speech
uses a lot of honorifics—

"—A Khampa never uses the honorific."

MONTHS WENT BY, and I continued to read, study, and prepare.
The tales I read about Khampa fighting skill and ruthlessness

were alarming indeed, and yet at the same time they were indescribably thrilling. One author was Michel Peissel, a French
anthropologist who befriended Khampa guerrillas in Mustang,
their Nepalese stronghold. Describing his first sight of them he
wrote,

> They walked like great robots, swinging their powerful
> arms and leading three tall horses with big silver-inlaid sad-
> dles partly covered with brightly colored carpets. These
> Khampas stood a good six feet in height, head and shoul-
> ders taller than the small, barefooted Nepalese, who sud-
> denly seemed minute and ragged in comparison. The
> Khampas wore great heavy boots and flowing khaki robes
> that flapped like whips as they walked, advancing with
> their feet slightly apart as if to trample the grass to extinc-
> tion. Like all Tibetans, they had the characteristic heavy
> gait of those used to pacing up mountains. Unlike Tibetans
> of Lhasa, their features were not Mongoloid, but straight,
> with large, fierce eyes set beside beaklike noses, and long
> hair braided and wound around their heads, giving them a
> primitive allure. They walked proudly, their posture erect . . .
> They were desperadoes, men destined to almost certain
> death, the only men to stand face to face with China.[3]

This was great stuff, although it made my blood run cold.
Another unforgettable tale was the story of Heinrich Harrer,
who lived in Tibet during the 1940s. He and companion Peter
Aufschaiter were Austrian escapees from a British POW camp
who made a months-long trek to the Holy City of Lhasa. Penniless and in rags, they suffered terrible privation while crossing
frozen steppe, eluding or hoodwinking Tibetan officials who
were under orders to turn all foreigners back. Among the
nomads the pair met, the Khampas were infamous. In his

3. *Mustang: The Forbidden Kingdom,* p. 27.

best-selling account *Seven Years in Tibet* Harrer says of Khampas, "You never heard the name mentioned without an undertone of fear and warning. At last we realized that the word was synonymous with 'robber.'"

Of course, I pressed on. The more I learned about the Khampas, the more fascinated I grew. Yet some accounts were contradictory, so I couldn't even be sure if the Khampa warrior tradition really existed or if it was just part of the romantic hyperbole that has grown up around "the Roof of the World." But if the tradition did exist, and if I did succeed in finding them, what I wanted to know was this: how would it *feel* to meet a Khampa? Would I be intimidated? Would I feel his warrior's mentality just standing face to face? And what would he think of me?

Finding and meeting Khampas might give me insight into the nature of warriorhood, something that I could use in my karate and my life—but that was a lot to hope for. Nevertheless, whatever the outcome of this journey might be, the quest itself was worth it, for the challenges it would bring would be a grand test of what I had learned.

"Hajime!" *With the crack of this whiplike word, enemies fall on us. Implacably we begin.*

2

IN TIBET

KUMBUM GONPA, THE Tibetan monastery where I had just arrived, lies in the northeast corner of the Tibetan plateau. Here at Tibet's fuzzy ethnic and geographic boundary, the highlands slope down to meet desert and Tibetans mingle with other races. Before the Chinese takeover, Tibetans divided their domains into Ü-Tsang (Central Tibet), Amdo in the northeast, and the eastern province of Kham; but Chinese cartographers have redrawn the map, rendering the Tibetan terms all but obsolete.[4] Kham was split among three Chinese provinces: Yunnan, Sichuan, and an eastern portion of Tibet Autonomous Region.[5] Ü-Tsang, which contains the capital Lhasa and the birthplace of Tibetan culture, takes up most of the rest of T.A.R.—or Tibet "proper" as it is drawn on modern maps. Amdo in the northeast is shared by the provinces of T.A.R., Sichuan, and Qinghai. I had come to Kumbum Monastery from the Qinghai provincial capital, which lay just three biking hours away.

4. See map on page viii.
5. Strictly speaking, T.A.R. should not be called a "province." Like Inner Mongolia and some other areas of China that are dominated by ethnic minorities, Tibet is officially designated an "autonomous region"—but this "autonomy" is pure fiction.

By now I was already a China cycling veteran, for I had just spent two months practicing. In the country's congenial southwest I rode up and down charming country highways, practiced speaking Chinese, collected rumors from the travelers' grapevine, and generally learned the ropes of China travel. If ever I was to slip around the barriers that walled off Tibet,[6] I would need this experience.

My original plan had been to bike through Yunnan Province's northwest corner into Kham. But it wasn't long before I heard that the *Gonganju*—Public Security—along that route was especially ruthless and vigilant. So instead I cycled from one popular backpacker haunt to the next, sampling Yunnan's fabulous ethnic diversity and meeting travelers from all over the world. And although hardly anyone had been to Tibet, it was the single most talked-about destination.

Tibet has always exerted an irresistible pull on romantic and intrepid adventurers. Historian Peter Hopkirk tells us about the late nineteenth and early twentieth centuries, when Tibet was independent and fanatically xenophobic: "The closing of Tibet's frontiers was not to deter for a moment those foreigners who had set their hearts, and sometimes their reputations, on reaching Tibet and—if humanly possible—its holy capital. Armed with sextants and theodolites, modern rifles and gold, and often in disguise, these determined trespassers sought out the secrets of its lonely passes and played hide-and-seek with the Tibetan border guards. Very soon it was to become a race, with travellers from nine different countries competing for the honour of being the first to visit Lhasa."[7]

And compete they did, risking all for the dream of reaching "the Forbidden City." Most were turned back, some lost

6. For brevity's sake, I will use the name "Tibet" to mean the whole of the Tibetan plateau and not just T.A.R.

7. *Trespassers on the Roof of the World: The Secret Exploration of Tibet*, p. 2.

their lives, but a few achieved their goal, returning home to receive public accolades, win geographic prizes, and write best-selling books. Then, in 1949, the Chinese invasion of Tibet closed down the competition, for the Bamboo Curtain proved more effective at keeping out foreigners than Tibetan border guards had ever been. Aspiring Tibet travelers could only gaze wistfully across the border from neighboring Nepal.

In the 1970s, China finally decided the time had come to show the outside world what socialism had achieved in this most backward corner of their domain. They began to admit a trickle of carefully controlled groups to Lhasa. Soon, well-heeled and intrepid tourists were flocking to see the long-closed city. Tibet's tourist industry soon showed potential for realizing enormous profit, so China gradually opened the doors further. By the mid-1980s tens of thousands of visitors were arriving yearly, their activities little monitored as they roamed freely over the plateau. But in 1987 a Tibetan rebellion against Chinese rule shook Lhasa. It was blamed on foreigners peddling separatist propaganda to overcredulous Tibetans, and Tibet tourism was promptly shut down.

By now, after three years of this, Tibet was again shrouded in the alluring veil of the Forbidden, the same cloak it had worn for centuries, and its holy capital was the most alluringly mysterious place of all. Many of my backpack-toting colleagues liked to imagine themselves sneaking into Lhasa, a feat accomplished by a lauded few. In cafés and hostels, people cooked up wild schemes; but only the most daring tried to implement them, and success was rare.

This was what I learned as I went about, like a good scientist, collecting data on Tibet travel. One of my best sources was a restaurant owner, an English-speaking Chinese called Jim. He told me: "It's been a long time since I heard of anyone getting into Lhasa. During the Asian Games last summer they opened it for a few days. Apart from that, backpackers just aren't going to

Tibet anymore. But two or three months ago I met some Germans who went to Lhasa on a group tour."

I knew about these tours. They were astronomically expensive. A couple of weeks of group-touring in Tibet would, in one shot, consume the Durfee Foundation money that was supposed to last me for months. The Chinese hadn't forgotten that Lhasa was a lucrative cow to be milked—but only if visitors had a sanitized, "politically correct" experience. The authorities tried to keep everyone under the watchful eyes of their guides until the tour was over, and then quickly hustle them out.

"From here you can go to Lhasa by road," Jim went on. "Of course you can't buy a bus ticket, but sometimes people try to hitchhike in trucks. Public Security nearly always catches them and fines them and sends them back. Right now, it's very, very difficult."

It was easy to collect Lhasa rumors like this. After all, more than the rest of Tibet, Lhasa had always been a place of passionate longing. Even the British army, which in 1903 shot their way to Lhasa in order to teach the Dalai Lama a lesson on respect for the British Empire, was not immune to Holy City's esoteric mystery. L. Austine Waddell, who accompanied the force, recorded:

> Here at last was the object of our dreams!—the long-sought, mysterious Hermit City, with the residence of its famous priest-god—and it did not disappoint us! The natural beauty of its site, in a temperate climate and fertile mountain-girt plain, with the roofs of its palatial monasteries, temples, and mansions peeping above groves of great trees ... one of the most delightful residential places in the world.[8]

8. *Lhasa and Its Mysteries, with a Record of the British Tibetan Expedition of 1903-1904,* p. 330.

Time had not attenuated Lhasa's reputation. Even in the 1980s travelers were still writing the words "Lhasa at last!" to culminate chapters full of hardship and travail just like their predecessors. No wonder nobody gave a damn about Kham. Soon I, too, had a mild case of "Lhasa fever," and sometimes I had to remind myself that Kham was my real destination. Anyway, the methods for foiling the Gonganju were bound to be similar no matter where you were going. And after I had seen Kham and found my warriors, if I had time and money left I would certainly try to visit the Holy City. It was undeniably the heart and soul of Tibet.

A couple of weeks later I met someone who had been there. Catherine was a short, plump, lively girl with long blond hair who had grown up in Hong Kong. She and her companion Han, who was Dutch, were both travelers of long standing, and Catherine was justly proud of their accomplishments.

"We looked around Chengdu," she said, "until we found an agent who would sell us a cheap one-way Lhasa tour." (Chengdu is the capital of Sichuan province and was the sole domestic air-link to Lhasa.) "Usually," she went on knowledgeably, "they make you buy a round-trip ticket so you have to return to Chengdu at the end of your five days or whatever. You can't get a refund on your return ticket, and you can't change it either. But we found someone who would sell us a tour with just a one-way ticket, so that we could stay in Tibet after the tour was over and buy our own return tickets when we were ready to leave. Agents aren't supposed to do that, and we heard that right after we left the *Gonganju* came and shut him down."

"So how long did you stay in Lhasa?"

"We were in Tibet altogether about six weeks, but not always in Lhasa. We went all over the place: Shigatse, Samye, Gyantse . . ."

"Didn't you have trouble with the police, not having permits for those places?" I asked, amazed.

"No—I mean, not *serious* trouble anyway. One time there were some bus station officials who didn't want to let us on a bus, but we went and stood in front of it and refused to budge until they gave in and let us on. The whole time we were arguing with those ridiculous Chinese, all the Tibetans on the bus were watching, and when we finally got on, they all cheered. They really love it when somebody beats the Chinese. Oh, and Public Security in Lhasa refused to extend our visas, so we had it done in Shigatse instead. But you know the funny thing . . ."

"What?"

"When we got to Lhasa there were a few tour groups around and some people who were staying on after their tours were over; but after us, nobody came. No one. The tours just stopped running. So after a few weeks the number of foreigners in Lhasa got smaller and smaller. By the time we left, there were only two or three people staying in the Yak Hotel—that's where everyone stays who isn't on a tour."

"What happened? Why did the tours stop?"

"Nobody knows. We certainly couldn't figure it out, except that it seemed the Chinese didn't want any foreigners in Lhasa during January and February. Maybe it has something to do with Tibetan New Year, which is in February. Sometimes the Tibetans try to hold demonstrations then. The Chinese don't like foreigners around to see how much the Tibetans hate them."

Catherine paused to let that moment of vehemence die away, then continued: "You know, of course, that if you go to Chengdu and try to buy a plane ticket to Lhasa, they won't sell it to you unless you have a permit, which you can only get by booking a tour. And if you somehow get hold of a ticket and get on a plane to Lhasa, there's a guy at the airport in Lhasa—the infamous Mr. Wang—who'll stop you right there and send you back."

"What about taking the bus from Golmud?" I asked. Golmud, a rail terminus north of Tibet, is the best jumping-off point for overland travel to Lhasa. From Golmud the Holy City is only two bus or truck days away.

"Same thing," Catherine replied. "First of all, you can't buy a ticket. And if you somehow get one, or if you hitch a ride in a truck, there are checkpoints all along the highway where they catch you and send you back. If they catch you riding in a truck, the driver gets a big fine. All the drivers know, so they won't pick up foreigners anymore."

So, for the time being anyway, I decided to forget about Lhasa. However, because part of Kham lies within Sichuan Province, in Kham the authorities might be easier to outfox. However dim the prospects, I *had* to try to enter Kham. I had come much too far to turn back.

I had already racked up a lot of miles but still knew nothing of cycling on the Tibetan plateau. What were the roads like? The weather? What sort of food and shelter would I find? Was I strong enough to pedal a loaded bike over high passes? I decided to research these questions in Amdo, in an area open to independent travelers. Exploring Amdo would be good training for the challenges ahead.

THAT'S HOW AND why I had come to Kumbum Gonpa. The monastery was founded some 400 years ago on the site of Tsong Khapa's birth. Tsong Khapa was the founder of the Gelug Sect of Tibetan Buddhism,[9] which is nowadays by far the most prevalent and powerful on the plateau. It was the Gelugpa who popularized the notion of "incarnate" lamas, or *rinpoche*, who are supposed to be either human emanations of supernatural beings or reincarnations of great teachers. (The Dalai Lama, Tibet's paramount spiritual leader, is the most famous *rinpoche*,

9. Tibetan Buddhism has four major sects, Nyingma, Sakya, Kagyu, and Gelug, each slightly different in doctrine and method.

but there are hundreds of others.) The Gelugpa have been so successful that their leader, the Dalai Lama, came to wield ultimate power in Tibet.

On that first afternoon, my bicycle safely stashed, I hiked above the monastery to get a bird's-eye view of the place. Kumbum's buildings have a curious mix of styles: traditional Tibetan roofs—flat, militant, and ringed with parapets—mixed among curving tile-covered gables that are strongly Chinese in flavor. In the courtyards and alleyways, shaven-headed figures draped in burgundy robes scurried to and fro, their zens (outer wraps) pulled tightly against the cold.

Strolling around Kumbum, I was reminded of Alexandra David-Neel, someone whose example contributed to my case of Lhasa fever. Alexandra David-Neel was a French scholar and explorer, renowned throughout Asia as an accomplished "lady lama." During the 100 years of her life she wandered all over the continent as an itinerant Buddhist priest. Her most astounding feat occurred in 1924, when at the age of fifty-six she made the long and brutal trek through Kham to Lhasa. Disguised as a Tibetan beggar woman and accompanied by her adopted Sikkimese son, she conquered snowy passes and crossed great stretches of uninhabited high plateau, she dodged authorities, fended off bandits, and subsisted on food that at home even her dog would have refused. Her courage and persistence paid off, for she became the first European woman ever to visit the Holy City. When she came out she was a celebrity overnight.

Prior to her famous Lhasa trek, Alexandra David-Neel had lived at Kumbum for three years. It was a happy time for her, alternating brisk mountain walks with study and scholarly seclusion. As I walked around the *gonpa* I was undoubtedly following a path she knew well.

I'm sure that those who knew me as a child never dreamed that I would grow up to emulate someone like Alexandra David-Neel. As a girl I was not the least interested in philosophy, sports, or Asia; instead I had a passion for the stars. I devoured astronomy books by the dozen and peered for endless hours into the nighttime sky. Later on, as a plump, unpopular teenager I spent all my spare time reading science fiction, for the real world held little charm.

My life changed completely when I started college. Being part of a student body in which men outnumbered women six to one brought me instant popularity, and quickly built up my self-esteem. Added to that were the twin challenges of classes (unbelievably difficult) and karate. I was unaware at the time, but it was during those years that my training for this journey really began.

As I stood musing and looking down at the monastery below, a cold wind swooped down over the hills. It snatched up sand from the ground, throwing it like a veil over the monastery. Below me, maroon figures disappeared like startled field mice into temple buildings. I watched them for a minute, then hurried back to the hotel.

In my room a fire was burning brightly, but its heat hardly reached beyond the stove's iron walls. Outside, the wind gusted and wailed. Sitting miserably on my thin mattress, huddled by the stove, I wondered how many more storms might cross my path on all those roads I had yet to conquer.

3

KUMBUM

BY MORNING THE storm was over and the air was completely still.
I was awakened well before dawn by a sonorous sound, a melancholy note that hovered mournfully in the air for a long minute
before finally dying away, only to resume a moment later.
Alexandra David-Neel wrote of this early-morning ritual:

> A few lads stand on the flat roof of the assembly hall, they
> have hastily recited the liturgic formula and, simul-
> taneously, lift the conches to their lips. Each of them takes
> turn at breathing, while his companions continue to blow.
> And so is produced an uninterrupted bellowing whose
> sonorous waves, rising and falling in successive crescendi
> and diminuendi, spread over the still sleeping monastery.
> Above the peristyle of the hall the young novices, wrapped
> in the clerical toga, are silhouetted on the bright starry sky
> like a row of unearthly dark beings who have alighted to
> call the dead from their slumbers. And, truly, the silent
> gonpa with its many low-roofed whitewashed houses
> appears, in the night, as a vast necropolis.[10]

10. *Magic and Mystery,* p. 94.

Seventy years later, despite interruption by war and revolution, the ritual described by David-Neel survived. I knew that the call of the conches was meant to wake the monks of Kumbum and summon them to prayer, but I also took it as a personal call. Inspired by Kumbum's atmosphere of peace and contemplation, I had decided that each morning I would make a kata practice.

A kata is an ordered sequence of karate moves, normally performed by one person alone, that reproduces in a stylized way a fight. The kata I have been taught were refined by Japanese masters of the past century, and have been faithfully transmitted by generations of diligent students. A kata is thus more than a rehearsal for an engagement; it is a vessel for preserving ancient knowledge—and a dictionary of techniques.

My thirteen years of training was hardly enough time to master even one kata, for the lessons instilled in kata are deeply buried and some need tens of thousands of repetitions to unearth. Kata movements sometimes seem absurd: one-legged stances, slow-motion attacks, impossible choreography. Like a Zen koan, which can take many years of meditation to unravel, to understand kata needs strict, sustained, wholehearted practice. Itinerant Buddhist monks of medieval Japan alternated their wanderings with spells of Zen meditation. Burdened as I was with the romantic notion of being a martial arts pilgrim, I was determined to keep up my kata practice even while I trotted around Tibet.

But in the bone-cracking cold of a Tibetan winter morning, I wished I could forget the whole ridiculous thing. I lay in bed for a while engaged in fierce inner debate before, inexplicably, Romance got a painful joint lock on Laziness and tossed him whining from the room. Shivering, I wriggled out of my sleeping bag. The fire had long since died, and the room had frozen into necropolistic silence. Over my thermals I pulled on socks, pants, sweater, down jacket, hat, scarf, gloves, and hiking boots. Thus encased, enfolded, and enmuffed, I pushed open the creaking door and went out.

Apart from a feeble bulb in the courtyard and the silver-indigo sheen of the nighttime sky, it was pitch black. The place I had selected for my karate dojo ("way-place") was a stretch of hardened dirt behind the hotel. I had just waddled to the spot when suddenly the silence was annihilated by a disembodied roar—a noise so close and fierce that I nearly jumped out of my boots. Whirling around, I could just make out a dim snarling figure on the slope behind me, perhaps thirty paces away. If any barrier lay between us, it was invisible. Immobilized by fright and clothing, I stood rooted to the spot, expecting at any moment to feel the beast's hot, fetid breath. . . .

Wait a minute. What was happening? The barking kept on but grew no louder—the dog was staying put. He must be chained up, I told myself, but it was a long time before I breathed normally again.

My scheduled workout was twenty-five repetitions of a kata called *Jutte*.[11] The name means "ten hands," which implies a multitude of attacking enemies. Some minutes after I began the dog gave up and quit barking; Kumbum regained its graveyard quiet. But the silence didn't last long. Half a dozen kata into the set I heard faint murmurs—cabalistic whispers from some netherworld. They seemed everywhere and nowhere, and however much I peered into the blackness, their source was invisible.

No, it was not my imagination. Now the voices were louder. I turned and squinted at the space above and beyond the dog, but saw nothing; the origin of these unearthly emanations was still cloaked by darkness. After a minute of futile peering, I gave up and went back to doing kata.

Time passed, and the mutters grew still louder. Then came a few voices slightly above the rest, little bubbles of sound rising out of the froth. They sounded, most improbably, like "Hello, hello!"

11. This and other kata practiced by the Shotokan school may be found in *Karate-dō Kyōhan: The Master Text,* by Gichin Funakoshi.

I turned around again. By now an azure watercolor wash was leaking from the eastern horizon. By its dusky glow I made out a long line of monks standing on a footpath up the hill. They were lounging against a wall while they looked down at me, talking and laughing. I paused, on the verge of waving to them, then resolved not to be distracted. Soon afterward the monks went away.

But the distractions were not over. There was a little footpath running past my dojo, and now I realized its *raison d'être:* it connected the hotel's first-floor rooms to the toilet block. Presently, one by one, guests and staff began to emerge for their morning calls. As each appeared in the doorway he would stop, momentarily startled by the sight of a flailing apparition. Then, seeing that I was harmless, he would continue up the path to a place where he could watch me safely from behind. For some seconds I would feel eyes drilling into my back. Then the drilling sensation would disappear, soon replaced by the muffled sound of peeing. After a moment the dark-coated figure would reemerge, spurt quickly past me, and disappear into the hotel.

People continued to go to the toilet. I continued to practice. Slowly the sky grew light, silhouetting a jumble of trees, power lines, temple roofs, and the pinnacles of *chörten*. Although it was winter, Kumbum was home to many birds, and as daybreak grew near their singing intensified. At seven o'clock came a rude reminder of whose country I was in: from loudspeakers mounted on telephone poles a chirpy Chinese voice began bleating news and information. I sighed, and went on doing kata. Medieval Japan could not have been like this.

KATA PRACTICE AT Kumbum Monastery was full of interruptions, but still the atmosphere there was wonderfully cleansing. After two months of roaming around southwest China, scarcely stopping in one place for more than two or three days, I needed some time out.

Getting used to China was a big enough project, but facing it alone, from the seat of a bicycle, made it even harder. Back home, cycling needed only determination and sweat; but here in China there was a whole new psychological dimension. Everywhere I went the bizarre sight of a bicycling foreigner created a monstrous sensation; learning to cope with that sensation was the first test of my karate skills.

To be sure, Chinese people taken a few at a time are as courteous and hospitable as any in Asia. But en masse China stares at foreigners like no other nation in the world. Set foot outside your hotel and, up and down the street, a hundred heads swivel to track your line of motion. Step into a shop or restaurant or railway station and it intensifies: a sea of faces pressing their eyes like suction cups onto your field of view. If you read, they stare; if you write, they stare; if you stare back, they stare; if you sit and do nothing, they stare; and if—heaven forbid!—you bring out a camera or some other foreign toy, they crane their necks and stare harder.

If you can contrive somehow to be a moving target, then the staring crowds can't accumulate; but people will still regard you as prime entertainment. As if you are a sleeping bear, they want to toss a rock at you, just to see what you will do. And everybody in China is armed with two words of English ammunition: "hello" and "okay." As I bicycled highways in Yunnan province these two words were constantly fired at me, sometimes in a friendly way, sometimes as a provocation.

At the beginning of a ride, when I was fresh, it was easy to take it all in stride; but as my energy decreased those fatuous "hello"s and obstreperous "okay"s began to get to me. On one especially bad day, when I had many villages to ride through, it went on for unbearable hours. By noon I was no longer interested in making contact with Chinese; I only wanted to escape from them. I wanted to be blind and deaf, and just mindlessly pedal my bike. But no matter how much I tried to ignore their hooting and rocket past as fast as I could—no matter how thick

I built my armor, there was always someone who could pierce it—like packs of adolescent girls who would call "hello!" and then burst into shrieking laughter. Trying to wall myself off from them wasn't the answer. Somehow I had to come to terms with the bombardment.

Then I remembered a grain of martial arts wisdom, a teaching about soft and hard. Proponents of the "soft" martial arts sometimes refer to karate as a "hard" style of fighting. Yet this is mistaken, for a stiff, hard technique is brittle, and is therefore easily broken. Hardness, by itself, does not signify strength, it augurs weakness. A hard body is neither flexible nor subtle nor quick. To become a truly strong human being, one should cultivate a soft, supple exterior laid over a core of tempered steel. A person with these qualities is open and yielding, sensitive to shifting intentions, yet impervious to harm. As Ohshima-Sensei often says, strength is not measured in extremes of hardness or softness, but in the *distance* between the two.

The principle, I realized as I rode the highways of Yunnan, applies to feelings as well: a stiff, hard shell is not a sign of strength. Chögyam Trungpa, a noted Tibetan lama, wrote "Human beings should be tender and open . . . [The] bravery of a warrior is like a lacquer cup, which has a wooden base covered with layers of lacquer. If the cup drops, it will bounce rather than break. It is soft and hard at the same time."[12]

As I shrank from the Chinese peasants hooting at me from the roadside, I realized that the thicker I built my shell, the weaker I became. This was precisely opposite to what I had learned in the dojo. So the next time I spotted some peasants, I didn't wait for them to call to me; I hailed them from afar as I approached. It didn't take much, just a friendly wave and a shouted "*nihao*," but it made all the difference. "Hello, hello!" they cried back, waving in return. Suddenly everything changed: they weren't suspicious or mocking anymore. That's

12. *Shambhala, the Sacred Path of the Warrior,* pp. 49–50.

it! If I can show them a heart that is courageous and open to everyone, then they can't hurt me! I thought of some of my karate teachers who, far from being distant and forbidding, are the warmest and most approachable people I know, people whose inner strength makes them utterly unafraid to meet any-one head-on. A soft exterior, a big heart, makes one strong and happy; a hard exterior, a shrinking heart, makes one weak. This was a grand discovery, and the more I applied it, the more fun it became. My bicycle journey went from an endurance test to a gala goodwill tour. And the lesson learned on the roads of Yun-nan would, in the future, serve me in good stead.

AFTER PRACTICE I breakfasted on the food stash I kept in my room, then went to explore the neighborhood. The whole town reeked of sulphur from the hundreds of coal-burning stoves, and black smoke curled up from many chimneys. Just outside the monastery was a lively street market with dozens of restaurants serving the Muslim staple of *la-mian*—"pulled noodles"—cooked up with beef in a chili fired broth. A bowl of this hearty, homemade spaghetti along with sweet Muslim tea was the per-fect combination to drive away winter cold. To supplement this fare, bakeries offered flat rounds of bread, shops carried canned fruit and milk powder, and stalls sold wizened little apples and pears.

The street approaching Kumbum was lined with dozens of shops catering to a pilgrim's every need: prayer beads, offering bowls, filigreed prayer boxes, Panchen Lama buttons, bright-colored woolen cloth for trimming Tibetan robes, long black hair pieces, hats of fox fur and silk brocade, sheepskin-lined coats, pelts, knives, jewelry, cassettes of Tibetan folk songs, and more. Under the glass counter of one shop I spotted a five-inch-long piece of squarish iron—an antidog weapon like the one Ahrin had shown me back in Los Angeles. Remember-ing the great snarling creature on the slope above the hotel, I bought it, tied a length of green cord to the end, and henceforth carried it with me.

Later on I walked the pilgrim's trail that encircled the whole of Kumbum Gonpa. It followed a winding path high up on the hills—a route that Alexandra David-Neel herself doubtless had strolled many times, for circumambulating sacred places is an integral part of the practice of Tibetan Buddhism, a form of pilgrimage. Keith Dowman, author of a book on Tibetan places of pilgrimage, explains: "Circumambulation, or korra, may appear to the Western mind as a simplistic practice for the credulous devotee. [But] to the pilgrim . . . korra can be a potent method of heightening awareness. Korra is usually performed clockwise around an image, a chörten, a temple, a gompa [monastery], or a sacred mountain or lake."[13]

And how does korra contribute to understanding? Dowman says, "the physical exertion and the sensual feast that is an integral part of pilgrimage in Tibet can become the mode and the means of attaining the Buddha's enlightenment. The rarity of the Tibetan atmosphere stretching the lungs to the limit; the sense of immense space and isolation; the unpolluted purity of the environment; and the unfiltered rays of the sun making a critical but undefined contribution: the body and mind are transformed and cleansed."[14]

Although no one had ever told me this stuff about circumambulation and heightened awareness, I still knew that in some indefinable way walking Kumbum's sacred path was good. And besides, I met all kinds of strange and wonderful people on these trails.

On that day, as I came around the back of the monastery, I overtook two women and one man lying on their stomachs, arms outstretched before them, their faces in the dust. They were circling the monastery in the most difficult—and there-

13. *The Power-Places of Central Tibet: The Pilgrim's Guide*, p. 5.
14. *Ibid.*, p. 1.

fore the most meritorious—way possible, by prostrating its entire length. I stopped to watch them. Each began the sequence standing, palms pressed together in sublime obeisance; then knelt to the dirt and stretched out at full length, chanting all the while as if bowing to a sacred statue or god. Then the prostrator got up from the ground and walked to the farthest point touched by his or her fingertips to begin the sequence again. They were, in effect, measuring the whole six-kilometer trail in outstretched body-lengths, touching every inch of ground on that sacred ring.

Every explorer's chronicle of Tibet mentions its incredible prostrating pilgrims, so I wasn't surprised to see them. But reading about them and meeting them are two different things, and no book could prepare me for the bizarre sight of human beings laying themselves on dirt. I couldn't just walk past. I stopped: awed, fascinated, and perplexed. What on earth was happening in the minds of these people? Were they aware of me looking at them, or were they in some kind of trance that removed them from ordinary perception? What was the proper thing to do? Bow? Greet them? Or just walk quickly past?

No, they didn't seem to be in a trance. As they pumped up and down, their eyes momentarily rolled toward me and smiles flickered across their faces. One or two prostrations later the smiles had broadened into beatific grins, as if six kilometers of push-ups were just a walk in the park. They seemed buoyed by something internal, lighter than air, that made them oblivious to pain.

Anyone who has completed a karate special training can't help being fascinated by extreme sports, triathlons and the like. Superficially, a marathon of prostrations is like many such endeavors, but in the prostrators' faces I saw something that was light-years away from our Western athletic mentality. Their motivation was nothing like the competitive drive or yearning for physical perfection that makes us punish ourselves with hours of pounding, monotonous exercise. Their faces did not wear that marathoner's look of glazed determination laid over endorphine-drowned pain. In their eyes and smiles I saw something altogether different—enthusiasm, piety, cheerfulness?

No, it was more than good cheer; it was pure joy.

Interesting, I thought, but certainly these prostrators had nothing to do with the warriors I was looking for, and would soon head down to Kham to find. Mentally, I filed them alongside the other odd phenomena I had seen so far in Asia.

NO MORE DUST storms came, but genuine sunshine was rare. On the few sunny afternoons I sat on a lookout above the monastery to watch its comings and goings, or on the hotel balcony to write or daydream. Tibetan New Year was approaching, and the monastery's tourist enterprises were officially closed. The usual stream of Chinese sightseers stopped; only a few odd backpackers and Tibetan pilgrims arrived from time to time. The monks were secreted away preparing for the New Year. There was little for me to do. I had resolved to stay at Kumbum to witness the New Year ceremonies, but the days until that time seemed infinite, and I grew restless and bored. I sat for hours in my room pouring over maps, tracing over and over again the highways that led south to Kham.

My impatience put me in mind of a karate instructor I had once, a compact, muscular, square-jawed man named George. He had little tolerance for halfhearted training, and he was always devising obstacles to discourage us. His class was at an unpopular day and time, so that only the most motivated people would show up. George was an avid boxer, so he taught karate with the gritty, in-your-face pugnacity of a boxing coach. If he thought your techniques or your mentality was below par he let you know, quickly and bluntly. His insults made people angry—and got them to perform.

One thing George taught is that effective training has neither variety nor excitement: "Tedium—," he once declared, "you've got to have tedium in your training. Pick a favorite technique and do it over and over and over again, two hundred, three hundred, a thousand times a day. Every day. For years. If you do that, you can whip anybody."

George's classes usually began with jabbing practice. For thirty or forty minutes, we'd move across the dojo making front-hand punches at imaginary opponents. During those endless trips back and forth across the floor, whenever I thought my punches were finally getting good, George came around to shatter my illusions, easily evading my fist and showing how vulnerable I really was. Yet over the years that I was George's student that tedium paid off in solid improvement.

So while I fretted at the boredom and pined to be on the road, I knew that to leave too early would be to run from whatever Kumbum had to teach. "When you are ready, a teacher will appear," goes an ancient Asian proverb. Indeed, it would turn out that the lessons I had in Amdo would be crucial. But I didn't know that yet; I only knew that I had to let my longing for excitement fall away, to wait for the subtle and beautiful things that would appear after the noise was gone.

ON MY FOURTH morning at Kumbum Gonpa, I woke to the sight of a clean, silver-white blanket tenderly clothing the earth. I decided to skip kata practice and to go hunting for photos instead, before the snow was spoiled by footprints. In the gray-blue twilight of an overcast dawn, the gonpa was perfectly still; no longer a bare and brooding place, the snow covered it like a down comforter on a child's crib. I meandered among silent temples, at length finding my way into a courtyard through a door that someone had left ajar. Inside, a rectangle of perfect, untrodden snow covered the ancient stone paving. As I

was angling for a photograph, I was startled to hear a voice calling to me in Chinese, "Come here, come here!"

Looking around, I saw a stubble-headed Tibetan face peering at me through a little window. It called again, "Come here!
Come inside! The door's over here." The way he indicated led
into a small cozy room, complete with a potted plant, sleeping
cat, and radio blaring Chinese opera. On a carpet-covered *kang*
(heated brick platform) an old monk sat cross-legged, wrapped
in robes of burgundy, magenta, and brown. He had an impish
face, ears that stuck out from his head, and a grizzled crew cut.

"Sit, sit sit!" said the monk. "Here, have some tea." From
a thermos he poured steaming liquid into a porcelain bowl and
offered it to me. I took a sip. It was hot and salty—not unpleasant. "Eat some *momos*," he said, motioning at a bowl of worm-
like fried dough. "No thanks," I said, but he waved the bowl
under my face saying "Eat, eat, eat!" until I took a piece. I tried
to bite the thing, but it was rock-hard. Having satisfied the
requirements of hosting, the monk sat back comfortably on his
crossed legs and rearranged his robes. He looked as if he was
accustomed to holding this posture for hours.

"So!" he said, "What country are you from?"

"America," I replied. This was the beginning of a script I
had rehearsed countless times, with practically everyone I had
met in China.

"Where in America?"

"Los Angeles."

"Are you alone?"

"Yes, I'm alone."

"Are you a student?"

"No, I'm a tourist."

"How old are you?"

"Thirty-two."

"What is your job?"

"Scientist."

"Are you married?"

"No."

"Thirty-two years old and still not married! Why not?"

"Too busy!"

Now it was my turn to quiz him. I asked him his name and age. "Tenzeng," he replied. "Fifty-eight." With a face full of wrinkles and a mouth full of decaying teeth, he looked older than his years. Further labored exchanges told me that his job was to sit in that room and to keep an eye on the visitors out in the courtyard. Soon my store of Chinese was exhausted, and the conversation lapsed. I'll bet this monk has studied Buddhism for decades, I thought to myself. Maybe he can explain how those prostrators can be so cheerful with their faces in the dust. I was just thinking how to frame the question in my limited vocabulary, when suddenly he said, "How much money do you make in America?"

So much for philosophy. Back to the script. I gave him my standard speech about how our salaries, which seem astronomical compared to Chinese wages, are just in scale with living expenses in the West.

"Ah," he said, and moved on to the next order of business: "Do you want to change money?"

No, I told him; I had bought all the Chinese *renminbi* I needed from black marketeers on the way here.

"Your boots," he said, pointing. "How much did they cost?"

I thought of a plausible number and gave it to him.

"What about that camera?"

Another number.

"Your watch? Your bag? Your jacket? . . ."

And on it went. I gave up any hope of learning about prostrations from this business-minded monk. Both of us had exhausted our mutual vocabulary and I was about to leave when the old man asked one last question:

"Are you going to Lhasa?"

Lhasa. Suddenly my face felt hot. The name conjured

images of Alexandra David-Neel slogging over snowy passes, of Heinrich Harrer outwitting soldiers and bandits alike in his trek to the Holy City. Lhasa was the ultimate challenge; it was something I hungered for; yet it was also something forbidden.

"Um, er—" I stammered. "I don't know. I hope so. Maybe."

4

TEACHERS

LATER THAT MORNING, in front of the hotel, I met some aliens from another dimension: two Western women, clean and unrumpled, wearing immaculate coats of virgin white. White! Obviously they hadn't been in China very long. They were both rather older than the usual run of backpackers. One of them had black dancer's leggings and a scarf tied pirate-style around her head; the other had bleached blond hair, makeup, and wore monks' robes under her coat. Groupies—I thought to myself—from California. They were certainly newcomers, for they looked quite bewildered. We introduced ourselves.

"Hi. My name's Pam. Did you two just get here?"

"I'm Anne, and this is Delores," said the one with the scarf. "We came on the bus from Xining this morning. We've checked into the hotel here all right, but the manager there doesn't speak any English, so we're looking for someone who can answer some questions—"

"I've been here for four days and I haven't yet met anyone in this whole town who speaks English. You don't know Chinese or Tibetan at all?"

"No."

"Well, I don't think you'll find any English speakers around here; but I know a little Mandarin. If your questions are simple maybe I can act as interpreter."

Now Delores, the woman in monks' robes, spoke: "You mean there aren't *any* monks who speak English?" she said, dismayed. "But I was told there would be English-speaking monks here! I'm a member of the Order!" she said indignantly. "I need to see the Abbot, to find out how to join the classes, the meditation, the chanting—all the things monks do here. Back home they said I could do this. That's why I've come!"

"I'm sorry, but I haven't the slightest idea about how to join the meditation or where to find the Abbot. When I arrived here, nobody ever asked me if I wanted to join in the services. The few foreigners I've seen here have all been tourists."

Perhaps what Delores was asking for was normal in Buddhist monasteries where she came from; but somehow I sensed that it wasn't here. I just couldn't picture her hobnobbing with Kumbum's shaven-headed Tibetan males. Luckily I had good reason to stay out of it. "Sorry, but I don't think my Chinese is up to the level of your questions. But I do know where to get a good hot bowl of noodles. Do you want to go to lunch with me?"

They did, and soon we were chatting over *la-mian* at one of the restaurants down on Pilgrim's Row. It was the beginning of a long and curious friendship. They were, I learned, not Californians, but from Colorado, though Anne had left the U.S. years ago to come to Kathmandu, the place that she now called home. Delores and she were old friends, and had undertaken this trip both as a pilgrimage and as a chance to renew their friendship, which had languished for many years because of the distance that separated them.

Of the two, Anne was the Asia expert. She had never been to this part of China, but after years of living in Nepal she knew all about the foibles of Asians. She had studied Tibetan Buddhism for a decade or more, and although she said little, she knew much. She wore her long black hair in a single braid down her back, had an expressive yet somehow tragic face, spoke softly, and moved with the grace of an athlete.

Delores, on the other hand, was a newcomer to the continent. Her knowledge of Asian culture was the sort acquired from "New Age" philosophy books. Years ago she had rejected Western spirituality, but in making this nonconformist gesture she had, it seemed to me, only transferred her conformity to a different clique. Early in our acquaintance she wanted to know my sign of the zodiac. To her, happy coincidences were "synchronistic," and people she approved of were "real." In her long and colorful career Delores had walked many spiritual paths—Zen, est, even Christianity—before coming home to Tibetan Buddhism. Now, after fourteen years of study and a Kalachakra initiation, she was an accomplished scholar and had made Tibetan Buddhism an inseparable part of her self. Yet in the absurd contrast of her painted face and monkish robes, in the way her skinny shoulders never seemed to settle completely onto her tall, bony frame, I sensed Delores was still a seeker; her life's koan was still unsolved. I could easily imagine a teenage Delores as a bookish misanthrope. Yet she had blossomed as an adult: she knew how to make herself look beautiful, and she wielded a deadly intellect.

The two of them, although knowledgeable about Buddhism, didn't seem to be on my track of warriorhood at all, and in a way I regretted the distraction they represented. But being here alone had been lonely, too, and even if Anne and Delores didn't share my obsession (about which I never told them or anyone else), at least they were somebody to talk to.

TIBETAN NEW YEAR was fast approaching. I waited eagerly for some sign of oncoming celebration; but for a long time there was nothing whatsoever to break Kumbum's monotonous quiet. Then we heard rumors of something—we weren't sure what—about to happen on the plaza in front of the monastery.

Full of eager anticipation, we arrived at the appointed hour to wait by the eight *chörten*.

Crowds of Tibetans were streaming down footpaths from the surrounding hills. Men and women wore traditional Tibetan coats: long, dark, and lined with sheepskin. To this heavy garment the women added a clanking load of amulets and jewelry, much of it fastened to their long black braids. As the people filed past me I caught the pungent aroma of yak butter—staple of the Tibetan diet and indeed the Tibetan way of life, so much so that rural people's hair and clothing generally reek of it. They joined the crowd of townspeople milling around the plaza.

Suddenly, from the path leading into the monastery, there came a clash of cymbals and a blast of horns. Like everyone else we began running up the path, and came upon a crowd of monks playing a melange of ceremonial instruments: bronze cymbals, drums held aloft and struck with curving mallets, and enormous copper horns that dangled from each trumpeter's mouth like a bull-elephant tusk, so heavy it required an assistant to carry. The elder monks were accoutered in all their finery: layer upon layer of burgundy fabric wrapping their bodies, and upon their heads golden coxcomb hats—the trademark of the Gelugpa "Yellow-Hat" Sect.

The monks banged and smashed and blew their instruments. It wasn't exactly music, but it certainly was loud. In the midst of this, several monks emerged from a nearby temple carrying curious pyramidal effigies. The effigies were elaborately decorated with colorful *torma* (dough sculpture) and crowned with fake skulls that had fake flames shooting out of their ears— a bit cartoonish but no doubt steeped in mystic symbolism. Then they all paraded down the muddy path to the plaza, trailing an excited crowd.

The ceremony that followed was long and inscrutable. To the caterwauling of horns and cymbals, dancers hopped and lurched, ritual implements held aloft in their hands. Elder lamas delivered long incantations in tones of mumbled gravity. Diabolical goggle-eyed creatures in flowing multihued silk, their masks topped by a crown of skulls, stalked portentously. One old lama poured a goblet of water onto the ground. As the music reached a deafening crescendo, a pile of straw was lighted and the effigies cast into the flames.

That was the end of the ceremony. With no further fanfare the monks and spectators quickly dispersed.

That night, back in the Golden Pagoda, I asked Anne and Delores what it was all about.

"I guess it was a New Year's Eve ceremony," said Anne. "Have you ever seen anything like it, Delores?"

"No," her friend replied. "We never did anything like that at the temple back home. The Rinpoche didn't teach us the ceremonies, just the philosophy."

"Those effigies they burned up at the end—do you suppose they represented the old year?" I suggested.

"Perhaps," said Anne. "Or it might have been another way to remind us of the impermanence of all things—the endless cycle of life, death, and rebirth."

"Oh," I said. Every conversation I had with these two inevitably ended up in the Twilight Zone. I had always disliked fuzzy, unprovable, superstitious claptrap. From an early age, my mathematician father had taught me to love logic and reason, rewarding my good grades with a subscription to *Scientific American*. Despite the stirring memories I had of Tibetan-style monasteries in Nepal, and despite the faith's inseverable link to Tibetan culture, indoctrination into the Byzantine psychic machinations of Tibetan Buddhism was a fate I hoped to avoid. Nevertheless, in the spirit of research, it was probably safe to ask just a few questions, as long as they were practical. "What's the point of all those terrifying masks—all those skulls? What do all those horrible monsters have to do with enlightenment?"

"The skulls are there to remind us of the certainty of death," Delores replied in the facile tones of an expert. "That's why so many of the Tantric deities are shown with knives or bone ornaments or even severed heads. After all, everyone dies. There's a Milarepa quote on the subject that I particularly like; it goes,"—here she began to intone darkly—"'Impermanence is like the spreading shadow of a mountain at sunset. No matter how hard you run from it, the darkness will finally overtake you. Therefore I find no escape.'"

Anne continued, more gently, "From contemplation of the certainty of death we go on to contemplate the fact that not only are we all going to die, we don't even know when death will find us. That's supposed to motivate you to begin the practice of dharma immediately."

"So you see," Delores said happily, "it all begins with death. Much of the teaching is about death: understanding it, preparing for it, and so forth."

Weirder and weirder, I thought.

"That probably sounds very negative," Anne broke in, no doubt because she saw the look of skepticism on my face, "but really it isn't, because the teachings show you a way out. That's one of the Four Noble Truths. You know what those are, don't you?"

Oops, she had me there. Years ago, thanks to the influence of martial arts, I had done some reading on Zen. Zen Buddhism was acceptable to me because it is philosophy utterly without any fancy window dressing. Devoid of the mystic and taking nothing on faith, Zen is harmonious with the strict, minimalist mentality of both a warrior and a scientist. Yet somehow, even while I was scanning the pages and mentally nodding my head, it never really sunk in. I knew that the Four Noble Truths are basic to Buddhist thought, but for the life of me I couldn't remember what they were. "Uh, I think I've forgotten. Remind me."

Anne replied, "The Four Noble Truths are: one, that man's existence is inseparable from suffering; two, that the cause of suffering is desire and attachment; three, that we can be liberated from suffering by extinguishing desire; and four, that the route to liberation consists of eight parts: right understanding, right aspiration, right speech, right conduct, right effort, right mindfulness, and right concentration—"Anne had been ticking them off on her fingers, but now she stopped, puzzled. "That's only seven. What did I leave out?"

"Right livelihood," Delores answered promptly, and continued with effortless smoothness, "From the idea of death you work backward to reincarnation, the law of Karma, respect for all sentient beings, and the importance of compassion, which is central to Mahayana Buddhism . . ."

Seeing that Delores was again drifting toward some far philosophical horizon, I tried to bring her back to solid ground. "What about performing prostrations?" I asked. "Ever since I saw those pilgrims on the trail the other day, I've been wondering what it's all about. There must be more to it than mere idol worship."

Anne answered patiently, "It isn't idol worship at all; it's a way to gain merit for yourself and all sentient beings. But it's not the physical effort that's important; it's the mental effort that matters. Prostrations are a way to free ourselves from pride, one of the most difficult attachments to overcome. Beginning students usually undertake a regular program—say, two hundred a day. Some people use the number of prostrations you've done as a measure of your spiritual development. For instance, they might say that if you complete a hundred thousand prostrations then you are eligible for initiation and advanced teaching—"

Aha! Here was something I could relate to. Performing prostrations was like making a karate kata, like the sequence called Jutte that I was doing twenty-five times each morning behind the hotel. Every Shotokan karate student is expected to choose a favorite kata and practice it intensively, above all others. Over years of practice and thousands of repetitions, imperfections are pared one by one; the kata is carefully polished until it shines like a jewel. As you eliminate increasingly minute errors of form, the techniques contained in the kata gradually become both realistic and deadly; but that's not all: you also come to express the strongest, purest, most beautiful mentality in the kata's movements. Developing self-expression through kata is a long and arduous task, for the road is full of false summits and beguiling byways. Five thousand repetitions are generally considered enough to make a kata "yours." Fifty thousand repetitions are said to be a minimum on which to claim mastery, to—perhaps!—solve the koan. Those few of my teachers who have reached this level have taken decades to do it.

"—Of course, the prostrations have to be sincere," Anne was saying. "Otherwise, it's just pointless exercise."

I thought: it's also like martial arts bowing. In the karate dojo we bow to our teachers, to our training partners, and upon entering or leaving the dojo. It's a lot more than just exaggerated politeness, as karate master Shigeru Egami wrote: "There are few persons who can make a perfect ceremonial bow, but one who can do this has to a great extent mastered the art . . . Without sincerity, the bow is meaningless. Rather than be concerned about its outward appearance, put your heart and soul into the bow; then it will naturally take on a good shape."[15]

Bowing is a part of a carefully designed system of dojo etiquette that, like kata, has been passed down from senior to junior over many generations. The purpose is, as one of my teachers put it, to train the unconscious mind. The Tibetan practice of repeated prostrations must also train the unconscious mind, but how this happens and what it feels like I could only dimly guess.

Delores added: "Performing prostrations is a way of developing right mindfulness and right concentration; meditation is, of course, the primary method. Once you have taken refuge, you can begin meditation on impermanence, the preciousness of human rebirth, the misery of *samsara,* and the illusionary

15. *The Way of Karate Beyond Technique,* p. 18.

nature of the 'self.' When you have a good grasp of the basics you can begin the development of *bodhichitta,* that is, a compassionate orientation ..."

Delores went on at length, her train of thought quickly disappearing into a choppy sea of unfamiliar ideas and Sanskrit terms; but I was already starting to realize that the methods she was talking of might be effective indeed. And regarding the similarity of karate kata and Buddhist prostrations, I didn't know it yet but I had just blundered onto a powerful idea.

EARLY THE NEXT morning, instead of the conches' usual distant, mournful call, I was blasted out of bed by a burst of blaring cacophony—horns and cymbals coming from somewhere nearby. What was going on? I quickly dressed and ran out of the hotel. A few minutes of searching brought me to the likely source of the noise, for in front of the Great Prayer Hall were piled heaps of shoes. The doors, which before had been always locked, were now standing open. Through them wafted the many-layered sound of chanting voices. There was no one standing at the threshold to stop me, so cautiously I stuck my head in and looked around.

The room was large, with a high ceiling, and dimly lit by chandeliers and flickering butter lamps whose aroma, even in the cold, was strong. The walls and columns were bedecked lavishly with *thangkas* (religious paintings) and intricate decorations, as if someone had flung a bucket of Mandelbröt fractals on every surface. From the ceiling hung a forest of silk banners made from glittering brocade. Long, low, carpeted platforms were arrayed on the floor, extending from where I stood to the front of the room where sacred statues stood behind rows of offerings. On the platforms sat cross-legged monks, young and old, buried deep inside their drapings of crimson cloth. Their chanting voices—from bass to soprano—rose and fell, lapping gently around me like wavelets on a warm, embracing sea.

After a few minutes I grew bolder and walked all the way into the room. Some Tibetan pilgrims were standing or sitting or prostrating in the back, not far from where I stood. Nobody seemed to mind me, so I settled down to watch the ceremony. On closer inspection, I saw that some monks looked utterly bored, while the novices in back whispered and giggled and fidgeted like regular children. Periodically other boys came around with great steaming casks of butter tea to pour into each monk's bowl.

After an hour the service ended and I was nearly trampled when the young monks sprang to their feet and sprinted out of the room as if the place was on fire. Adult monks followed at a more sedate pace. The aged came last of all, hobbling slowly and taking an eternity to lift each shriveled foot over the high wooden doorsill.

I found out that these services would go on for several days, so the next morning I brought Anne and Delores with me. We left the hotel well before dawn. The campus was deadly quiet, and so dark that I could hardly make out the twists and bumps frozen into the muddy path. Delores, shuffling along in her robes, adhered to my side like an overgrown but frightened child. When we arrived at the assembly hall I went in first, while the other two followed hesitantly.

Just as they had been yesterday, the monks were chanting in their places. We three stood silently for a few minutes, watching and listening. Then Delores sidled up to me and whispered, "Where do I sit?"

I whispered back, "How should I know? Over there on the floor I guess, with those pilgrims."

"No," she said confidently. "I don't have to sit with them. I'm a member of the Order. There should be a place for me with the monks." She looked up and down the rows of chanters. There were lots of vacant places, but none had a sign over them labeled VISITOR AREA. Although Delores was convinced that she ought to have a place to sit, she was not bold enough to take one uninvited. After a while she gave up, and joined Anne in examining the *thangkas* and other treasures displayed in the room.

I watched the scene, lost in daydreams of distant places. Certain features of the monks' intensive prayer session reminded me of karate special training: an early rising . . . shivering in the cold . . . young and old assembling to accomplish a task that was, in some way, larger than life. The resemblance is not accidental, for karate special training traces its origins ultimately to Buddhist practice. In medieval Japan, samurai warriors had a great affinity for Zen, and the two traditions exerted profound mutual influence. The first recorded martial arts intensive training was completed by two master swordsmen about four hundred years ago at Japan's Kashima shrine and was strongly religious in inspiration.[16] Starting from a formal sitting position, the two samurai rose, drew their swords, and cut imaginary opponents 113,870 times over fifty days. This incredible feat, which must have required some twenty-two hours a day of intense physical exertion, has never been equaled.

Almost 150 years ago Yamaoka Tesshu, chief kenjutsu instructor to the Shogun (military ruler of Japan), made a ten-day "standing special training." Ten students took turns attacking him, each being required to score 100 points a day. From six in the morning until six at night they trained, and one by one the students began to pass out from exhaustion, but Tesshu himself continued without pause. Subsequently Tesshu's pupils were made to complete three-day standing special trainings, and his school became famous for the practice.

By the early twentieth century special trainings were held regularly by kendo and judo schools for their students. At that time, karate had only a very small following compared to these two martial arts, and most karate instructors were also kendo or judo black belts. Thus the method of special training was soon

16. Tsutomu Ohshima, *Notes on Training,* Idyll Arbor, Inc., Ravensdale, WA, 1996, and personal communication.

adopted by karate. From Japan it was brought to America and Europe, where it has been honed by my instructor Tsutomu Ohshima. It has evolved from being a practice reserved for only the very elite to one aimed toward the fit, prepared but otherwise ordinary student.

The special trainings I had attended had no intentional or overt religious component, for in modern times Buddhism and martial arts have largely gone their separate ways, one emphasizing internal spiritual struggle, the other outward explosion of spirit. Nevertheless I could see in these Tibetan monks a few elements of the tradition I knew.

It was good to think of special training, for soon my days at Kumbum would end, and I would face the challenge I had been anticipating for so long: biking the mountains of northern Tibet.

5

—

A HARD RIDE

THE NEXT DAY I was out.

The manager at the Golden Pagoda had given me sage advice on where I was going and how I would get there. I assumed that he understood my situation: that bicycles are slow, that dirt and gravel roads make them slower, and that winter days allow only six hours or so of travel. Little did I realize that he had grandiose illusions about the powers of foreigners and our magical foreign machines. So, like a fool, I believed what he told me.

The destination was Labrang Gonpa, a projected five days' cycling away. Delores and Anne were also going to Labrang, but they were going by bus and train, by a different route. Labrang Monastery is larger than Kumbum, and is famous for its spectacular Mönlam Festival that would begin in about a week. Labrang was also the starting point for my journey south—to Kham.

On the first day I rode from Kumbum back to the Qinghai provincial capital, which had been my jumping-off place nine days earlier. The city's sprawl of industrial-gray concrete boxes offered no temptation to stop, so I kept on riding, turning east to follow the Huangshui River downstream. It was an easy journey. In midafternoon I reached the town of Ping'an, little more than a cluster of shuttered noodle shops and drab rectangles nosing around a single intersection. By the time I checked into a hostel it was getting cold, gray, and windy.

Only one restaurant in town was open. Inside its dim, dingy interior, the walls boomed with television din and flickered with blue-gray light. The other diners, all bearded Muslim males, eyed me from their tables while I wolfed down two bowls of *la-mian*. When I left that place at dusk, the street had been swept clean of humanity by a howling winter wind.

That was the easy day. Tomorrow promised to be harder. Hualong, the next town, was seventy-six kilometers distant. By tracing the rivers on my Chinese highway map, I deduced that a pass lay in my way, although how high it was I had no idea. But I wasn't worried. After all, a month and a half earlier in Yunnan Province I had ridden 130 kilometers in a single day....

Of course it hadn't been planned that way. But after six hours of cruising scenic Yunnan countryside, I still had three hours of daylight left and only sixty kilometers to my destination. And it was not just any destination; it was Dali, a backpacker refuge par excellence, a town famous for its "banana-pancake" restaurants catering to their Epicurean needs. Drawn by the promise of orange juice, brown bread, peanut butter, and other delights untasted in weeks, I just couldn't stop riding.

That day, as afternoon gave way to evening, my weariness grew, but still I kept on pedaling. Then darkness fell, and I forgot all about being tired for now I had a worse problem. Oncoming trucks, previously benign, now were monstrous behemoths. They thundered out of the night, as if on purpose to terrorize me. As each approached its headlights slowly brightened to blinding intensity; then, as the monster blundered past, the blaze instantly extinguished, leaving me in sudden, utter blackness—a shock so violent it felt like a kick in the stomach. Each time I winced and gasped, and swerved uncontrollably along the invisible edge of the road. "This is crazy!" I thought, and kept going. I reached Dali safely; but afterward vowed never to ride at night again.

That was in northwest Yunnan, where the roads are paved, hills moderate, and weather agreeable. Qinghai Province would be harder; but even so (my reasoning went), a mere seventy-six kilometers, no matter how steep, just couldn't be too difficult.

The day began gray and overcast, without a breath of wind. As before, everything was barren and monotonous: brown hills, frozen farmland, distant ridges dusted with white. The road sloped steadily, relentlessly upward. I dropped down to my lowest gear and stayed there. Then it began to snow. My glasses, already streaked with sweat, became fogged from my breath and clouded with melting snowflakes. Wiping them was hopeless, so I resigned myself to near-blindness and rode on. There was little enough traffic; and, anyway, the drivers always honked.

The few people who were out walked with heads bent and eyes to the ground. A few looked up to stare at me as I rode by, for certainly a foreigner on a bicycle was an unheard of phenomenon in these parts. Back in sunny Yunnan, it had seemed wonderfully easy to smile and greet such strangers, but now I was hard put just to keep the pedals turning and front wheel on course.

I was carrying only a little food, figuring to buy some along the way; but the buildings that I passed intermittently along the road were all shut tight. When at last an open store appeared, the snow was falling thickly and I was ready for a break in a sheltered place. Dismounting first, I pulled my bike off the road and through the portals of the promised sanctuary.

The place was large, dusty, and achingly drab—all the more so for the sullen gray light that dribbled through the doorway, the room's only illumination. Behind the counter was a young male clerk who jumped up from his stool the moment I came in. A few idlers had trooped into the store behind me, eager to see what I might do.

I set the bike on its kickstand, took off my hat and gloves, and looked up to regard my hosts. At first they numbered just six or seven, but word quickly spread, and in a few minutes they multiplied into a mob. They collected around me in a silent ring, following my movements with darting eyes as I wearily checked over my vehicle. When I walked away to look at the items under the counter, they closed in on the bike, pointing and chattering. But I was too tired to worry about them; I just wanted to find some food and quickly move on.

The clerk accepted my water bottle and went to fill it from a kettle he had brewing in back. Meanwhile I perused the merchandise. Like every country store in China, this one was loaded with cigarettes, batteries, and booze; it also had cloth, washbasins, shoes, thermoses, matches, and hard candy. I already had plenty of candy, and there was nothing else to eat. By the time the clerk returned with my bottle, I had given up in despair.

As I approached my bike the crowd gave way. Now they stood gaping at a safe distance, treating me like some rabid animal that had wandered in from the hills. Whispering among themselves, they edged closer and closer—until I pulled a sack out of my handlebar bag, and they jumped back as if I had bared a set of fangs. By now the snow and ice outside were starting to look positively tropical compared to these frigid people. I ate a few handfuls of raisins and peanuts from the sack, then started for the door, scattering startled peasants who had to leap out of my way.

As if that wasn't bad enough, now I discovered that in those few minutes the sweat-soaked linings of my gloves had frozen. There was nothing to do but put them back on—they felt like blocks of ice. The sky was grayer than ever, and snow continued to fall. I had covered less than a quarter of the distance to Hualong. How could I ever make it before dark?

ONWARD AND UPWARD I rode, my rear tire sometimes spinning uselessly on the slick highway. Houses were becoming scarce, but it was nearly noon and I needed a sheltered place to stop. At last I came to a tidy building of gray brick, conspicuous for its uncommonly literate sign saying *fandian*—restaurant. The door stood open, and at that moment two men were just going inside. Visions of sweet Muslim tea filled my head, halting my machinelike slog up the mountain. I dismounted, turned the bike off the road, then pushed it through the welcoming doors.

It was a spacious concrete-floored room with pink curtains hanging before ample windows. There were no customers, just several black-coated men squatting on stools by the great iron stove in the center. They weren't eating; they were just resting and talking and warming themselves in the usual unhurried rural way. Recalling the horrid crowd in the shop, I warily counted my potential tormentors: only four. Maybe it would be all right.

Of course, when I appeared they all looked up, utterly astonished. An old man with high, brown cheekbones, a white skullcap, and a Muslim's bristle of hairs on his chin was the first to speak. His dialect was a far cry from the Beijing Mandarin that I had learned, but the message was perfectly clear: "Oho! What's this? Who are you? Never mind! Come here and sit down and get warm. Come, come, come—take this seat." He gestured at one of the stools. "Do you want tea? Brother, get this poor thing some tea. Now tell me, where in the world can you be going in such awful weather?"

I haltingly explained who I was and what I was doing. After each sentence they burst out babbling, marveling at the perfect lunacy of my story. When I was done they were full of incomprehensible advice that could only mean one thing: I absolutely, positively, must not continue today.

It was easy to agree.

This being settled, I made that stool my home for the rest of the afternoon: hunching over the stove, sipping bowl after bowl of tea, and receiving all the neighbors who came to meet the Fantastic Foreigner and her Marvelous Machine. Slowly, the hot coals dried my clothes and warmed my blood. Surrounded by good people, I began to feel human again.

After dinner I was led into a house behind the restaurant and ushered onto a *kang* (brick platform). Around me, six adults and two toddlers sat leaning against the walls, warmed by the coal fire that burned beneath the carpet-covered brick, our legs tucked under a communal quilt. They talked and we all watched television while the children crawled on our laps.

This room was obviously the center of family life. Besides the *kang,* an iron stove and a few shelves, it was bare of furnishings. The walls were papered in newsprint and decorated with photos of famous mosques and framed samples of knotty Arabic calligraphy. Around me faces glowed, as nuggets of homely conversation were traded back and forth. I understood little of what they were saying, but the simple act of sitting as one family, young and old together under the same blanket, convinced me that here were family ties of uncommon strength.

When it was time to go to sleep, I was taken to another room, spotless and furnished with nothing more than a large bureau and another *kang.* There I bedded down with an old woman, a teenage girl, and a toddler. It was the warmest, coziest night of my whole Asian adventure.

Early the next morning, well before dawn and with the sky still black as pitch, I was awakened by an unamplified tenor voice intoning a minor key with expressive and haunting grandeur: *"Allaaaaaahu . . . akbar! Allaaaaaahu . . . akbar!"*—the Islamic call to prayer. Before now, these words had always evoked a picture of a scowling mullah hunching over a microphone. But not this voice: it was young, virile, and rich with triumphant power. No one in my bed stirred. I lay there gazing into the darkness, listening to the call and contemplating the fate that had brought me among these generous people.

A FEW HOURS later I was on my way again, pedaling under a brilliant blue sky and breathing air so clean that it cracked like a whip in my lungs. The lower snowdrifts were already melting, but as I climbed toward the pass, snow lay thicker and colder until everything was pure white. The road's summit was marked by a crude cairn decorated with prayer flags. Having won that spot with such toil, I rejoiced at the sight, and silently saluted the defiant Tibetan spirit that moves them to erect such monuments.

Optimistically, I imagined that from the pass it would be downhill all the way to Hualong. Indeed, as a reward for the hard climb, there followed thirteen kilometers of unceasing, breathtaking descent. But euphoria soon changed to dismay, for the frozen air blasting over me felt like liquid ice. At the bottom was a crossroads and a small noodle shop where I had to stop and thaw out my frozen fingers.

Now cycling became hard work again. The terrain tortured me with pass after pass—not high but dismayingly frequent. In the valleys the road was fine, but in the intervening hills I had to wrestle with gravel and mud. A few kids threw rocks at me, making me nervous about everyone I saw. The hours dragged, yet too soon the sun was dipping toward the horizon. I began to wonder if I would make Hualong today after all.

I did make it, but only because I cheated, hitching a ride on a tractor for five kilometers up to the last pass. Confronted now with the true difficulty of this Tibetan "special training," my lofty notions of crossing the plateau unaided were beginning to crumble. It was a humbling look at my own true face, but I was too tired to care very much. I reached the town at dusk, wanting only a bowl of noodles and a warm, safe bed.

In the morning I set out for the next stop, Xunhua, an easy downhill run. The road skirted a frozen lake, then needled into a rocky defile. After twenty-five kilometers of euphoric cruising through a snow-filled gorge, I was released by spreading canyon arms onto more farmland, now below the snow line. Tibetans were scarce, but Muslim farmers were already out breaking up the dirt for spring planting. I crossed the Yellow River, a mighty roiling mass of dun-colored water, and half an hour later was in Xunhua.

Tomorrow, I knew, would be the hardest day of all, for I had to climb over the range that divided Qinghai and Gansu provinces. It would be some seventy kilometers of horizontal distance, but that meant nothing. The real measure of difficulty was the height of the pass, call Darja La.[17] I had no idea how tough it might be. There was nothing to do but make an early start.

On a blazingly clear winter morning I started up a wide valley checkered with farms. Every half hour was a village of mud-brick houses, often with a quaint country mosque in their midst. After some twenty kilometers I reached a restaurant—a plain stone hut with a dark cloth for a door and a few stools drawn up to the stove. A motherly old Muslim woman got me tea, then heated up some sticks of fried bread by holding them over the fire. Once they were hot she urged them on me, but I could hardly stomach the greasy bars. Still, her house was warm and her tea replenishing; I hated to leave that place.

By midafternoon I had climbed a fair distance, yet the hardest twenty kilometers of ascent was still ahead. I came to a village that the map told me was the last in Qinghai. It was a humble place of mud houses and mired footpaths. As I bumped along their rutted mud road, a dog burst out after me, barking

17. I later learned that it's a piddling 3,470 meters.

murderously. In a flash he had caught up and seized my rear tire between his slavering jaws. My iron antidog weapon was within easy reach, but I didn't dare take even one hand off the handlebars. Instead, a bolt of adrenaline pressed my feet into the pedals, and after a few meters the snarling beast was forced to let go. Heart in my throat, I fled like a wraith out of town.

Once I was safely clear of that place, I stopped to rest and consider my situation. Darja La was far away, but there was still a chance I could make it before dark and get down far enough on the other side to find shelter. It was a risky proposition, though, because the next village might be hours away, yet once I crossed the pass it would be heartbreakingly difficult to pedal back the way I had come. But on this side of the pass at least, I could always roll back down and seek shelter in the village with the dog. And perhaps there would be enough daylight left to continue into Gansu. Or, failing that, maybe a bus or truck would appear to carry me to safety.

So I went on. Houses became fewer and fewer, and then none. The valley walls loomed ever higher, steeper, and closer. The snow grew thicker and patches of ice covered the road. Before long I had to get off and push. But I didn't feel worried or downcast; on the contrary: the land was exultation itself: gargantuan twin ridges funneling a cascade of white that tumbled into the far distance.

The sun got lower and the mountains got higher, and I knew that eclipse would bring instant cold. A breeze sprang up, gentle at first but ominously insistent. The pass was still ten or fifteen kilometers away. Still I trudged on.

Then I heard a distant groan—a bus approaching from behind, probably my only chance to get to Gansu today. I retreated to the side of the road and raised my hand to flag it down. Closer and closer the bus came, and then, to my shocked dismay, it roared on past. In disbelief, I watched it shrink to a dot.

After having come so far, to be ignored by that bus felt like a cruel blow. But there was no help for it now. Gathering myself up, I checked the sun and calculated: two or three hours left. Perhaps someone else would come to pick me up. I decided to keep on going, pushing my bike uphill. It was warmer to be moving, and besides, if no more traffic came then at least I'd be headed in the right direction.

Now as I walked my ears were sharply tuned, listening for the sound of some approaching vehicle—someone, anyone, to get me off this ridiculous highway.

Hark! What was that? I whirled to scan the pencil-line of road snaking down the valley. Nothing there; just wind whistling through bicycle spokes. Wearily, I turned to face forward—

Wait! Another sound. But when I stopped to look behind me, all was motionless and the sound had ceased. Must have been my imagination. I started to walk again, and the noise resumed—just my own tires crunching on snow.

Prospects for crossing the pass were looking bleak, but I wasn't worried. The scenery was grand, and I could always go back down. An hour or more later Darja La stood before me at the summit of three enormous switchbacks that cut a colossal letter Z in the mountainside. Behind me was a breathtaking vista of mountains and glittering snow. The breeze had turned into a biting wind, and little more than an hour of daylight remained.

Would I find shelter on the other side? How far away? At that moment I knew I had to turn back; return to one of the villages below and ask for shelter. Already I was starting to shiver uncontrollably and my movements were stiff and clumsy. Yet coasting downhill in this icy wind would be even colder. By now I was talking to myself, commanding my numb fingers to open the saddlebags and pull out every bit of extra clothing. Fumbling, I put it on. Then I began the treacherous descent.

A few minutes of rolling undid an hour's pushing. I was looking out for potential shelter when, in the far distance, I spotted a blue speck moving up the road, shimmering and miragelike. Unbelieving, I blinked to see if it would vanish. It didn't; instead it continued crunching up the highway toward me.

A minute later the station wagon skidded to a halt on the shoulder beside me. The driver rolled down his window and looked at me in amazement. Despite my weariness and cold, somehow I got my Chinese working: "Hello! I'm going to Linxia, but it's too far to finish today. Can you give me and my bicycle a lift?"

"I can take you," said the man slowly, looking me up and down, "but there's no room for your bike."

I peered into his car and saw four passengers: a young woman with a toddler on her lap, and two husky, leather-jacketed men. The cargo area held only a few small bags. "No problem! No problem!" I said quickly. "Look, it comes apart." I demonstrated with gestures how the wheels and panniers could be taken off. The man began to look less like he wanted to roll up his window and drive away, and more like he might help. He got out of the car, as did his two male friends. I saw that he was tall, somewhere in his middle forties, with thick black hair that flowed from behind a receding hairline to the nape of his neck. His face was not especially handsome but sharp-eyed and effective. He was nattily attired in an immaculate knee-length overcoat of dark gray wool. His car was brand new and spotless. This fellow in the overcoat was clearly a man of means.

The three bent over my bicycle, jabbering excitedly. They seemed to have forgotten all about me, until suddenly the man in the overcoat looked up and said, "If you're going to Linxia, why are you headed back down? You're going the wrong way!"

To explain this apparent contradiction was a test of my Chinese, but in the end he seemed to understand. "I see," he said. "So you want me to carry you and this bicycle to Linxia." His face and his voice were hard, but in his eye I detected the beginnings of a twinkle.

"Yes, please."

A long pause.

"Okay, let's put it in the back."

It was a struggle, but we managed to squeeze it in. The engine fired up, and off we went, climbing slowly to Darja La.

As we ascended the snow got deeper, and after we crossed the pass it was deeper still. As the car wallowed and fishtailed, I said many silent thanks that I was not cycling in this goop. While I gazed out of the window, the others in the car were chatting amiably back and forth. Then suddenly I realized: they were speaking Tibetan.

I interrupted: *"Nga pö-ke detsi shing-gi yö"* (I know a little Tibetan) and they all exclaimed in delight. Now they began to ask questions: where did I come from, what was I doing on this road, and where on earth did I learn Tibetan? I was embarrassed to reply in Chinese, but Mandarin words came much more readily to my tongue.

Fortunately, they soon ran out of patience with my bad Chinese, and I was allowed to relax into a silent stupor. It was all perfectly unreal, to be plucked from a mountainside in the wilds of Asia and then dropped into a peculiarly familiar environment: blue vinyl upholstery, five-speed gear shift lever, controls labeled in English—as if a tesseract had sucked me out of Tibet and spat me out on the freeways of Los Angeles. But instead of palm trees and burrito stands, outside was an ocean of blue-gray snow, rapidly going dark.

After a couple of hours we turned left onto a major highway. Labrang lay on the right fork, and I should have gotten out to search for lodging in the town at the junction; but I was content to surrender all decision-making to the man behind the wheel, who would surely take me someplace good. An hour later we came to Linxia, a city of big buildings and bright lights—dazzling to my tired eyes. He drove us to an uncommonly nice hotel. Inside, he secured first-class accommodations for himself and his wife, while I opted for a less opulent room but one that still had a bath with hot running water.

Finding myself in a tub of hot water was a fairy-tale ending after that long, grueling day—not to mention the weeks that had passed since my last shower. But I couldn't linger; my benefactor had instructed me to meet him and his companions for dinner. When we stepped through the restaurant door I knew my host was someone important, for the staff leaped to attention. The food quickly came. In between slurps of noodles, I was able to find out a little more about this mysterious but forceful man.

"I live in Lanzhou, Gansu Province's capital," he told me genially. "My family home is in Xunhua, and I have a store there. I have three stores altogether; the other two are in Lanzhou and Lhasa. Are you going to Lhasa?"

Every corpuscle I possessed had been rung dry by the exhausting journey, but somehow at the sound of the word "Lhasa" my heart quickened. "I hope so," I answered. "It's difficult for foreigners you know—"

"Yes, I know. But you should definitely go to Lhasa; it's the most wonderful place in all the world. We have a house there, which you can come and visit."

"Yes, and you should visit me in America."

"Oh, I've already been to America!" he said gleefully. "I even know English: *Thank you very much!*" he added as a demonstration. "*Thank you very much! Thank you very much!*" he repeated, his face aglow with satisfaction at this linguistic tour de force. He added in Chinese, "Good, eh?"

Then he remembered something: "Look at this—" he said, pulling out his wallet. He withdrew three U.S. one hundred-dollar bills and gave them to me to examine. I was astounded. It was a weighty sum of money for anyone to be carrying around, let alone a citizen of the People's Republic, especially a Tibetan. I wanted to ask him where he got it, but now the others had finished eating and were waiting impatiently to leave. I gave back the money, gulped down the last of my noodles, then jumped up to follow them out the door.

"Tomorrow," said my benefactor, when we had returned to the hotel, "I will take you to the bus station and help you buy a ticket for Labrang."

Somehow I still cherished a vague notion of continuing to Labrang by bike. This notion I now quickly dropped. The man in the overcoat was not one to be contradicted; and besides, I had had rather enough cycling.

"Okay," I said. "Thank you. Good night."

"Good night."

6

LABRANG

AFTER THE QUIETUDE of Kumbum, arriving at Labrang Gonpa was like dropping into a maelstrom. Everyone, it seemed, had come to see the Mönlam Festival, part of the monastery's *Losar* (New Year) activities and its most important annual event. In the town next to Labrang sheepskin-clad nomads promenaded up and down the streets, gaped at foreign tourists, leaned on shop counters, and haggled endlessly with vendors. At the monastery, a never-ending vortex paced the trail that encircled Labrang's walls. The hotel where Delores and Anne were staying was full of junketing politicos from the Gansu provincial capital. Gangs of photographers from the Chinese press roamed everywhere, converging like black-snooted flies on groups of prostrating Tibetans. The town was abuzz.

After my tiring journey, the swirls of people and whirls of activity were just too much to face. Delores and Anne invited me to move into their four-bed hostel room where I could get some peace.

"Don't worry," said Delores. "The festival doesn't start for a few days yet. There's nothing to do except go and watch the morning service at the monastery. You can take a day or two to rest up."

"But you really ought to go and see one of the services," said Anne. "The nomads all go; it's a great chance to meet them."

The next morning I walked with Anne down the town's main street to Labrang's gates. From both sides of the entrance extended a line of prayer wheels that curved around the monastery walls; the creaking of the wheels and the stream of circumambulating pilgrims ceaseless. Nearby, peddlers camped on the dirt, selling snacks and useful items such as rope, cook-pots, and woolen scarves to passing Tibetans.

We didn't pause, but walked straight through the gate and into the monastery. It was a small city in itself, and before we could get to the main temples we first had to pass by a maze of low mud-walled compounds—dwellings where monks live and study. As these humble habitations were left behind, the heart of Labrang rose majestically on our right, a matrix of gold-roofed turrets atop imposing rectangular fortresses built of rammed earth, clay, and stone. Designed for defense, the buildings' thick heavy walls had but keyholes for windows, and their flat roofs were rimmed with parapets. It was easy to imagine the time when armies of Muslim conquerors and bands of desperadoes flung themselves against these very walls. These looming, impregnable giants fitted well the rarefied air and great open spaces of the high plateau.

Labrang Gonpa, constructed in 1708, is the largest monastery outside Tibet Autonomous Region and one of the six great centers of the dominant Gelugpa Sect. Labrang is renowned for its scholarship, and its student body numbers some six hundred monks. The monastery is divided into six colleges, each specializing in a branch of Buddhist knowledge. At least fifteen years of study are required to attain the rank of *Geshe* (Doctor of Divinity), equivalent to a doctorate and the highest degree awarded.

Threading our way between the massive colleges and

chanting halls, we came to a plaza in front of a tall temple building. In front was a great colonnade where an old man in a yellow peaked cap and voluminous robes sat on a thronelike platform. Below and facing him, on a lower platform, sat a row of high lamas, each one wearing a striped sash that proclaimed his exalted rank. Below these men, on the ground level, sat two or three hundred ordinary monks in their humble robes and zens. Behind the monks sprawled a sea of pilgrims: young and old, men and women, many dressed in the garb of nomads. Anne led me to a spot among them, and we sat down.

It wasn't long before the Tibetans around us began to take an interest in us. They stared curiously at our faces and clothes, murmuring to one another in gentle amazement. A hand reached out to touch the fabric of Anne's jacket, and she responded by extending her arm so that they could take a closer look. Other Tibetans reached out to touch the long braid in Anne's hair, and I felt someone gently lift my braid from my back. I heard giggles behind me, and then an animated discussion.

Anne was talking in sign language to an old lady nomad who was examining the red cord around Anne's neck. Anne pointed to it, then to herself, and then pressed her palms together in an attitude of prayer to show the woman that, like her, Anne was a practicing Buddhist. Then Anne pointed to her eyes and said "Dalai Lama," meaning "I have seen the Dalai Lama." The woman understood, let out a long "oohhh!" and nodded admiringly.

All the while, far away in the front, the lamas droned on. Chinese photographers hovered around the perimeter, seeking out prostrating Tibetans and pointing cameras at their honest, devout faces.

"Look at them taking pictures of the Tibetans while they're prostrating!" Anne declared in disgust. "Those Chinese photographers have no respect whatsoever for these people.

They think nothing of pointing their cameras in the Tibetans' faces, and there's not a thing the Tibetans can do about it. It makes me sick to watch."

I looked at the photographers' subjects. They seemed passively indifferent to the cameras, probably with the same fatalism that they endured the parasites on their bodies and every other scourge of worldly existence. I wanted to photograph them myself, but not wanting to be rude like the Chinese, I kept my lens cap on.

After a while the ceremony was concluded. The high lamas began to rise and file off the platform, followed by ordinary monks, and then the rest of the crowd. "Where is everybody going?" I asked Anne.

"To the main chanting hall," said Anne. "Come on, let's follow." We threaded our way through the maze to one of the largest and most imposing temples. By the time we arrived all the monks had disappeared inside. Extending from the entryway was a queue of pilgrims. "There's something going on in the prayer hall inside, and these people are lined up to walk around the edge of the room," said Anne.

"Let's go inside and take a look." We got in line. It didn't take long to reach the vestibule where a couple of monks stood looking over the people in line. I knew that photography would be forbidden inside and had already put my camera away, but nevertheless one of the monks approached us. He touched my sleeve and, with a look that left no room for argument, he pointed toward the door. Evidently we weren't allowed inside at all. I was crushed. I reasoned that probably too many rude foreigners had preceded us, snapping forbidden photos and talking loudly in the presence of sacred images—but that knowledge didn't assuage my hurt feelings. Sadly, we left that place and walked back toward the hotel.

By the time we were walking through the town, my disappointment was beginning to fade. "Let's stop and get some lunch," I said as we passed by a little cafe. We went in and took a table in the corner. The place was full of exotic characters: well-dressed Tibetan businessmen, lean and weathered Muslims, a couple of monks, and some swaggering young nomads. Two Muslim youths wearing blue Mao caps presided over the dough-kneading board and the wok, working furiously amid rising clouds of steam.

While we waited for our noodles, Anne and I chatted about the events of the morning. I asked her, "Why didn't Delores come with us? Isn't she interested?"

"I think she's mad at me about yesterday. Whenever I try to teach her a little Asian etiquette, she takes it as a personal affront. You see, we were talking with this monk we met in a shop, and Delores"—here Anne's voice assumed a tone of righteous horror—*"put her hand on his shoulder!"*

Being inexperienced myself, I didn't know this was a major sin. I tried my best to look shocked while Anne continued: "So later on I had to explain to her that you never, ever touch a monk."

"Was the monk offended?"

"Oh, he was quite a gentleman about it. He acted like nothing had happened."

"So Delores is still mad?"

"Oh, it's not really that. I think this trip is getting to be a bit much for her. It's not hard to understand why. Here she's spent fourteen years studying Buddhism and she thinks she knows about Tibetan culture. But her teachers back home—although they may be Tibetan, they speak English and are thoroughly Westernized in a lot of ways. Now she comes here and finds out that most Tibetans are nothing like her teachers. She doesn't fit in like she expected to. It's something of a crisis for her."

"The nomads are certainly interested in her. People are always approaching her, and they completely ignore us."

"Yes, they're trying to figure out what she is. She wears the robes, but she also has long hair and even wears makeup, so she *can't* be a nun. They've never seen anything like her before."

"Why *does* she wear the robes?"

"All I know is what Delores herself has told me," said Anne. "She says that last year one of her teachers told her that she has a special relationship with Palden Lhamo."

"Who?"

"Palden Lhamo. She's a wrathful tantric deity—a fairly important one. She's in a lot of temple wall paintings—the one with the blue face, riding a mule across an ocean of blood, and wearing a crown of skulls."

"And why is she so horrible-looking?"

"The wrathful deities represent violent transformation— cutting through ego and turning confusion into wisdom."

Anne, who had strong elements of earth-mother/teacher in her makeup, was going into guru mode again, but I was used to that by now. Although much of what she said in this mode went over my head, I could usually glean a few useful nuggets. And despite my skepticism I was starting to sense a hidden world of wisdom lying behind her words. "So Palden Lhamo is a god?" I asked.

"No, not in the Judeo-Christian sense. The tantric deities are personifications of various qualities of Buddhahood—for instance Avalokitesvara for compassion, Manjusri for wisdom, and so forth. In tantric practice you seek to integrate the special enlightened qualities of a particular deity into your own person- ality. This is done by visualizing the deity, contemplating the virtues that the deity represents, making offerings, and reciting the deity's mantra. The ultimate goal is to become one with the deity so that you take on all of his or her enlightened qualities, which is the same as achieving Buddhahood."

Before I met Anne and Delores, Tibetan Buddhism looked to me like a watering down of Buddhist philosophy into a sim-

ple folk religion revolving around the dozens of deities like
Palden Lhamo and their "magic" attributes. And among many
uneducated people it is probably just that. But to those who
study it deeply, Tibetan Buddhism is not a religion at all, but a
complex system of spiritual exercises designed to pry open the
psyche and operate on its contents. Practitioners examine in
detail their states of mind, emotions, ego, perception of self,
sensual desire, fear of death—every element of their mental,
emotional, and spiritual existence. Through a long course of
meditative practices, negative mind-states are overcome or
rechanneled into positive directions. In this process, the many
deities, mandalas, bells, drums, and other paraphernalia are symbols and aids to visualization—not objects of worship in themselves. The real action is not in the ceremony or ritual objects,
but within the human mind.

But at this point I was only beginning to have an inkling of
all this, and was indifferent to diving in any further. I just wanted
to know why Delores was so peculiar. "So Delores is contemplating Palden Lhamo?" I asked, trying to draw more out of
Anne to help me understand.

"Yes, but not only that—Delores seems to think that she's
her reincarnation."

This made me sit up in my chair. "No kidding! Delores a
real incarnation?"

"I don't know if it's true; all I have to go on is what Delores
herself has told me. Whether it's true or not, I know that whoever compared her with Palden Lhamo knows her really well,
because it's a perfect fit. You've seen how she does so many pro-
fane things: she smokes; she wears other clothes with her robes;
she even wears makeup. It all fits her Palden Lhamo identity. Of
course, no monk or nun would be permitted to do the things
she does, but incarnations are allowed a lot of leeway."

"Yes, and every time one of those things comes up—for
instance yesterday when you were asking her not to smoke in

front of the nomads—she excuses herself, saying 'it's the rebel in me that makes me do it.'"

"I wish she wouldn't smoke in front of the Tibetans, but I can't stop her. Anyway, that's why she wears the robes. Incarnations are obligated to do that."

Anne's words certainly gave me something to chew on. Delores an incarnation? Incredible!

BACK IN OUR hotel room we found the woman herself sitting cross-legged on her bed by the door, sparkling with roguish good humor. As soon as she saw us she said, "You should have been here. You missed some good fun."

"What happened?"

"I was meditating, and in the middle of it the attendant brought over a new roommate for us. You know those hotel people; they never knock or anything. The attendant just unlocked the door, and there I was face to face with this French woman. So I said, 'Hello. Are you here for *Losar?*' Well, she took one look at me sitting here meditating and she looked around the room and saw Pam's bike standing there in the corner, and she just freaked out. She said, 'Excuse me, I think this room is full,' and pulled the door closed. I guess we're just a little too weird for her!" Delores giggled gleefully.

Anne and I gave Delores a rundown on the morning's adventures. Eventually the conversation came back around to the subject of prostrations, for I still had unanswered questions. At last Delores said, "We can try to explain it, and you can read books about it, but there's no substitute for actually doing it."

"We can teach you how if you want," added Anne.

"Well . . . um . . ." I stalled, not wanting to get *this* deeply into Tibetan Buddhism. But surely there could be no harm in learning this one little thing. "Okay."

Anne stood up. "First you put your palms together like this, with your thumbs tucked. Then you touch them first to your forehead, then to your neck, and then to your chest," she said, demonstrating. "This symbolizes your desire to attain Buddha's body, speech, and mind, respectively. Then you put your knees and palms on the ground like this and bend low, so your forehead touches the floor—"

I copied her movements, feeling clumsy and self-conscious. "That's right," she said encouragingly. "That's a partial prostration, which is enough for most purposes. For a full prostration, once you're on the ground you reach out with your hands and stretch to full length. But it's important not to rest there on the floor, you have to get up again immediately."

"That's okay, I think a partial prostration is enough for me," I said quickly.

THE NEXT DAY brought the start of the long-awaited Mönlam festival. Despite cold gray skies, the town was humming with excitement. We went down and joined the crowds heading toward the western end of the monastery. Several blocks were lined with onlookers, as if to view a parade. Chinese photographers had taken up choice positions, while villagers perched on roofs and nomads thronged the streets. I separated from the other two and found my own spot by the road.

After a long wait, I heard a distant clash of cymbals and blast of horns that signified the start of something. Before long a line of elder lamas and young monks carrying ceremonial silk banners marched in a stately procession down the street. Then came a slightly disorderly crew of cheerful, muscular young monks shouldering a thick tubular yellow bundle, about twenty meters long. As they passed, onlookers left their stations and began following the monks, joining hundreds already in tow.

I trailed them out to a huge field directly beneath a sloping valley wall. The monks with the bundle crossed the valley and then climbed its far wall. At the top of the ridge they formed a long line, silhouetted against the sky. Then, to the accompaniment of clattering music, they slowly unrolled the cloth—an enormous *thangka*—on the side of the mountain. It took a long time, but the crowd, now numbering in the thousands, was enthralled, and the field was bobbing with prostrating nomads. When the *thangka* was completely unrolled, its protecting orange cloth was hoisted to reveal Buddha Sakyamuni rendered in enormous appliqué.

A line of instrument-playing monks emitted a wailing cacophony and no doubt liturgical formulas were intoned by the high lamas; but the crowd was too thick for me to get close. After a time the *thangka* was rolled up again, and the crowd dispersed. Now that the excitement was over, the bitter winter wind became uppermost in my thoughts. I hurried back to the hotel to warm up and to compare notes with my roommates. When I arrived the room was empty, but at length the door opened and Anne burst in, full of news.

"I've met an English-speaking monk!" she announced proudly.

"Really? Who? Where?"

"I was standing by the gate to the monastery and he came right up to me," said Anne. "He said that he's looking for someone to give him English lessons. His name is Jinba."

"So are you going to do it?"

"Yes, we have an appointment for three o'clock this afternoon, in his quarters. You want to come along?"

7

COMPASSION

LATER THAT DAY Anne and I walked through the maze of one-story windowless stone fortresses to Jinba's residence. Uncharacteristically, Delores was off on some solo adventure. We two knocked on the heavy wooden door, and after a pause it was opened by a young novice who led us across the courtyard to Jinba's room. The boy invited us to sit on the carpet-covered *kang* while he went to fetch Jinba. While we waited, I looked around the room. The window and door frames, as well as the trim around the walls, were made of carved blond wood. The walls had patterned paper on them, and were decorated with photographs of the Dalai and Panchen Lamas. Muted but pleasing sunlight entered through the window.

The door opened, and in came a smiling round-faced monk. "Hello, Hello! Welcome!" said Jinba eagerly. "Oh, no one give you tea yet. I bring tea. Wait one minute here." He disappeared again. A few minutes later he returned, his arms full of a kettle, a leather drawstring sack, three tea bowls, and a fancy lacquer box. He offered each of us a bowl and poured tea into them. I tasted mine: it was salted in the customary Tibetan style, which by now I had come to like. "You eat butter?" asked our host as he opened the sack.

Anne and I looked at each other. We both knew that Tibetans regard tea to be incomplete without butter, but neither of us were that eager to go native. "Just a little," I said. Jinba took my bowl and dropped a walnut-size lump of butter into it, a modest serving by Tibetan standards.

"Give me about half that amount," said Anne, but Jinba was already depositing an even bigger lump into her bowl. We both sat and dubiously watched the lumps melt in our bowls, forming little yellow slicks. I tasted mine. As tea it was horrible stuff, but as broth it was hot, rich, and sustaining.

"This is my friend Pam," said Anne. "She wanted to meet you, so she offered to help with your English lesson."

"Very good! Welcome you visit my home," said Jinba. We exchanged some pleasantries. Jinba was nothing like the introverted, studious, house-bound monk that I had expected him to be. He seemed quite at ease with us, and he spoke confidently —indeed forcefully—looking his listener right in the eye. He was thirty-one, had a fleshy, boyish face, and a comfortable belly. He had been a monk for twelve years.

"You are hungry?" Jinba asked when we had drunk down our bowls to the half-full state. "You eat *tsampa*. Here—" He opened the lacquer box to reveal a partitioned interior containing *tsampa* (flour of roasted barley), sugar, and some crumbled, gravelly white stuff.

"You know how to make *tsampa*? No? No problem, I make." He took Anne's bowl and lofted a few scoops of *tsampa* into the remaining tea. "Sugar? Cheese?" Anne nodded, so smaller amounts of those materials were added. Then he began to knead the mess skillfully, spilling not so much as a crumb over the sides of the bowl. When the dough was well combined he molded it into a ball, then pinched off a wad and pressed it inside his closed fist into a curvaceous lump. "This is best way to eat," he said, handing the lump to Anne.

She took a bite of her lump, chewed introspectively, swallowed, and then pronounced, diplomatically, "Very good. Thank you, Jinba. It's just too much for me; I don't think I can finish it all." But Jinba was already hard at work mixing up another bowl for me. I took an experimental bite. It tasted like greased sand. Once in my stomach it seemed to expand like a tsunami rolling into a lagoon. After two or three bites I set the rest down in hopes that Jinba would forget about it.

An hour later the lesson was finished, but Jinba would not let us leave. "I want you see something," he said. He went away briefly and then returned with a roll of canvas. "It is a *thangka*. I paint," he said as he unrolled it. The *thangka* was small but finely done in vibrant watercolor highlighted with gold. The central image was a delicately shaped green-skinned female seated on a spreading pink lotus, surrounded by a field of flowers. Her face had a purity that shined through the garish coloring, a transcendental beauty that reminded me of something completely un-Tibetan: the Virgin Mary.

"Beautiful! Who is that?" I asked.

"Green Tara," said Anne.

"In Tibetan we call her Dolma Jang," said Jinba.

"And what is her role?"

"Oh, my English is not enough good to explain. Anne, you tell her," answered Jinba.

"All right, I'll try. Tibetans are Mahayana Buddhists, which means that to them the goal of Buddhist practice is not to achieve enlightenment just for oneself alone, but in order to help all other sentient beings. Compassion is the supreme virtue. Avalokitesvara is the Buddha of Compassion, the one invoked by the mantra 'Om mani padme hum' that you hear everyone chanting and that you see carved into rocks all over Tibet. The Dalai Lama, incidentally, is considered the incarnation of Avalokitesvara—which explains why he's the supreme spiritual leader of Tibet. Green Tara represents Avalokitesvara's female aspect; that's why Green Tara is loved and revered by Tibetans. Did I get that right, Jinba?"

Yes, Anne, you say very well," said Jinba approvingly. "You

like this *thangka?* You want to buy?" He went on to explain how
he was trying to get money together to go abroad to study English. Jinba's plan seemed pretty far-fetched, but no matter: I
liked the *thangka* so I bought it. That exquisite face with its glow
of infinite divine compassion spoke to me somehow, and I
wanted to take it home.

UPON OUR RETURN, we went with Delores to eat dinner. We three
were joined, as usual, by Pat and Catherine, a British couple
staying in the same hotel as us. The two were intellectuals and
perpetual travelers; their hotel room was a marvel for the quan-
tity of books stacked on every surface. While I pitied them for
the weight of their luggage, I admired them for the breadth of
their minds. Catherine had worked in Taiwan and spoke ser-
viceable Chinese. She was slender, had boyishly short blond hair,
and a lively, pretty face. Her husband Pat was very tall, a little
gaunt, fair-haired, and seemed older than he was. Beneath the
scruff of travel his face was that of an aristocrat. He had an intel-
lectual's irreverent disregard for conventionality, and although
he came from a wealthy family, he cared nothing for the life of
vapid luxury enjoyed by others of his class. He knew a lot about
history, politics, and philosophy, and could expound with savage
brilliance on most any topic of import.

On this night, as on most nights, we ate at a low table,
shouting our conversation over the din of the restaurant's television set. As usual, the gang of Chinese photographers sat at
another table enjoying the camaraderie of professionals engaged
in a common enterprise. As an aspiring photographer myself I
could easily relate to them and what they were doing, but there
were never more than a few terse words exchanged between
our two tables. Anne had declared war on all Chinese photographers, and had vowed to interfere with their work whenever
possible. As soon as they were seated she gave them a sidelong
hostile look and remarked heavily: "There they are! You see that

guy on the end? He's the worst of them; I saw him pointing his camera right in the face of a poor old lady nomad today. She kept turning away, but he just wouldn't let her alone. So I went right up to him and gave him a piece of my mind. I cussed him out pretty good, and I think he understood some of it, because he got all huffy and walked away."

"Keep your voice down," I said, glancing at the other table. "Some of those guys might know some English." Although I sympathized with Anne and her cause, I had no stomach for confrontation. If the Chinese photographers were insensitive, it was because of the society that had reared them. The wheel of karma ground on them as finely as upon the Tibetans. If loving compassion—personified by the Green Tara I had rolled up back in my room—is the ideal, shouldn't it be extended to them, as well?

Soon we got away from this hopeless topic and on to upcoming events. Pat and Catherine had been here before and seemed to know everyone and everything. Pat explained: "Tomorrow is the second day of Mönlam, which means Lama dancing. There will be music and dancing, but the real show is in the costumes. They're utterly spectacular—and highly symbolic."

"Symbolic of what?" I asked.

"I was afraid you were going to ask me that!" chuckled Pat. "In fact someone once explained some of them to me, but that was quite a while ago now. Do you remember much of what Lama Tenzing told us, Catherine?"

"I might a little," she said modestly.

"That means she knows them all," said Pat. "She's a master of understatement. Anyway, the day after tomorrow, in the evening, there will be an exhibition of butter sculpture. These things are absolutely astonishing—the monks spend weeks creating them. They're made from butter, but the shapes are so delicate and the colors are so bright that they look like wood or plastic."

"That night the pilgrims will keep up an all-night vigil," said Catherine, "circumambulating and prostrating before the sculpture."

"At dawn the sculpture will be tossed into a bonfire and melted down," continued Pat, "a reminder of the impermanence of all things. On the last day of Mönlam a statue of Maitreya—"

"The Buddha to Come," explained Anne.

"—will be taken from its vault and carried in procession around the monastery walls. That's the end of Mönlam," he concluded.

IN THE MORNING I awoke to a fall of fresh snow. Following the crowds of nomads that streamed down the main street, I went out to the monastery and joined the huge waiting audience that had formed in front of the main chanting hall. They were squatting on the ground, impervious to the cold and damp, in their heavy sheepskin coats.

After an eternity of waiting, half a dozen monks emerged from the temple carrying the usual horns, drums, and cymbals. Then came dancers dressed like demoniac skeletons—attendants to Yama, the Lord of Death. They made formations, hopped up and down, turned, waved their arms, changed places, and did it all again. After that opening there followed a nonstop parade of voluptuous costumes, esoteric symbols, and fiendish masks. For hours they danced while the orchestra banged and smashed in staccato accompaniment.

When the dancing was over I returned to the hotel to find Delores alone. She was sitting on her bed reading, and I noticed a bottle of *baijiu*—Chinese rice whiskey—on the table beside her. By dinnertime, the bottle was half empty, and that white-hot lubricant was loosing Delores's demons. As we sat in our favorite restaurant conversing with Anne, Paul, and Catherine, she began to talk as she never had before. The first subject she picked was innocuous enough:

"Tantric sex," she declared airily, "is something that captivates the Western mind. People want to be Buddhists because they've heard about tantric sex, and they think that orgasm is enlightenment. And that's basically true, but it's a terrible oversimplification. You see, normally we try to get beyond carnal desire, to eliminate attachment to pleasure and aversion to pain. These things are illusory and normally only hinder spiritual development. But in tantric practice these drives are recognized to be a form of spiritual energy that needn't necessarily be suppressed. With training, you can learn to control the energy and channel it toward a more powerful level of consciousness."

Seeing that her hooks were going in, Delores continued smoothly, "In tantric symbolism the male represents compassion and action; the female represents wisdom and understanding. For spiritual liberation to occur, the two halves have to be united. Orgasm is equated with enlightenment—but you're not supposed to take that literally; it's just something to be visualized during an intense course of meditation. And it's not for beginners; first you have to transcend your ego and acquire a perfect compassionate orientation before you're ready. It takes years to get that far. There's a lot more to it than just fucking your way to nirvana. . . ."

On and on Delores went, the sharp blade of her intellect ever more gleaming and dangerous. When it grew late, we adjourned reluctantly and walked back to the hotel.

Despite the hour, Delores still wasn't through. She found her *baijiu* bottle, poured herself another drink, and sat back on her bed, cradling the cup in her hands. Soon her tongue was loosened even more. She began firing barbs at Anne—first rehashing every dispute since the start of their journey together, and then, when that well was dry, she began needling Anne for mistakes Anne had made in her life years earlier. As I listened to her hateful words, a deep pain spread through me until my whole body was stiff and aching.

Once, Delores's assault on Anne was interrupted by a noise outside—other hotel guests returning from a late-night party. Delores became incensed. She jumped from her bed and flung open the door; in a stentorian rage, she commanded the entire building: "Shut up! Just shut up! You're waking everyone in the whole fucking place! Just shut up!" Then she slammed the door closed again.

Provoked beyond endurance, at first Anne had been defending herself, but now she fell silent, probably hoping that Delores would tire and give up. But Delores didn't. Instead her tone changed from castigating to soothing, as she remarked with elaborate casualness: "Do you remember, Anne, when we were at Kumbum and you were watching Pam do her karate in back of the hotel, and you said that she's not bad, but that she has no sense of balance? I really think Pam should know that you said that, don't you?"

No sense of balance! Anne said that about me? That hit me where I lived. I felt my blood becoming hot. How dare she?! What does Anne know?!

In my throat was poised a shocked retaliation, but before it came out I suddenly remembered Green Tara's shining face— the face of infinite compassion. Compassion! Delores is sick; that's why she behaves this way. I swallowed my words at their source and resolved, somehow, to forgive her. With that change of heart, the acid suddenly seemed to go out of Delores's poisoned mouthings. Ten or fifteen minutes later I drifted into exhausted sleep.

THE NEXT MORNING I woke feeling stretched and ragged. Delores lay in her bed in the corner, still ranting faintly. I got dressed and went outside.

Down the road, past the shops and restaurants of the town I walked, through the monastery gates, past the monk residences, finally arriving at the plaza and the morning service, where, as they had every morning since my arrival, a crowd of nomads sat listening. I squatted down on the ground among them, and, amid their simplicity and contentment, cauterized by the blinding white light of a Tibetan winter morning, I began to heal a little.

When the service ended I followed the crowd to the temple. I got in the line to go inside, and when I came to the monk at the entrance who had stopped me from entering days before, I pressed my palms together to show him I had come not to gawk, but to pray.

This time he didn't stop me.

Into the dark interior of the temple I went, pushed along by the shuffling line around the edge of the room to the front, where, behind a row of flickering butter lamps, stood a sacred image ensconced in carvings and offerings and draperies that once seemed so gaudy and exotic, but now seemed so beautiful and reassuring. In front of the statue was a wooden floor worn smooth by the sliding hands of countless pilgrims, where each visitor stopped to make prostrations.

I put down my bag. Three times, as Anne had taught, with suppliant hands I brushed my forehead (Buddha's body), neck (Buddha's speech), and chest (Buddha's mind), then bent low and touched my forehead to the floor.

And out of the extremity of my weariness and heartsickness at the ills of the world, from that physical act of reverence, I found catharsis—soaring, liberating release.

8

"KNOW THE ENEMY, AND KNOW YOURSELF"

ANNE AND DELORES were gone. Pat and Catherine were gone. The Chinese photographers were gone and so were the junketing politicos from Lanzhou. The nomads had packed up their tents and returned to their distant homes. What was I doing still in this horrible hotel?

I lay in bed, weakened by a fever, drowsy from decongestants, alternating between fitful sleep and dazed wakefulness. Meanwhile, from loudspeakers on the street outside, the screech of a female pop singer drilled into what was left of my brain. It was way past time to leave, but I wasn't going anywhere. My bicycle stood in the corner, a reproachful reminder of what I had come to do; but I might as easily have climbed Mount Everest as cycled out of town. Trash accumulated in a corner; the maids had not cleaned the room since I had arrived. For two days I was too sick even to go out foraging; I subsisted on stale bread, candy, and a bit of granola that Anne had left behind.

But it was not a life-threatening illness, and by dosing myself with medicaments brought from home and sleeping most of the time, I got slowly better. After three days I was strong enough to eat in a noodle shop and to buy a bus ticket out. I had had quite enough of this town. To leave was my only thought, illness or no. I was sure that my health would quickly return if only I could just get somewhere—*anywhere!*—else.

My first destination was Hezuo, a town of no special attraction that just happened to be on the way south, toward Kham. I put my bike on a bus roof, and together we rode over brown, barren countryside that was broken only rarely by clusters of mud houses. I was still unwell, and now, as the bus groaned along under leaden skies, my left ear began to hurt. The miles rolled by, and it got steadily, spitefully worse.

Hezuo turned out to be a small, dilapidated town, gray and muddy. By the time we rolled in it was midafternoon and my ear was throbbing. I checked into the first hotel I saw, stashed my bike there, and then returned to the station to buy a ticket for tomorrow's bus south. By now the pain had squeezed my vision into a long dark tunnel, and far away at the end of it was a girl shaking her head: *"Meiyou,"* she said brusquely. None available. What about the day after? *"Meiyou,"* she repeated, and turned away, banishing me and my woebegone foreign face instantly from her mind.

Friendless and anguished, I went back to my miserable concrete-floored cell with its dirty walls and cracked windowpanes. I couldn't face the prospect of hunting down a restaurant, so I went to bed hungry.

At midnight I was awakened by excruciating pain—and now it was in *both* ears. This must be, I reflected, the sort of pain that makes animals gnaw off diseased limbs. As I lay listening to my heart pump pounding clods of pain through the twin bottlenecks in my head, my only thought was how profoundly tired I was of this whole enterprise. With passionate longing I contemplated the simple wonders of home: my little bungalow seven blocks from the beach, a pitcher of orange juice in the fridge, convenience stores on the corner, washing machines, my own lovely bed, and—most of all!—the sense of security that comes from being pretty sure what on earth will happen next. I fervently wished not to have this blasted bicycle. Riding it into Kham seemed a ludicrous proposition, a notion belonging to a fantasy world from which I was now permanently evicted. I was certainly not interested in Tibet anymore, nor in China.

The hours ticked slowly by, and the pain grew worse. In near delirium, my mind tried to distract itself. I tried to think of all the regular characters who ever played on the series *M*A*S*H*. I tried, mentally, to explain the plot of the movie *Hair* in Chinese. Nothing worked. Then I went back in time, dredging up memories of my father's death from liver cancer two years earlier. As if a melodrama played before me on a wide screen, I relived every detail. We had never been close, although in the last year, when we both knew he did not have long to live, I was visiting him more and more frequently. His illness was already advanced, but he was still taking care of himself, for he had always been a loner and fiercely independent.

One afternoon I called his home in southern Arizona and found him incoherent. My mother and he had been estranged for many years, and my brother was unable to come, so I flew out alone on the next plane to Tucson. After an emergency-room ordeal the doctor diagnosed an overdose of morphine, which had been prescribed to combat pain. I stayed with him for three days until the crisis was over, then flew home, having left him in the care of a nursing home and intending to return in a week or two. But perhaps the ignominy of sterile, alien surroundings was more than he could bear, for the next day he died. My return to the Arizona desert was a dry-heaving nightmare that left me drained, regretful, and a child no longer.

In the morning when a feeble gray light came to illuminate my prison-cell room, my self-pity reached an apex. I had not one single friend anywhere within reach, only the barest ability to speak the language, and was enduring agonizing pain. If my quest was to have a nadir, I hoped earnestly that this was now it. After a good cry, I got out my dictionary and looked up the Chinese word for "doctor." Then I went downstairs to make inquiries.

An office assistant took pity on me and led me to a tiny clinic around the corner. Inside, a middle-aged man sat behind a beat-up desk eating breakfast. A wifely looking woman of the usual short, rotund proportions stood by the stove presiding over a pot of something. They quickly got over their surprise at seeing me. The man put on a white coat and went to work.

"Sit down, sit down," he said in Chinese, offering me a stool. "Now, what's the problem?" I pointed at my ears. He got out a little flashlight and peered into one, then the other. "Hmm. Not good," he said, shaking his head. He got out a thermometer and took my temperature, then he measured my pulse and looked down my throat.

Meanwhile his wife was busy over the stove. Presently she offered me chopsticks and a hot steaming bowl of, well, something. It was yellowish porridge, lumpy, strewn with bits of fat and swimming in hot broth. It was revoltingly tasteless, but I ate it anyway, for I was starved—for food, yes, but also for human kindness, an ingredient wonderfully abundant in that humble bowl of mush.

I don't know whether it was the porridge or the penicillin I received in that office, but two days later I was up and about— and on the bus for Zoige. It is a town in the heart of Amdo's grasslands, and would be a good place to resume cycling. From Zoige I planned to ride south, eventually arriving in western Sichuan Province and—at long, long last—Kham.

Crossing the grasslands south of Hezuo the sky was blazing cloudless blue, and by noon the air was warm. The landscape looked like some titanic janitor had raked it clean of hills, piling them in the distance as a wall of snowcapped peaks. Grazing sheep and yaks were like specks of salt and pepper flung over the withered yellow plain. Every now and then I saw a nomad tent: black rectangular affairs made of woven yak hair.

For my first few days in Zoige I did little besides sleep. On
the third day, as a test, I biked out about six kilometers along the
highway, then stopped. A stone's throw away were some yaks
and sheep, quietly grazing. After standing immobile for a minute
my mind quietened, and I awakened to the sound of teeth ripping grass, the smell of moist spring earth, a dot of a human figure crossing the plains in the distance, vultures wheeling in the
vastness overhead.

It was magnificent, but I was deeply tired—both physically
and spiritually. It would be 133 kilometers to the next town,
with no chance of succor along the way except what I might
find among the nomads. And this was not even Kham; the first
place where I might see Khampas—a town called Barkam—was
another 185 kilometers further.

The question was, did I come here to ride a bike or to
meet Khampas?

My heart answered, and so decided my future course. I
went back to town and bought a bus ticket onward.

TWO MORNINGS AND 318 kilometers later, awakened by a cheerful light streaming in the window, I reflected that here at last was
a truly pleasant place. Barkam was warm: 700 meters drop in
elevation from the grasslands. It was clean and pretty: a torrent
of clear water flowed through town, and greenery-covered
mountains rose up to embrace it. It had conveniences: well-
stocked shops and restaurants that served real vegetables. And
it had Tibetans, too; about one-third of the people on the street,
judging by their clothes. But never mind all that. What I wanted
to know was: is this Kham?

"*Kang? Kang?* Please say again," said the young Chinese
man in the starched green uniform in between drags on his cigarette.

"Kham. The place where Khampas live. Is this it?"

"I'm sorry, I don't know this 'Kam.' For three years I am policeman here in Barkam, but I never hear about this 'Kam.' "

That was strange. Kham was the Tibetan name for eastern Tibet. We were due east of Lhasa and at the edge of Tibetan territory. It had to be around here somewhere, yet he had never heard of it. Guess you just can't expect Chinese to know about these things, I concluded.

In fact Barkam, while technically in Kham, belongs to a different cultural milieu. It is home to Jarong Tibetans, who occupy a thin strip squeezed between Kham proper and the Han-dominated lowlands. The Jarong Tibetans have their own speech, distinct from other dialects of Tibetan, although I often heard them speak Chinese among themselves. Jarong women wear black Tibetan dresses, and their braids are wrapped around their heads to secure an embroidered bonnet. Despite Barkam's nearness to Kham I saw no one who looked like a warrior.

Officer Li, although uninformed, was nonetheless a pleasant chap, and about as eager to practice his English on me as I was to have someone to talk to. He was the first *Gonganju* officer I ever cultivated as a friend, and the effort would be rewarded.

His office was in my hotel, so it was inevitable that Mr. Li would find out about my bike. To my relief, he wasn't worried about its potential for mischief; he even suggested several places around town to which I might easily ride. I took his advice, and by exploring the scenic highway that ran east and west through Barkam, I slowly regained both my strength and my enthusiasm for cycling.

After many sociable visits over the course of days, I was ready to ask Officer Li a favor—but it had to be approached delicately. One morning, as I sat sipping tea in his smoke-filled office, I wistfully remarked, "Barkam is such a beautiful place, I'd like to see more of this area. They say that Aba is quite interesting. Can you give me a permit for Aba?"

"Oh no," he said quickly. He sucked on his cigarette, exhaled, then went on, "Sorry, I cannot. Aba is closed."

"I know it's closed. That's why I need a permit. Can't you find a way to give it to me?"

"No, I am not allowed to give permit for Aba. So sorry."

He was, it appeared, genuinely sorry, so I continued hopefully: "Then how about Serdar? I'd like to visit Serdar."

"Sorry, I am not allowed to give permit for Serdar. It is closed."

"Well then, what about Danba and Kangding?"

"I cannot give permit for Danba and Kangding."

"But I just met some foreigners who came from there, and they said they had permits."

"Danba and Kangding are not in Aba Prefecture. If those foreigners went to Danba and Kangding, then they did not get their permits here. We can only give permits for Aba Prefecture."

"Then what places *can* you give me a permit for?"

"How about you visit Guanyinqiao? I can give you a permit for Guanyinqiao."

This caught me by surprise. "Guanyinqiao? What's that like? I never heard of it."

"Guanyinqiao is very interesting. It has an important monastery. Many pilgrims go there."

"Where is it?"

"Not far. Just seventy-six kilometers west of here. You can buy a bus ticket the night before."

West? This was an auspicious direction; it would take me closer to Kham. "Oh, I don't need a bus ticket. If it's just seventy-six kilometers I can ride my bicycle."

"Ha, ha," he laughed warningly. "No, you cannot ride bicycle. The road is very bad. Besides, it is not allowed."

"Why not? Barkam is open, and I'll have a permit for Guanyinqiao."

"You are allowed to stay in Barkam and you are allowed to stay in Guanyinqiao, but the road in between is closed."

"I'll ride fast and I won't stop anywhere along the way."

"No," he said with finality, dropping his cigarette to the floor and grinding it with his shoe. "You must take the bus."

Having put up a token struggle, I thought it was now best to acquiesce graciously. "Okay—if you say I have to take the bus, then I'll take the bus."

"Good." He had done his duty; but I didn't mind. It was all for the best. Now if I was caught breaking the rules it wouldn't be his responsibility.

EARLY IN THE morning, well before Officer Li would be coming to work, I wheeled my loaded bike through the front door of the hotel and rode quickly out of town. Slick as a whistle! I thought triumphantly. It was another idyllic day in paradise. Leaves and pine needles were aflame with sunrise radiance. The road slipped beneath gray cliffs of twisted rock, past evergreens springing out of vertical walls of dirt, and postage-stamp-size fields where I saw yaks pulling plows and Tibetan farmers dropping seeds into the rich black earth. It all unfolded to the merry jangle of the Somo River, which tumbled over boulders and cut into cliffs on its helter-skelter cascade down from the highlands. After so many weeks in the desiccated cold of the plateau, this moist green valley was intoxicating. Smooth black asphalt rolled like silk under my tires. Few people were about, and I had the road to myself.

The natural scenery was charming enough, but even better were the houses of the local folk. Gone were the squat mud-brick huts of Kumbum and Labrang; gone were the tents of the grasslands. These houses were not just homes; they were castles—three stories high with stone walls more than two feet thick. Some villages even had stone watchtowers, each twenty or thirty meters high, planted on strategic lookouts. It was all so quaintly medieval that I fancied at any moment one of Tolkien's hobbits might come stumping along the road, or a fire-breathing dragon might alight on a hill above me.

If there was any rule against foreigners cycling here, no one was around to enforce it. I rode forty-five euphoric kilometers on that buttery-smooth asphalt before coming to a fork in the road. Turning right and crossing a bridge, I was now following a tributary to the Somo. My destination, Guanyinqiao, lay another thirty-one kilometers upriver.

Now the holiday was over. No more downhill on asphalt; now the slope was up, and the highway was gravel. It was fun to trade waves' with women working in the fields, but I also desperately needed that mental boost to keep up my spirits for cycling. Constantly veering between stones and dirt; constantly being walloped by bumps; and the constant agony of going uphill—after a couple of hours I ached in every corpuscle.

At last, after six hours of cycling, I reached Guanyinqiao. When I rolled up parched and panting to the turnoff, a crowd of people stood waiting at the intersection. They had come to see off a truckload of pilgrims who stood parked nearby, ready to depart. There was a sparkle in the air, for Tibetans are never happier than when on pilgrimage, and these people were undoubtedly headed for Lhasa. Tomorrow they would be continuing west into the heart of Kham, traveling the road that was the object of my dreams and longing. And I envied them—people who belonged to this stupendous land, people who could go to Kham or to Lhasa so freely. For here at Guanyinqiao I had come to a day of reckoning.

Sun Tzu, in *The Art of War,* says, "Know the enemy and know yourself, and in one hundred battles you will never be in peril."

By now I knew my enemy. First, he was long distances, high passes, bad roads, and uncertain weather. Second, he was those men in green, bent on keeping foreigners out of Tibet. The Guanyinqiao townspeople took me directly to Public Security, where my permit was carefully checked before I was allowed to stay. Third, my enemy was the ticking clock, for I could not stay in China indefinitely.

And by now I had come to know myself. I had to face the truth: that I was not strong enough to cycle solo across Tibet. If I tried to follow those pilgrims west, even if I aimed merely for Derge—a Khampa town another 460 kilometers—there was little chance that I would make it before illness or exhaustion or one of the many obstacles erected by officialdom would stop me. And Lhasa—well, it lay 1,500 kilometers beyond Derge; to bike that mighty distance was an impossible dream.

No, this bicycle of mine was more a burden than a help. But there was another way.

9

—

KHAM

AFTER TEN DAYS of rest in Chengdu, Sichuan's provincial capital, I was ready to go back to the plateau. After my retreat from Guanyinqiao it had taken a week of devouring cheese omelets, letters from home, and English-language newspapers to restore my explorer's mettle; now I was eager to get out of town. My research was complete, and it was time to set my sights on Kham in earnest. The first step was a bus headed west.

In the fertile Sichuan countryside, spring was in full swing. The air was balmy and heavy with the scent of flowers. Rice paddy and vegetable plots stretched as far as the eye could see. I felt revitalized, full of energy to meet the challenges ahead. My bicycle was safe and out of the way. My pared-down kit, now carried in a compact blue backpack, was riding on the bus roof.

I was embarking on a new style of travel, one whose rules I didn't yet understand but would gradually learn through an ad hoc combination of research and instinct. The first one is, when straying into closed areas, stay in small hostels whenever possible, because larger ones are likely to report your arrival to the police. If asked, say that you are headed toward Chengdu or some other open place. When told to leave a closed area do so quickly and graciously, and don't get caught in the same place twice. Be compassionate of cops, for they have to answer to their superiors. And most important of all: keep moving.

The bus ground slowly upward, gradually leaving the populated lowlands and ascending into mountain jungle. We crested a pass, and I caught sight of a row of snowy jagged peaks in the southwest, the mightiest of them Gongga Shan, so impressive that early European explorers thought it to exceed even Everest in height. My heart beat faster knowing that soon I would be back among Tibetans in the highlands.

At last we pulled into Kangding, an important border town also known by the Tibetan names of Dartsendo or Dardo. In former times explorers, missionaries, traders, and thousands of tea-carrying coolies made their way from China to Kham on a caravan trail that passed through this famous city, which is still considered the gateway to Tibet. But it little resembled the wild and rustic outpost I had read about, for in Kangding the Chinese presence is strong. Gone are the city walls and ancient gate; instead the approach is lined with cafés and tawdry hotels. The city center, formerly a warrenous labyrinth of ramshackle wooden houses, is now a tidy district of concrete. On the highway are neither coolies, yaks, nor mules, just trucks rumbling up and down past the main bus station.

Officially, Kangding was closed, but the travelers' grapevine had assured me that I would have no problems here. I stayed for three days. Despite its tamed and developed appearance, there remained a wild edge to this town. It was in the high-voltage blue of Kangding's sky; it was in the cold wind that gusted through Kangding's town square; and it was in the barely contained whitewater torrent that ran between Kangding's two main streets. Most inhabitants were unremarkable: Chinese, old and young, dressed up for business meetings or going about their shopping; truck drivers seeking little more than a good meal and a few hours of video entertainment after a hard day's work; and plenty of Jarong Tibetans like those in Barkam.

But then there was a new sort of character: men who wore

Tibetan coats, knee-high boots, and felt hats. Each one carried a long dagger stuck in his belt, and wore his hair elaborately braided and tied up with a wad of red silk string. They walked down the streets slowly and purposefully, seldom glancing to the right or left.

They were Khampas. At last I had found them.

I WAS THRILLED, but I hung back. It wouldn't do to walk up to one and introduce myself saying, "Hi! I hear you're a warrior!" Kangding was only the edge of their territory. I had to get deeper in before I could see what they were all about.

This wasn't going to be easy, for Kham was designed as if on purpose to keep out intruders like me. The eastern Tibetan plateau is sliced by mighty rivers: the Yangtze, Mekong, and Salween, all flowing north to south in deep parallel tracks. The valleys they gouge support immense forests as well as agriculture, and have made Kham into Tibet's breadbasket. Between the valleys are mountain summits rising to nearly Himalayan elevations. But the greatest land area belongs to treeless highlands, where nomads still tend their herds in classic Tibetan fashion. Thus Kham is a land of dramatic topography, with prosperous valleys, alpine pasture, and frigid, snowy heights.

Kham's history has been shaped by its topography, for invaders have been hard-pressed to conquer such a rugged, inaccessible land. In the last century or so, two outside powers—Lhasa to the west and China to the east—have vied for control of Kham. Until China's 1950 invasion of Tibet, the boundary line shifted back and forth, but tended to gravitate toward the Yangtze River, which divides Kham neatly in half. However, those two distant capitals had little real influence; Kham's *de facto* rulers were petty chiefs. They governed feudal kingdoms centered on towns and monasteries. In eastern Kham—places like Barkam and Kangding for instance—Chinese warlords from neighboring Sichuan had easy access, carving out miniature empires for themselves and competing with native rulers for land and influence.

In Kham (as elsewhere in Tibet) political intrigues were often centered on the monasteries, and it was not unknown for lama chiefs to wield armies of monk soldiers in defense of their perceived interests. These wars were usually not sectarian in nature, but were fought over wealth and power.

Whoever they were, the rulers contending for various pieces of Kham made alliances with each other, with Lhasa, and with assorted Chinese factions according to strict self-interest. Besides fighting over local resources, they competed for the lucrative right to tax the tea trade. Officials dispatched by China or Lhasa were, more often than not, just corrupt opportunists determined to rake as much profit as possible from the taxes they were charged with collecting. Outside cities and towns, however, the force of law was weak, and most "taxes" were probably collected by brigands.

With the 1950 invasion of Mao Zedong's forces, that chaotic era ended, although the changes were not obvious at first. Within a year, Kham was flooded with Communist cadres come to advise the Tibetans on how to achieve "self-determination and self-rule."[18] As the decade advanced, however, the Chinese occupiers made more and more changes to the Tibetan way of life: redistributing property, organizing communes, preaching class struggle, discouraging Tibetan religion, and imposing the culture of "the Great Chinese Race." Tibetan leaders were merely figureheads; it was their Chinese advisers who really ruled, taking cues from Communist party directives handed down from Beijing. Khampa discontent grew and grew, leading to the formation of guerrilla bands and sporadic bloody revolts.

In 1959 Tibetan discontent boiled over into a general rebellion. In Lhasa a battle broke out, and in the confusion the

---

18. Jamyang Norbu, *Horseman in the Snow,* p. 71.

Dalai Lama, then twenty-four years old, escaped and fled to India. Subsequently the Chinese began an all-out effort to bring Tibet fully into the Communist fold; however, it wasn't until the Cultural Revolution was launched in 1965 that damage to Tibetan religion and culture accelerated to near-holocaust proportions. Monasteries were looted, and many razed to the ground. Monks were defrocked, traditional dress and customs outlawed. It was, without a doubt, the darkest period in Tibetan history.

By the early 1970s, the Cultural Revolution over, Tibetans were given limited freedom of religion. Monasteries were gradually reopened, and the government even financed some repair. Slowly, conditions were normalized—although Tibetans never lost their fear that those evil days might return, and the Chinese never relaxed their policy of ruthlessly stamping out any movement for Tibetan independence.

BUT HISTORY, POLITICS, and topography were not on my mind as I prepared to leave Kangding. I had just one thought, and that was how to sneak past the checkpost at the west end of town. On the morning of my planned escape, I rose a couple of hours before dawn and tried to steal out of the hotel, but was stopped at once by a locked gate. I banged on different doors until I had woken up everyone; only then did the gatekeeper come and release me. So much for stealth, I thought ruefully.

After that fiasco, I had to walk through dark streets past legions of barking dogs. I kept my canine defense weapon in hand, but luckily none came to attack. At the checkpost I found the guard inside his shack with his back to the window, and I tiptoed safely past. I walked on a kilometer or so before stopping to wait for passing traffic. It wasn't long before a pickup full of Tibetans and one or two Chinese stopped at my waving hand.

"Where are you going?" one of them asked in Chinese.

"Tagong," I replied.

He consulted with others in the truck. "Ten yuan."

That was reasonable. "All right."

"Get in." They made room for me in the back seat and we took off. The sky was getting light now. We crawled like an ant at the foot of ice-topped mountains, themselves crouching beneath sun-flamed clouds, all crested by limitless purple-blue. Soon the last houses were behind us, and there was nothing but desolate hills and scrub. The ribbon of asphalt led us up and up, at length to Tsheto-la, a pass marked by a *chörten* and a clutch of ragged prayer flags.

As we came over the top, the Tibetans in the car let out a triumphant whoop: *"Lha so, Lha so!"* they cried as the labored groan of the car's engine was replaced by a throaty *va-room!* The driver shifted into high gear and the car leaped forward as if it had suddenly taken wing. Down, down, down we went—into another world.

IT WAS A different sort of place. Gone were steep mountain walls. Gone were the Chinese institutional buildings and the terraces crowded with vegetables. This place was wide open, but not flat like the grasslands of Amdo; here the stubble was laid over a vertigo-inducing panorama of gently rolling hills. Presently we came to a house, a great stone fortress set like Noah's ark on a mustard-colored ocean. A little way further was another house, then two together, then two men on horseback riding at a lazy walking pace, with no sign of where they had come from or where they were going.

We drove an hour or two to a fork, then turned north onto a gravel road. Now the highway followed a clear stream that bubbled over gray and white stones, sliding past stands of pines on the steeper hillsides. I must have been dozing, for I was awakened by a touch on my shoulder.

"Tagong," said the woman sitting next to me, and pointed ahead to where some houses lay clustered around a bend in the highway.

The driver asked, "Where do you want us to let you off?"

In stark terror, I gazed at the stone buildings by the highway. You mean this is it? This town is so tiny—can it really be the place I was told of? What if there's nowhere to stay, nowhere to buy food? What if the people are unfriendly? What if I get arrested?

But then, the lesson of special training is: if you want to learn, you have to take that leap.

"Take me to the monastery."

In a flash we were at the other side of town, where a rectangular tile-roofed colossus sat surrounded by a high wall. We pulled to a stop in front of the gate. I got out of the car, gave the driver his ten yuan, and pulled my backpack out from where it had been wedged.

The door slammed shut and the car took off, disappearing around a hill and leaving me in a cloud of dust.

I looked around. No people in the vicinity, but the monastery stood before me, its gate wide open. There seemed nothing to do but go in.

Timidly, I walked through the gate and across the plaza to the steps in front of the main assembly hall. I took off my pack and set it against a pillar of the colonnade, then sat down beside it and waited for something to happen. Before long a couple of monks came out and noticed me. They summoned their friends, and quickly a whole crew of shaven-headed youths was crowding around to inspect me and my exotic paraphernalia.

This place might be Kham, I reflected, but its monks were like monks anywhere: playful and curious. I took out my Tibetan grammar book for them to see, and in no time the ice was broken. After they had taken me around the precincts, I was brought to a dark sitting room where I sipped their tea and choked down some *tsampa*.

After a time my labored Chinese began to pall, and the number of monks attending me dwindled. It was time to bring up some practicalities, like where I would be sleeping that night.

"At the hotel. Ahtsong will take you," replied one young man, nodding toward the earnest monk sitting beside him.

Ahtsong had been so quiet until now that I barely noticed him. "We go now?" he asked.

I rose and picked up my pack. "Yes. Let's go." Thanking the others and bidding them good-bye, I followed Ahtsong out the door.

At the other end of town we turned off the highway and walked to the front door of an ordinary stone house with a crudely lettered sign on the balcony saying "hotel" in Chinese and Tibetan.

"Halloo!" Ahtsong announced our presence as he led me through the door and up a ladder to the second floor. "I have a guest for you, an American woman."

From upstairs, a delighted voice answered. At the landing I was met by a petite, energetic Tibetan matron. "Come in, come in," she said, practically lifting me up the stairs. "Sit down. Put your things over there. Where did you come from? Where are you going? How long will you stay?"

After I was settled, had drunk some tea, and talked my way out of eating more *tsampa*, Ahtsong invited me to his home. It was right next door: another stone fortress. When I entered the living room I gasped, for the walls were painted in a boggling array of designs: flowers, snow lions, auspicious Buddhist symbols—no two panels the same. Along one wall a great cabinet displayed rows of cook-pots behind glass doors. A pleasing light entered the room through papered wooden lattice in the windows.

Still dazzled by the sumptuous decor, I sunk onto a carpet-covered couch. Already Ahtsong was installing another bowl of tea in my hands—my umpteenth bowlful that day. On the table were platters of hearty bread. Ahtsong saw me scanning the food and said, "Have some bread—take all you want. Would you like *tsampa*? How about some butter for your tea?"

One thing was certain: I wouldn't go hungry or thirsty in this town. To ward off the prospect of more *tsampa,* I tried to change the subject. "This is a beautiful house. Is it very old?"

"No, not at all. It's only two years old."

"Who lives here?"

"Me and my two sisters. My older sister is a doctor, my younger sister is a teacher."

"They must be very smart. And do your parents live here also?"

"They're dead."

"Oh!" Ahtsong seemed very young not to have parents. What had happened to them? Could they have been casualties of the Khampa resistance movement? I was afraid to bring up such a politically sensitive topic, for I didn't want to do anything that might endanger this kind young man. Moving onto safer ground, I asked him the inane questions that my small vocabulary permitted, and he answered gravely. He was tall for an Asian, bony and plain, and the stubble on his head showed threads of gray.

Tagong Monastery (Lhagang Gonpa in Tibetan) belongs to the Sakya sect, an older "unreformed" sect who do not follow such a rigid code of dress as their Gelugpa counterparts at places like Labrang and Kumbum. Sakya monks are even permitted to marry, but if they do so they may not reside in the monastery.

"Why don't you live in the monastery?" I asked Ahtsong.

"It's better to live at home," he replied. "I still go to study at the monastery every day." He looked at his watch. "In fact, I have to go there now."

"Then I'll return to the hotel," I said, rising.

Together we went downstairs. When we reached the road, Ahtsong said shyly, "I will see you tomorrow?"

"Yes, see you tomorrow." I answered. "Good-bye."

"Good-bye."

★   ★   ★

THE NEXT MORNING after breakfast I walked to the town square. The night's frost was melting fast, and sun glared harshly on the parched brown earth. A dozen horses were tied to posts by the highway, their backs weighted with carpets and saddlebags, the bells at their throats emitting an occasional jingle. Dust lay thickly on the road and jumped in the air at the slightest breeze or touch. I felt as if I had time-jumped a hundred years back to Tombstone, Arizona—or else wandered onto a Hollywood movie set. In the square men were circled around two pool tables, intent on games in progress.

Around one table were young monks—a swaggering, motley crew and not exactly the picture of piety. The other table was full of Khampas—wild men from the hills. Khampas! The ones I had come so far to see! I stood for a while taking in their outlandish outfits: felt hats[19] *racked* at a jaunty angle, hair elaborately braided with turquoise and ivory, swashbuckling Tibetan coats belted at the hip, and long daggers in silver sheaths.

Despite the Khampas' flamboyant dress, they were smaller and less imposing than I expected. I sat down, took out a pen and some postcards, and began writing. Soon the players abandoned their games and came over to have a look at me. I was quickly ringed by a semicircle of Khampas.

Now that they were close, I felt not the least threatened, their roughneck outfits utterly at odds with their gentle, smiling faces. One fellow leaned over to get a look at the postcard I had on my lap, so I passed it to him, explaining that the subject was Gongga Shan, a mountain not far from here. Before long my

19. The "cowboy" style of felt hat was introduced to Tibet by a real American cowboy-turned-Asian adventurer named Fred Schroder, who was sent to Kumbum Gonpa on behalf of Mongolia to negotiate with the Panchen Lama in 1913. The august lama so admired Schroder's crush-center Stetson that Schroder gave it to him, and it was subsequently copied in local felt. *China Caravans: An American Adventurer in Old China*, Robert Easton, pp. 9, 77.

entire collection of postcards was circulating among the men. But even when they had tired of the photos, a few remained behind to stare at me. Later, curious eyes followed me down the street to lunch. As the day passed the watch changed every half hour or so, but the watchers rarely flagged no matter what I did.

Around midafternoon Ahtsong came walking down the street toward the monastery. He turned to look at me, and when we exchanged shy smiles I felt some odd kind of resonance that left echoes after he had gone.

10

A TIBETAN FRIEND

I HAD BEEN told that Tagong had a sacred mountain in the neighborhood, but by now had forgotten all about it. In late afternoon I took a stroll up the highway, rounded a corner and suddenly came upon a sweeping vista dominated by a craggy massif whose five closely spaced peaks rose like a shark's fin out of the plateau. There was no mistaking it—this was Wild Yak Mountain, an inspiration to pilgrims who come to Tagong to complete the holy circuit around its base. It was easy to understand their attraction, for although I was not much of a Buddhist, I felt drawn to this mystical summit.

That night, when Ahtsong came to visit me, I asked him: "What is the name of that mountain?"

"Which mountain?"

"That big one, over there." I gestured out of the window to where the mountain lay invisible behind a hill.

"It's called 'Shatak.'"

"What?"

"Shatak."

"Please write it," I said, handing him my notebook. He wrote two syllables in careful Tibetan cursive. They looked nothing like the name I had heard.

"I heard it was called *Mogetso*," I said. "That's what they told me in Kangding. Is "Shatak" the Tibetan name or the Chinese way of pronouncing the Tibetan name?"

"What?" said Ahtsong, leaning forward and looking at me quizzically. "I don't understand."

I repeated my words, then showed him the characters that someone had written for me; but somehow we couldn't connect. Did the mountain have more than one name? Or was there another mountain? Asian people can be maddeningly indifferent to precision in factual matters. While I was growing frustrated, Ahtsong seemed hardly perturbed at all.

I gave up on figuring out the mountain's name and changed the course of my investigation. "How far to the mountain?"

"Three days on horseback," he answered.

"How far to walk around it?"

"It's two hundred kilometers. Many days walking. No villages, no people. It's very difficult."

"Oh." That seemed formidable. But perhaps I could go to the base of the mountain and then return. "Can I go to the mountain?"

"Very difficult. Many days."

"I mean, just go close to it, not around. Just to take a look, then return to Tagong. Is there someone in town who can take me?"

"'Take you?'" He was trying hard to understand me.

"I mean, uh . . ." I pulled out my dictionary. "A guide. I need a guide."

"A what?"

I showed him the characters.

"No, there is no guide here."

"Can *you* go with me?" I asked.

"No. In five days I am going to Lhasa."

Lhasa! A sharp pang made me forget all about the mountain. "You're going to Lhasa?" I asked, to make sure.

"Yes. I leave in five days."

"How?"

"On the bus. Aren't you going to Lhasa?"

I had told him before, but apparently he hadn't understood. "No. I can't go to Lhasa," I said sadly. "I don't have a permit. It's not allowed."

"You can come with me. It's all right; you don't need a permit."

"I do need a permit. All foreigners have to have permits," I explained slowly and carefully. "I'm sorry. I'd like to go with you, but I can't."

He looked hurt, and I wasn't sure if he believed me. After a lengthy silence he asked, "Do you have a photograph?"

"What?"

"Photograph," he repeated.

From my backpack I fetched out my little album of photos from home, and explained each picture. He showed little interest in most of them, but he kept coming back to one showing me in my research lab back in Los Angeles.

"Can I have this?" he finally asked, holding it to his chest.

"Well, um . . ." This particular photo I really wanted to keep. But what the heck. "All right."

He was enchanted. He studied it for a long time, then looked at me and said, slowly and earnestly, "I really, *really* like this."

This declaration left me at a loss for words, so I busied myself with returning the album to its place in my pack. When my hand fell on my Tibetan grammar book, I had another idea: "Ahtsong, will you teach me Tibetan?"

"Teach you Tibetan? Yes, of course."

"Now?"

"Yes, now, if you want," he answered. I brought out the book and together we turned the pages, repeating words and phrases. His Khampa accent was broad and nasal—not much like the voices on my language tapes back home. But after that night he was careful to use orthodox Lhasa grammar when speaking to me, and not the Khampa colloquialisms so popular around here that I couldn't make head or tail of.

Sitting side by side bent over the open book, reading by the light of a flickering candle (for there was no electricity in that house), I wondered just what was going on in the mind of my strange new friend?

THE NEXT AFTERNOON I spent on the steps of the restaurant watching nomads on horseback and their trains of yak sauntering down the highway. Sometimes a truck lumbered by, shattering the peace and raising a cloud of dust. This highway led from Kangding west, eventually going all the way to Lhasa. Several buses plied this road every day, and so when a bus roared past without stopping I paid it little notice. Then a few minutes later an excited call came from down the road: *"Waiguoren, waiguoren!"* Foreigners!

Gradually, the outlines of three figures appeared in the dust that hung in the air over the road. Slowly they expanded and grew clearer. A minute later they were standing before me: dirty, disheveled, and larger than life.

"Hello!" said one of them in a cordial English accent. "I'm Rob, this is Mike, and this is Pierre."

"I'm Pam," I answered slowly. Perhaps this was all just a dream.

"We've just come from Dawu up the road," said Rob. "We were trying to go to Lhasa in the back of a truck."

"The cops caught us in Dawu," said the one named Mike. He had an American accent, and his voice was softened by a southern twang. "We're supposed to go back to Chengdu, but we were so mad about getting caught that we couldn't stand the thought of running back to Chengdu like whipped pups."

Rob continued: "So when we passed this place and saw the monastery and all these great Tibetan houses, Mike and I both began to think of getting off the bus. And then when we saw you sitting next to the road, we thought if other foreigners are here then it *must* be a good place."

Mike said, "So I looked at Rob and said, 'Let's get off,' and Rob said, 'Right,' and before the bus was a hundred yards past the town we both stood up and yelled 'STO-O-OP!' at the top of our lungs—"

Rob broke in, "You should have seen the faces of the other passengers when we stood up and yelled. They must have thought we were mad. But the driver figured it out. He stopped a couple hundred yards down the road and let us off."

Mike added, "Pierre didn't quite know what was going on, but we pulled him off the bus with us. So here we are."

"Are you here by yourself?" Rob asked.

"Yes, I am," I said, overwhelmed by the torrent of English after so many days of straining to communicate.

"What is this place?" asked Mike.

"It's called Tagong."

Rob was looking up and down at all the buildings. "Is there some sort of hotel here, or are you staying in the monastery?"

By now I was starting to realize that these three weren't going to go away, and so I might as well accept this sudden shift in my circumstances. With that change of heart, I began to feel a touch of pride that I had "pioneered" this town, and so now I could indoctrinate these newcomers. "That's the hotel over there," I said, "and here's the restaurant. Follow me and I'll introduce you to the family that runs the hotel."

I led them down the road, still reeling from the surprise of meeting these new arrivals. It was nice having Tagong to myself, but it had been rather lonely, too. Lost in my own thoughts, I didn't hear the men's voices murmuring behind me. Then, as we passed through the gate, Rob touched my shoulder and motioned me to stop.

"Just a minute," he said.

I turned around to face them: three grave, honest faces.

Rob continued: "We just want you to know that, well, we realize that you were here first, and maybe you don't want other foreigners around getting in the way."

Mike broke in, "What Rob's saying is, we don't want to rain on your parade. If you say so, we'll be on the next bus out of here."

I looked at them. Rob was in his late twenties, quite nice-looking despite his spectacles and thinning hair. Although he spoke with an Oxford clip, with his dirty trousers he hardly fitted the stereotype of the overweening English snob. The second fellow, Mike, was the baby of the party, with winsome boyish features, blond hair, flashing blue eyes, and an accent that was sweetly southern and irresistible. Pierre was blond and rangy, said little, and stood slightly apart from the others.

As much as I wanted to explore Tibet alone, I couldn't send these nice fellows away.

"Of course you must stay!" I exclaimed. "I really miss having people to talk to. And Tagong is a great town; you'll like it a lot, I'm sure."

There was a predictable fuss at the hotel, but in the end the three were settled. Sitting with these Westerners gabbing at full speed, I couldn't help thinking of my strained—but somehow magical—conversations with Ahtsong and the other Tibetans. Before the newcomers had arrived I had been growing steadily closer to the people here, but now they had suddenly receded to distant, inscrutable figures across a great cultural chasm. My bubble of immersion was broken.

With Rob, Mike, and Pierre I had a lot to talk about. Rob and Mike were traveling companions of long standing, having first joined forces in eastern Europe. As I had thought, Rob was English and Mike was American; Pierre, it turned out, was Swiss. Pierre had joined up with the other two when they cooked up their plan to ride a truck to Lhasa. Later on, at dinner, I asked them how it had come about.

"I knew even before I left home that I wanted to go to Tibet," said Rob. "I called the Chinese Embassy in London, and they said no problem; Tibet is open. When Mike and I decided to go to China together, that was the one thing we definitely agreed upon; that we would go to Tibet. So first we went to Golmud expecting to take the bus to Lhasa, but the Golmud police said it wasn't allowed; we'd have to go to Chengdu and then fly. We were pretty annoyed about that, but we still wanted to go, so we took their advice and came down to Chengdu."

"That's where we got really screwed," said Mike. "First we asked about going to Lhasa on our own, but the *Gonganju* has a lock on all the CAAC ticket offices, so there was no way to go by air. They said we had to sign up with a group tour."

Rob continued, "Even though it was expensive, both of us wanted to go so much that we thought it was worth it. It took us a few days to round up enough people to make a group. There was Mike and myself, plus a Belgian guy and a Canadian. We thought that everything was all set, and the travel agent promised that we would get our permits and would be leaving in a few days."

"And it didn't happen?" I asked.

"No," said Rob. "Every day we went to his office and every day he said the same thing: 'Tomorrow permits come; day after tomorrow you go to Lhasa—don't worry!' But our permits never came."

"It made me so mad to have to sit in Chengdu and waste all that time," said Mike, his eyes blazing. "Those stupid Chinese! If they would just say 'no' in the beginning, we could have started looking for a truck ride much earlier, or given up and gone somewhere else. But instead they just kept stringing us along—"

"Finally," said Rob, interrupting Mike's impassioned delivery with his calm British tones, "after more than a week, they came back with the answer that our permit applications were denied. Why? Because there were too many different nationalities in our group!"

"What?" I said. "That doesn't make any sense."

"We figured it was just an excuse," Rob said.

"A typical lame, hypocritical Chinese excuse," added Mike scathingly.

"So that's when we decided to look for a truck to take us to Lhasa. The other two pulled out, but we met Pierre and decided that the three of us would go together."

Mike said, "So we found a middleman, a Chinese guy who spoke English pretty well and who also understood all the problems about permits and checkpoints and so forth. We paid him to find a driver for us and to explain to the driver that he would have to hide us in his truck all the way to Lhasa."

"You mean that none of you three speaks Chinese?"

"Only what we've learned since we arrived—numbers and a few other things," said Rob.

No wonder they are having so much trouble, I thought. Three foreigners traveling together can't possibly keep a low profile, and not knowing Chinese on top of it—well, they were doomed from the beginning. "So how did you get caught in Dawu?"

"It was the driver's fault," said Mike. "I can't believe he was so stupid. The first day we went to Ya'an, and that was fine. The next day—that was the day before yesterday—we drove all the way to Dawu. It was about sixteen hours, and when we got to Dawu it was past midnight."

"Sixteen hours in ze back of a truck, sitting only on shoes," said Pierre, with a shudder. "Ze truck was carrying shoes, and we were sitting on ze boxes."

"And by the time we got to Dawu half the boxes had come open and there were shoes flying around everywhere," recalled Rob, laughing.

Pierre was not amused. "Now you are laughing," he said, "but in zat truck it was freezing going over ze pass. It was night, and zere was a big wind in ze truck. I never thought Tee-bet would be so uncomfortable."

"Yes, it *was* fairly cold back there," said Rob wryly. "And it dragged on interminably. I thought we'd never arrive. When we finally came to Dawu, the three of us checked into one room of a hotel, while the driver checked into another. The driver said to be ready to leave at nine A.M. the next morning. So there we were at the truck waiting for him at nine o'clock sharp like he said."

"We waited and waited and he didn't come," said Mike. "That idiot just decided to sleep late, and he didn't even bother to tell us! So there we were standing next to a truck for three hours, and of course after a while somebody noticed. It took some time for the *Gonganju* to get organized and come after us—"

"And all during that time, if the driver had just turned up, we could have left and gotten away," said Rob.

"But no, he *had* to sleep in, and screw up our chance to get to Lhasa!" cried Mike bitterly.

Pierre added, "Still I don't believe zis. How can zese Chinese be so stupid?"

"Anyway, they caught us and told us we had to go back to Chengdu," said Rob. "I don't know what happened to the driver; we never saw him after that. We were allowed to stay one more night in Dawu, until this morning when there was a bus back."

"—And so here we are," said Mike, finishing the story. "All our cherished dreams ruined by that one idiot Chinese." Although Mike's words were hyperbole, the pain in his eyes was genuine. Then he recovered and said, "But there's no point in complaining about it now. What happened, happened. What about you? How long are you planning to stay? Where are you going next?"

"I'll stay here a day or two more and then I'll try to get to Litang."

"Litang?" said Rob. "Where's that?"

"It's west of here, on the southern route to Lhasa."

"Southern route? What southern route?"

"You know how there are two main highways going west —one going through Derge and one going through Batang . . ." They were looking perplexed so I stopped. "It's easier to explain if I can show you my map. Shall we go back to the hotel?"

Outside, the sun had just set and the temperature was swiftly falling. When we arrived at the hotel I found Ahtsong waiting for me. In my excitement over the three newcomers, I had forgotten all about him.

Of course Ahtsong already knew that more foreigners had arrived in Tagong, so he was not surprised to see them. I made introductions all around, but lacking any common language the two sides could only make well-intended but ultimately superficial gestures of friendliness. They may as well have belonged to different species.

Ahtsong followed us into the room and sat down on one of the beds. I got out my map and began to explain to the three about the different roads. As I babbled on, I felt Ahtsong watching us silently. What was he thinking? Of course he understood nothing of our words, but he must have felt the bonds of common language and experience that connected me so readily to these three strangers. Between Ahtsong and I, communication was slow and mostly nonverbal, but every idea exchanged was a jewel to treasure. Now as English sentences flew back and forth, I drank deeply of the sensation of unfettered communication— a thirst I hadn't known I had. But as the scene played on, my shy Tibetan friend seemed to grow shorter in stature before my eyes. His monk's robes grew shabby and alien, and the man inside more and more a stranger.

It was still early, but Rob, Mike, and Pierre were tired. Not only had they made a hard and unlucky journey, but they had climbed too fast and were consequently suffering from a touch of mountain sickness. After a while I left with Ahtsong so that they could get some rest.

Next door we resumed my Tibetan lessons, bending over the book together and reading by flashlight. In Ahtsong's cozy living room, the intimate circle of our friendship bridged for a moment the chasm between our worlds. A young cousin of Ahtsong's joined us with her own schoolbook, interrupting us to ask him questions. It was a beautiful scene, tinged with the spark of a new and budding friendship.

—Or did he have something else in mind? Knowing as little as I did about Tibetan cultural norms, I couldn't help but wonder if Ahtsong might be misinterpreting my behavior. The boundary between friendship and courtship is different in each society, and in this fact lies great danger of misunderstanding.

In the middle of a lesson on the future tense we came to the sentence, *"Khyerang sangnyi dir shugi-yinbe?"* Ahtsong read it out loud and I diligently repeated it, then began looking at the next example, but he pointed at the line again and gave me a penetrating, expectant look.

"What?" I asked, perplexed.

"Acha," he said reprovingly, using the Tibetan form of address that means 'older sister' and, in that instant, evaporating my worries. He repeated the sentence: *"Khyerang sangnyi dir shugi-yinbe?"*

I was nonplussed for a moment before I realized what he was driving at. The sentence meant, "Will you be staying here tomorrow?"

"La se, la se!" I answered, laughing. All right, all right!

After the lesson was over, Ahtsong brought out the photograph that I had given him, and said earnestly, just as he had before, "I really, *really* like this."

THE NEXT DAY was different from those that came before, for now instead of being alone in the center of everyone's attention, I had three companions to share the spotlight. I got to know the three travelers better. Mike, whom I had taken for a twenty-two-year-old college student, turned out to be twenty-seven and a practicing attorney. He had become disillusioned with his work and had found escape by signing on as an English teacher in eastern Europe, the starting point for his journey. Rob had left a successful advertising career in England to tour the world—particularly South America, toward which he was now slowly headed.

While we three chatted over our meals, the restaurant doorway was filled with curious faces. Every day a new batch of nomads came to town, so every day we had a new audience. I was used to it by now, and although I sometimes spoke to the watchers or pointed my camera, I could just as easily ignore them.

That fact made me sad. Were these shy, curious Khampas the warriors I had come so far to find? During my first days in Tagong I had been awed by their swashbuckling dress, their fine horses arrayed in colorful carpets, and the wild land in which they lived. But now I was coming to believe that the object of my journey—those courageous warriors on horseback who defended Kham against the invading Chinese army, the men who spirited the Dalai Lama out of Lhasa from beneath the very noses of the PLA, the infamous guerrillas who sallied from their Mustang stronghold to do battle on the windswept plains of western Tibet—if they or their spiritual kin still existed, it was not here, not in Tagong. The Tibetans of Tagong were beautiful and magical; but they were not the heroes I was looking for.

Little did I suspect that soon I would get a lesson on warriorhood that would change the course of my quest.

11

PILGRIMS

MY LAST MORNING in Tagong dawned bright and beautiful, with cotton balls of mist lying daintily about the valley and fresh snow dusting the hilltops. Having already said my good-byes (although Rob, Mike, and Pierre at least I might see again, for in a day or two they would be following me west), I set out hiking along the highway.

It wasn't long before a big green Dongfeng ("East Wind") truck picked me up. It was headed back to Kangding, and I wanted to go west, so at the crossroads I got out to wait for westbound trucks. Settling on a comfortable rock, I reflected how magnificent it was just to be on the high plateau, with tawny hills, blue sky, and a ribbon of road reaching out in three directions. It was high noon by now, and yet there was no sign of humanity. Apart from occasional passing traffic, there was nothing to interrupt the sound of birdsong and my musing thoughts.

Then, out of the corner of my eye, I caught a small movement toward the southeast. Just a momentary flicker, then it was gone. What on earth was it? Someone or something coming from Kangding? I squinted at the spot, but now all was again still.

Wait! Now it was back, something crimson peeking above the horizon where the road rolled over a hill. But before I could

see who or what it was, the elusive thing was gone again. By
now I was standing, squinting into the glare, waiting for the
thing to show itself again. Soon it reappeared, a little bigger this
time; then, just as quickly, it vanished below the horizon. I
couldn't quite make it out, but whatever it was, it was coming
slowly closer.

Two or three cycles later the entire figure was above the
blacktop horizon and in full view. It was a human being—a man
in monk's robes performing prostrations. I watched him alternately stand, then flatten himself on the ground, stand, then go
flat again. When he had moved a few body lengths closer a
second figure appeared behind him, also prostrating. They
advanced slowly in an inexorable rhythm, up, down, up, down,
up, down—a pair of caterpillars inching down the road.

I watched and waited, and presently there was a tableau of
seven figures bobbing up and down, all in dark, ragged clothes
with thick pads on their hands and heavy aprons. Their steps
were hurried, mechanical, as if they had been at it for a long,
long time. But despite their weariness, on every prostration each
person laid himself completely flat, arms stretched forward in a
posture of utter humility. The sight of human figures facedown
on the ground in the middle of open countryside seemed very
queer indeed.

Now they began to turn the corner, taking the fork that
led toward Tagong. I knew exactly where that road went. From
Tagong a day and a half of driving takes one to Derge; after
which one crosses the upper reaches of the Yangtze River into
Tibet Autonomous Region. Then comes Chamdo, the largest
city of Kham. Beyond Chamdo, a week of treacherous, often-
vertical terrain brings the traveler at last to Lhasa, the climax of
any journey in Tibet. The highway follows an ancient caravan
route, historically a conduit for tea, wool, and other goods that
were traded between old Cathay and the Roof of the World.

Now I suddenly understood where the prostrators were
headed: it could only be *Lhasa itself!* They were making the pil-

grimage of a lifetime, traveling from Kham some 2,000 kilometers to the Holy City. Their route would bring them across three great rivers: the Yangtze, Mekong, and Salween. Between these and other valleys the pilgrims would cross innumerable passes of 4,000 meters and higher, and march for weeks on desolate high plateau. On many days they would not see a single house or tent. And they had chosen to make this journey in the most arduous way possible: repeated prostrations. Every millimeter of the long, long road would be measured in outstretched body lengths.

In awe I watched them, wondering how long they had been on the road, and how many more months—or years—it would be until their journey's end.

But now something was happening, for when the lead man rounded the corner he abruptly left off prostrating. Standing erect, he wiped a sleeve across his forehead, then pulled the mitts from his hands and threw them down like someone who has just finished a hard day's work. Until this moment, the pilgrims had seemed to me like mindless automatons—alien and unfathomable; but now that the leader stood resting he suddenly became human, and a deeply tired human at that.

Before long the others had caught up, and now they all had left off prostrating and stood absorbed in discussion, apparently working out what their next move would be. Presently they walked to the edge of the road and disappeared, climbing down to an unseen field that lay below and behind the highway. One man remained behind, and as I watched, he set out walking, heading in my direction.

He was coming to talk to me!

When the pilgrim stood in front of me I hardly knew what to say, for my standard vocabulary of mime and pidgin Tibetan was ludicrously inadequate to the wonderment that I felt. The man was perhaps thirty years old, with a long, uncombed ponytail and bangs. His shabby black *chuba* (Tibetan coat) was tied around his waist by the sleeves, exposing a shirt that was faded, dusty, and torn. His face was strong and honest, and by the aquiline cut of his nose and shape of his eyes I knew that even though he wore no red tassel he must be a Khampa.

The pilgrim was smiling and curious—but not like the simple nomad folk who watched me through the restaurant doorway in Tagong. This man was neither childlike nor shy. According to his worldview there are lamas who can predict the future, walk for days without stopping, or dwell naked in mountain hermitages sustained by self-generated heat. To this pilgrim the power of Buddha's teachings was hardly a matter of faith; it was an incontrovertible fact—for if ordinary human beings can prostrate all the way to Lhasa, then for learned and holy folk surely nothing is impossible. To someone who is daily engaged in such a super-human task, the sight of a foreign woman sitting by the roadside is surely a lesser marvel. The pilgrim had come not to gape at me like a peasant, but to greet me as a fellow citizen of a most extraordinary universe.

He knew no Chinese, but with gestures and Tibetan words he asked me where I was from and where I was going. Stammering a bit on the Tibetan, I answered, and he smiled with delight at my use of his language.

In the middle of our conversation I remembered that pilgrims rely on gifts for their sustenance, and how such a donation brings the giver merit. I opened my pack and pulled out a sack of peanut candy to give him. Unlike ordinary Asians—who will invariably refuse a gift at least three times before accepting—the man didn't argue but simply smiled and thanked me.

Now he gave me a questioning look, raising cupped hands to his lips and saying, *"Ja tung? Ja tung?"* Did I want to drink tea?

I nodded yes, my awe giving way to puzzlement. How in the world are a bunch of penniless prostrators with no visible luggage going to produce tea?

The riddle was solved when he led me down the embankment to where his friends were resting. I was amazed to see the size of their camp: a small canvas traveling tent, an awning supported by poles, and a neat pile of sacks that no doubt contained *tsampa,* butter, meat, tea, and salt—standard provisions for Tibetans on a journey. Two pots were propped up on rocks over a fire. Those not helping with lunch sat resting in the shade on various threadbare mats and blankets. They must have brought all the goods here earlier, then repaired back to their starting point for the day's prostrations, I deduced.

The group consisted of six men (two of them monks) and one young woman, a nun. The oldest was perhaps forty-five and the rest considerably younger. Their clothes were worn and tattered and their shoes full of patches. Wisps of dirty hair hung about faces that were black from the sun. Yet beneath the rags and dust, their bodies were strong and centered, and the pilgrims moved about their camp with a perfect economy of motion. It must be the physical exertion—which exceeded anything I could ever imagine—of their holy undertaking that had given their bodies such grace. Yet even more striking was the inner strength instilled in their radiant faces. Despite their impoverished appearance, the pilgrims were remarkable to behold.

But it was not the mere shape of their movements that caught my attention, it was the aura of sacredness that attended everything they did. In the uncomplicated manner of one who has stripped away all that is false from his mind, one man measured out tea leaves with absolute attentive care. The pilgrims talked quietly while the tea simmered, betraying not a shred of impatience. One of the monks chanted for a while until the brew was ready. Then the cook took a bowl, ladled tea into it, and silently passed it to his neighbor. One by one, the bowls moved around the circle of pilgrims in an unadorned ritual that beautifully expressed the bond that these people shared. When everyone had his or her bowl they passed around butter and *tsampa.* Like a Japanese tea ceremony, the whole ritual was steeped in potent, eloquent simplicity.

My hosts surely had no idea what I was seeing, but the

scene moved and entranced me. Even in the ordinary business of eating *tsampa,* the pilgrims' extraordinary mentality was manifest.

Of course, as their honored guest, I had bowl after bowl of tea thrust upon me, and was given far more *tsampa* and butter than I could possibly consume. When everyone had had their fill, my sack of candy was brought out and reverently distributed.

After an hour or so I left them, but I could not easily throw off the spell of these amazing people, whose courage went beyond anything I had ever seen. They were light-years apart from the idlers who hung around playing pool in the Tagong town square. Their journey of prostrations had to be the ultimate special training. If I had been able to ask their purpose, the pilgrims doubtless would have said something about practicing right mindfulness and generating good karma for themselves and all sentient beings. But after my experience at Labrang I knew that there was more to it than Buddhist dogma; I had directly experienced how the act of prostration can release a torrent of cathartic emotion. Somehow faith and extreme physical practice join together to create—what? I wasn't sure. But whatever it was, I could see it plainly in the pilgrims' graceful movements, serene smiles, and glowing eyes.

I wished that I was Tibetan and could join them.

IT WASN'T LONG before I was in another truck bouncing west. Now that I was again on the move in territory closed to foreigners, I quaked with every vehicle and checkpoint we passed, but nobody seemed to care. Once or twice I tried to warn the driver that carrying a foreigner might get him into trouble, but he only scoffed. Surely America and China are friends, are we not?

In late afternoon the truck wheezed into Yajiang, which is set picturesquely beside the Yalong River in a deep gorge. My forebodings increased. Yajiang was much larger and more sophisticated than Tagong. Might I get arrested here?

The driver took me to a small hotel tucked in an alleyway off the main street. Apprehensive about being seen, I stayed indoors and out of sight. No one came to ask about my permit, and I went to bed in an optimistic frame of mind.

So far so good, I thought. I only want to get to Litang, just one more day west; then I will be in the heart of Kham.

The next day there was a long climb, then over a pass and onto undulating yellow hills that seemed to go on forever. The only signs of human life were the rare nomad tent and two or three small compounds by the road.

Staring out at the limitless hills and sky, I thought of the people of Tagong, the first Khampas I had found. Although Tagong's people have the same blood as those guerrillas who fought the Chinese from Mustang, and although Tagong's people carry a few trappings of their martial past, they were not the fearsome warriors I was seeking. I had come to Asia to test myself and to find inspiration for my martial arts practice, but it seemed that the inspiration I sought among the Khampas no longer existed—destroyed by the Chinese subjugation of Kham. Yet to my surprise and joy, I had seen another version of warriorhood: those pilgrims back at the fork in the road inching their way toward Lhasa. Perhaps, I thought, they are the truest warriors of all.

What should I do now? I wondered. Should I change the course of my quest? I cannot join the pilgrims, for my faith in Buddhism is far too shallow and immature to sustain an endeavor like theirs. Besides, I would surely be caught eventually, and get them into trouble. Still, the act of *pilgrimage* itself— surely there is something important here. Perhaps I should undertake a pilgrimage of my own . . .

But isn't that what I'm already doing? Am I not on a quest to find warriors?

Round and round I went. What am I looking for? Where

should I search? There was no easy answer to any of it. But there was one thing of which I was slowly becoming convinced: of all the challenges this land had to offer, the greatest was that forbidden road to Lhasa. Sooner or later I had to face it.

WE ROLLED ON for hours more, at last cresting a ridge. Below, on the rim of a broad plain, sprawled the city of Litang. A few steep switchbacks later we pulled into the outskirts. The driver let me off in front of the bus station, then quickly sped away.

Litang at last! This was the heart of Kham, a rugged town 4,000 meters above sea level—one of the highest permanent settlements on earth. Unfortunately, I suspected that my stay here would be short. The *Gonganju* was bound to find me and send me back. So after checking into a more-than-usually-dilapidated hotel, I set out to explore. There was no point in hiding anymore, for if I hid I would never see anything.

As I strolled down the dusty highway, past concrete boxes and Tibetan stone dwellings, Litang's people seemed remote and unfathomable. There were a number of Chinese and Tibetans in city dress, people who possessed the usual two-word English vocabulary:"hello" and "okay." As always in seldom-visited places, these "sophisticates," out of braggadocio or fun, shouted these two words at my back, making me hunker down and walk faster.

If Litang's city slickers were better-educated and better-dressed than their counterparts in Tagong, Litang's wild folk were wilder. The Khampas' coiffures were more elaborate, their clothes were scruffier, and they were taller, darker, and sterner-looking. Some were so proud and aloof in their wild-ness that they didn't deign even to glance my way. Whenever I saw a Khampa like that, my heart beat faster and a chill ran up my spine.

These Litang Khampas were not the sweet, ingenuous angels of Tagong; they were the ones whose reputations had brought me to the high plateau.

The sun set and the air quickly became icy cold. As I walked a wind sprang up. It carried gritty dust in a wave down the main street, driving it into my face and through the cracks of my jacket. From the darkness behind me came a hollow, mocking voice: "Hel-lo! . . . Oh-kay!" followed by a burst of cackling laughter. Back in my room, I found a mass of broken plaster had fallen off the decaying wall and onto my thinly padded bed.

Litang was a cold, eerie town. I didn't understand it at all. But I rather liked it.

12

THE MEN IN GREEN

IN THE MORNING, as the white-hot sun rose to illuminate Litang, my window became a stage across which paraded the hurly-burly of Tibetan life. From the transport yard opposite the hotel came the throaty rumble of trucks—the lifeblood of Litang's economy and its most vital connection to the outside world. On the street, pedestrians walked to and fro, many of them nonde-script Chinese and Tibetans in the usual baggy blues. But there were also Khampas—some modest, others flamboyant—saun-tering with an easy, unhurried gait. Nomad women jingled and glittered in their sumptuous chatelaines; around each woman's waist dangled nomad essentials: knife, flint, purse, and prayer box.

Litang was a cosmopolitan place compared to Tagong, but even so, motorized traffic still had to contend with the occa-sional yak train dawdling down the highway. I was watching the antics of one caravan leader trying to catch his fleeing animals when, out of the corner of my eye I saw three foreigners cross-ing the street. They were Rob, Mike, and Pierre.

A short time later I was sitting in their room listening to the tale of their journey. They had meant to stay a day behind me, but their driver had driven all the way from the crossroads in one twelve-hour marathon behind the wheel. At midnight they had arrived, cold and exhausted, with Mike still suffering vestiges of altitude sickness.

Later on, back in my own room, I had some most unwelcome visitors: two uniformed officers of the *Gonganju*. Their call was clearly not social in nature. "Hello," said the older one pleasantly in Chinese. "Your passport, please."

The officers were both Tibetan, and they were both smiling, but they definitely meant business. "Hello," I said, feeling queasy. I got out my passport and handed it over.

It didn't take long for them to read everything inside it that was written in Chinese: my visa and its three stamped extensions. So far so good. Then they turned to the front and peered at the English in perplexity. I waited apprehensively. Finally the leader closed the little book, looked up at me and asked, "What country are you from?"

"America," I said, trying not to smile. These unfortunate men, who were responsible for policing foreigners in Litang, obviously didn't know a word of English. "Here—" I said helpfully, pointing to the silver embossed words on the cover, *"United States of America."*

"Ah!" he said, beaming with pleasure. "Thank you! America, eh? Very good!" His smile hung in the air hopefully, awaiting my answer to his next question. "Now. Do you have a permit to stay in Litang?"

This was the perfect time to spin a fancy tale of stolen papers and a dissertation on Tibetan jewelry-making, but my brain froze. I've never been a good liar. It seemed better to throw myself on their mercy. "Uh . . . no," I stammered.

Despite my inauspicious reply, the men's smiles did not completely dim—I guess they just liked talking to foreigners. They had a set procedure for dealing with criminals of my ilk, including a long list of questions to ask and a big black book in which to record the particulars of my misdeeds. It was an enjoyable interrogation. They sadly informed me that Litang was *bukaifang* (closed) and that if I was still here tomorrow I would get a big *fakuan* (fine). Then, with obvious apprehension they got ready to go and interview the three men.

"Would you like an interpreter?" I volunteered.

"Yes, thank you!" they replied with relief.

Rob, Mike, and Pierre were a bit taken aback at first, but I hastily assured them that these were *friendly* cops. The trio was questioned and written up; then we were told sternly to be gone the next morning. But why weren't they just fining us on the spot and shipping us straight back to Chengdu? I certainly didn't want to ask, but I got my answer when the leader explained that we were actually *permitted* to stay in Litang for one night only, provided we were on our way somewhere else. Where might we be going? Well, Lhasa was one allowed destination . . .

Lhasa! That was certainly one place I yearned to go. These officers were mistaken, though, because two towns up the road was Mangkang, and Mangkang was supposed to be a most inhospitable place . . .

The account I had heard was firsthand, and it had come from two intrepid Australians whom I had met five months earlier. Peter and Steve were experienced adventurers who dreamed of crossing Tibet on horseback. Starting from northern Yunnan, their plan was to hitchhike to a village near the Yunnan/Sichuan border, buy a pair of horses, then set out for Lhasa. But one thing went wrong after another. First, there were no horses to buy, so they hired a guide and set out walking. Led by a succession of inept, thieving guides they walked in circles for many days, enduring hunger, cold, and agonizing doubts about where they were going. This ordeal brought them no closer to Tibet, so when at last they came to a road, they immediately gave up walking and found a truck. Now heading west toward Lhasa, they had to pass through Mangkang, and it was in this place that they were arrested and ignominiously thrown back.

Peter and Steve's anguished voices as they told me their story was now a deeply etched memory. Yes, the cops in

Mangkang knew that Lhasa was closed, and that all foreigners were to be fined and turned back. So the police of Litang just *had* to be wrong....

Or so I told myself. In any event, with only three weeks left on my visa, I would soon have to get off the plateau and take a quick trip to Hong Kong to pick up a new visa. Then I would begin my assault on the Holy City in earnest.

After the police had gone, we four had a quick conference. We had only one day to see Litang, so there wasn't a moment to lose. Minutes later we were headed for the street.

Outside, the sky was electric blue, and sunbeams knifed the air. Wedges of bright light and inky shadow drew sharp lines across Litang's buildings, like a cubist's jumbled rendition in geometric black and white. Arrayed at the edge of a great plain, Litang's concrete New Town gave way to a maze of Tibetan stone dwellings growing vine-like up the side of a gently sloping hillock. Beyond, a rambling monastery was surrounded by the remains of a high stone wall. Everything—concrete, dirt, and stone—was bleached to the color of bone. My eyes watered from the glare and from dust carried by the gusting wind.

All four of us had shopping to do, so we spent the morning walking from store to store. Then we visited the monastery. It was interesting enough, yet the whole time I pined to be on my own, on that dusty street at the edge of town where I had seen those chillingly proud Khampas. I wasn't ready to leave Kham— there was so much still undone! And Lhasa, a thousand or so kilometers up the road, still beckoned urgently.

That evening at dinner I asked the men: "I know you told those two cops that you're going with me, but really, why don't you try again for Lhasa? You're already nearly halfway there."

Rob replied, "I've been thinking about it all morning, ever since that Public Security man said we're allowed to be on the way to Lhasa. But after getting arrested in Dawu ... well, you have no idea how discouraging that was."

"We had been wanting to go to Lhasa for so long," said Mike, "and then to be caught so early—it just killed it for us."

Rob added, "And from what you say about Mangkang, we'd probably just get caught again. I for one don't want to waste any more time. We gave it our best and we lost. I'm ready to go on to something else."

"Right," agreed Mike, "and besides, I'm ready to get out of here and go somewhere where I can have a hot shower and some decent food."

"Are you serious, Mike?" I asked. "Don't you think that exploring Tibet is worth going without hot showers for a few weeks? After all, you can still wash."

"Of course it's worth it," said Mike defensively. "That place we were just at—what's the name?"

"Tagong."

"Tagong. That place was great," Mike said. "Those nomads were such sweethearts, and I loved that sacred mountain. A lot of what I dreamed about seeing in Tibet was in Tagong." That quixotic exposition delivered, Mike snapped back into practical mode. "But we couldn't have stayed much longer. So I say, if I can't go to Lhasa, I might as well go back to civilization."

"What about you, Pierre?" I asked. "Why don't you try again for Lhasa?"

"I have a ticket home to Switzerland," said Pierre. "There is not enough time. Also, before I leave China I must see Yunnan Province."

"Yes, Pam, you've been telling about Yunnan and all the different cultures there," said Rob. "I want to spend a few weeks there, then get out of Asia. China has been interesting, but I've had enough."

So much, I thought, for these guys. Clearly they were just tourists; not pilgrims like me. But before I could try again to reach the Holy City, first I would have to run down to Hong Kong and get a new visa, for the time on my first visa was almost up. Two more Tibetan towns lay along the route back to the lowlands. Xiangcheng was an agricultural town—utterly tame; after a day of exploring we pushed on to Zhongdian. It was a harrowing but beautiful ride, for the road had been cut from near-vertical walls of rock. We arrived in Zhongdian hungry and elated; but our pleasure was short-lived. After dinner we found three *Gonganju* officers outside the door to our room, waiting for us grimly. The mood was ominous as they marched us to the police building.

The scene that followed was like something out of Dragnet. In a dark, bare room, we were made to sit on a wooden bench before the interrogating officer. The man never smiled once. His stoney face and cold questions made me want to simply confess my crimes, pay the fine, and leave as quickly as possible; but the guys wanted me to put up a fight. "Tell them I'm sick," urged Mike with his usual flare for melodrama. "Tell them I've got dysentery and can't be moved."

So in my broken Mandarin I explained that Mike was ill, and pleaded for a rest day in Zhongdian. Mike had brought along a roll of toilet paper as proof of his unfitness to travel. Whenever he was able to catch the officer's eye, he pointed significantly at the roll and put on his most piteous puppy-dog look. But in the end it was all for naught, for the verdict was a fifty-yuan fine for each of us, and in the morning we had to leave.

It was not the money, nor the disappointment of missing out on Zhongdian, but the shame of being branded a criminal that bothered me to the most. Suddenly this cat-and-mouse game with the authorities wasn't fun anymore. Early the next morning, limp and dispirited, we boarded a bus for Lijiang.

From Zhongdian the highway runs flat to the edge of the plateau. Then we plummeted. Soon we were passing girls in pleated black skirts and quaint umbrella-like hats. "Yi nationality," I told the guys, for I remembered the costumes from my travels here four months before. I was back in Yunnan's ethnic cornucopia, but that was scant compensation for leaving Kham.

Don't worry, I told myself, and vowed: I'll be back.

AT THE BOTTOM of the descent we came to the Yangtze River, stately and colossal as it coursed through an immense valley of rich farmland. Just before crossing the river, Rob and I got off the bus. We would be taking the scenic route to Lijiang: a two-day walk through Tiger Leap Gorge. While we two were hiking, Mike and Pierre would proceed directly to banana-pancake nirvana, carrying our extra gear with them. We would all meet at the Number One Guest House in Lijiang three or four days hence.

Rob and I set off in high spirits. We were glad to be moving at last under our own power, unfettered by the whims of Chinese truck drivers—not to mention police. For two days we hiked Tiger Leap Gorge. Most of the thirty-kilometer trail has been hacked—or dynamited—out of vertical slabs of stone, giving us a stupendous view of the whitewater fury below. It was beautiful, but we both agreed that it couldn't compare with Tibet. Nevertheless, the Yangtze's thrashing violence and thunderous roar as it battered its way downstream were fitting reminders of the pettiness of our problems.

By the time we emerged from Tiger Leap Gorge, Kham was far away and seemed to have happened to me a long time ago. Crossing the Yangtze in a small wooden boat, we came to the outskirts of a hamlet called Daju. Many hale and hearty farmers were in the fields harvesting winter rice as Rob and I walked the final distance.

For two days we were stuck in Daju, for there was no transportation out. When at last the mini-bus arrived from Lijiang it was carrying a load of eager hikers, Mike and Pierre among them. For the last four days the pair had been stuffing themselves with Lijiang's haute cuisine; now they were full of energy to tackle the gorge.

Quickly—for soon the bus would depart—Rob and I briefed them on the trail conditions. The two were about to set off when Mike exclaimed, "Oh! I almost forgot to tell you. I've been thinking, and I've decided I'm not going to let the Chinese beat me. I'm going to try again for Lhasa—and this time I swear I'll make it!"

"What?" I was amazed. This was a mighty big turnaround for someone who talked of little but hot showers, banana pancakes, and coffee the whole time we were together on the plateau. "Are you serious?"

Mike apparently saw nothing inconsistent, and he replied matter-of-factly, "Of *course* I'm serious. I was discouraged before, but that was before. After I got to Lijiang I realized that I can't give up."

"How are you going to do it?"

Mike must have lain awake for many nights scheming, for he spoke like a man obsessed: "Golmud. Golmud is the only way. From Golmud it's just two days hiding in a truck to Lhasa—just two fucking days! All I need is a driver with guts and brains enough to keep me hidden while we go through the checkpoints. If I offer enough money there's bound to be a driver who'll do it."

I was astonished. This mercurial Southerner had made a complete about-face. Was this new resolve of his for real? Why in the world did Lhasa mean so much to him anyway? He hadn't even read the stories of Heinrich Harrer and Alexandra David-Neel, yet he had a full-blown case of Lhasa fever. I wanted to talk to him some more, but the mini-bus was leaving. Rob and I exchanged embraces with the other two before we got on board. As the bus began lumbering away, Mike and Pierre were already far down the street, striding toward the river with quick, determined steps.

IN LIJIANG I ruminated for two days. Then Mike and Pierre came back. They had walked the gorge at a record pace it seemed, not even glancing at the scenery in their mania to keep moving. I went to see Mike, who was lying in bed about to go to sleep. His roommates were out. He was exhausted from the trek and annoyed with me for interrupting his well-earned rest, but I put everything out of my mind except the business on which I had come.

"Mike, are you still serious about going to Lhasa?"

"Of course I'm serious," he said impatiently.

"Then what do you think of this—" I swallowed, reflecting on the fateful consequences that my next words might have. "How about we join forces. We go to Lhasa together."

"Together?" He looked puzzled, as though the idea had not occurred to him. "I can see why that's good for *me*—you speaking Chinese and all—but what's in it for *you*?"

"It's better having company. Traveling by myself is lonely."

He didn't seem very impressed by this argument. "Oh . . . well . . . I don't know," he stalled. "I'm so tired that I can't think. I never considered going with someone else. I'll think about it. Ask me again tomorrow."

Ask him again tomorrow! Curtly, I said good night and left. So much for *him,* I thought.

Soon after that I went to dinner. When I came back to my room much later, I found a note. It was short and to the point:

PAM—

LET'S DO IT. RE:LHASA.

M

New Year's ritual at Kumbum: monks in costumes and masks.

The author approaching a pass on the way from Kumbum to Labrang.

Two nomad men and a baby, visitors to Labrang Monastery's Mönlam festival.

Monk at Guanyinqiao Monastery.

Stone homes at Guanyinqiao, an area inhabited by Jarong Tibetans.

Man with prayer wheel walking beneath wild Yak Mountain in Tagong.

Handsome Khampa with rings
on his hair, Litang.

Khampa nomad woman
of the Derge region.

Tibetans loading themselves and baggage on a truck in northwest Sichuan.

Pilgrims stop at a simple chörten during their circumambulation of Palpung Monastery.

Members of a rinpoche's honor guard.

Khampa horseman.

Palpung Monastery.

Monks on the roof of Ganzi Monastery.

Women cross a perilous
bridge over the Hunza
River in Pakistan.

Magar porters carrying
trek equipment up the
side of the Seng River
Valley, Nepal.

Kirgiz man tries out the author's mountain bike.

On the Karakoram Highway south of Kashgar,
at the edge of the Taklamakan Desert.

13

ATTACHMENT

SIX WEEKS LATER Mike and I were on a train, going clackety-clack across the great sandy waste of Qinghai, due north of Lhasa and getting closer every minute. There was no turning back now. So far, ever since I had met up with Mike after renewing my visa in Hong Kong, he had proved to be an outstanding ally and companion; but I still secretly wondered if inviting him along might turn out to be a big mistake. Perhaps I had merely fallen for his sweet way of talking and good looks; for truly, in the game of outwitting China I was much the better equipped.

By now Mike and I had had lots of time to get to know each other and to hear each other's life stories. While it was true that Mike was attractive, too often I felt the age difference between us. Mike revealed his romantic résumé, describing his past girlfriends. There had been two of them, spaced a few years apart, both beautiful, and both devoutly Christian. Besides them, Mike had had dozens of close women friends.

When Mike talked like this, he seemed not like a twenty-seven-year-old law school graduate, but an adolescent grappling with the raging passions of youth. He also cherished strong views on certain issues of the day—such as gun control and abortion—that ran directly counter to mine, and our debates were sometimes fierce. However hot his passions burned, though, they always ran their course in an hour or so. The rest of the time Mike was sweet and understanding and easy to talk to. No wonder girls fell for him.

Despite my forebodings, on the day we left Hong Kong together it was clear that as traveling companions Mike and I were perfectly in sync. Having him around was wonderfully convenient. Now I could use train station toilets without having to drag my baggage into the stall with me. And when I felt too lazy to chase after black-market tickets, Mike was there full of energy for cutting our expenses. My ability to speak Chinese was perfectly complemented by his genius for wordlessly charming the pants off people. Everything went like clockwork. It seemed a good omen.

Our backpacks were bursting with the stuff of dreams: warm clothing for the high passes; food to eat for the two days we would stay hidden in a truck; camping gear so we wouldn't be dependent on hotels. Later on we planned to go to Rongbuk Monastery at the foot of Mount Everest, so we had brought a full complement of trekking paraphernalia. Last but not least, we had a guidebook telling us what to do and where to go in the Holy City. I spent hours reading about the places we would visit: the Jokhang Temple, holiest shrine in all of Tibet; the Barkhor, a circumambulating path around the Jokhang and the hub around which Lhasa turned; Norbulingka Palace, tranquil summer residence of the Dalai Lama; and, in the hills outside city limits, the three great monasteries of Drepung, Ganden, and Sera.

Most of all, I dreamed of seeing the Potala Palace, the greatest and most acclaimed building in all of Tibet. For three hundred years, until the fourteenth Dalai Lama fled in 1959, the Potala had been the seat of Tibetan government, witness to history and backdrop for endless intrigue. The Potala was also a repository for the scrolls, armor, and other priceless treasures generated by the wealth and power of the Tibetan Empire. In its countless labyrinth chambers were hoarded thousands of sacred objects, many made of precious metal and studded with diamond, pearl, turquoise, agate, and coral.

Visitors to Lhasa are invariably awestruck by the sight of the Potala standing high above the city: its massive walls and countless windows, its many wings, and the long, steep staircases that are the only means of entry. How much more moved were Heinrich Harrer and Peter Aufschnaiter, who had escaped from a World War II prison camp in India. Wretched, impoverished, and pursued by bandits and authorities alike, the two fugitives had been months on the road to the Holy City. When they first spotted the Potala from a distance: "We felt inclined to go down on our knees like the pilgrims and touch the ground with our foreheads. Since leaving Kyirong we had covered over six hundred miles with the vision of this fabulous city ever in our mind's eye. We had marched for seventy days and rested only during five. That meant a daily average of almost ten miles. Forty-five days of our journey had been spent in crossing the Changtang—days full of hardship and unceasing struggle against cold, hunger, and danger. Now all that was forgotten as we gazed at the golden pinnacles—six miles more and we had reached our goal."

Harrer and Aufschnaiter did more than reach Lhasa, they lived there for nearly five years during the city's apogee. They learned fluent Tibetan, mingled with the aristocracy, and even attended the court of the Dalai Lama. I had read Harrer's book so many times that his impressions seemed almost like my own. Now, with Lhasa getting closer every day, all those sensations were more powerful than ever:

I smelled the pungent aroma of yak butter on the Barkhor, Lhasa's great market and principal pilgrim circuit, where traders, monks, and beggars jostle with pilgrims from all corners of the Buddhist world.

I heard the bellow of horns and the clamor of cymbals overlaid with a tapestry of chanting voices in the halls of the three great monasteries.

I tasted the dust kicked up by horses' hooves as the Dalai Lama, accompanied by all his court, servants, and guards, marched in procession from the Potala to his summer home at Norbulingka.

I felt the excitement on Lhasa's streets during Mönlam, when twenty thousand monks from surrounding monasteries and an untold number of pilgrims came to stay in the Holy City.

But these sensations, these images, all belonged to the past. Now I saw scenes of violence: shells falling on the Norbulingka . . . the Dalai Lama's secret escape to India from the very jaws of the Chinese invaders . . . imposition of alien rule on the people of Tibet . . . thousands of destitute, ill, and starving refugees pouring over the Himalayas . . . protests, imprisonment, forced labor, executions . . . and, most horrible of all, desecration of the one thing Tibetans hold dearest: Buddhism.

It was a terrible parade of images. Yet despite it all, somehow Lhasa had survived. Tibetans and their religion had survived. Shoppers and pilgrims still jostled on the Barkhor. Vendors still shouted their wares. Again there were prostrators at the Jokhang. Again pilgrims from outlying provinces—like those I had seen inching along the highway back in Kham— were coming to the Holy City. Despite everything, Lhasa lived.

I had an aching thirst to see it.

MIKE AND I were keyed up, for the car carrying us to Golmud was full of uniformed police. It was all too easy to imagine what business they were on. Just a few weeks ago, on May 23, the fortieth anniversary of China's "liberation" of Tibet had been observed. It had been a tense time in Lhasa, for the independence movement was determined to hold a demonstration against Chinese occupation, and the Chinese authorities were just as determined to prevent any disturbance from marring their "celebration."

In Hong Kong, Mike and I had anxiously followed the news as it filtered out of Tibet. None of it was good. The planned large demonstration was canceled at the last minute when its leaders were arrested, and the small demonstration that did take place was swiftly quashed. The very few foreigners staying in Lhasa then were either confined to their hotels or being escorted everywhere they went.

But now, several weeks later, we hoped that all the trouble was past. Perhaps Lhasa would even be opened to backpackers like us, so we wouldn't have to outfox the authorities. Five months before there had been an article in *China Daily* saying that Lhasa was to be opened to individual travelers. So far that announcement had been shown to be a lie, but perhaps the authorities in Beijing would change their minds and open Lhasa for real. It was a vain hope, especially as we sat on the train surrounded by policemen, for surely Golmud was not their final destination.

Evening came, and the sun dropped behind distant, jagged hills. Our compartment mates went to sleep. Mike and I lay in our upper berths talking through the night. In the darkness of the room, lulled by the train click-clacking over the endless Qinghai plateau, we spoke of places far away. Mike told me of growing up in Arkansas: about trout fishing, redneck cops, Sunday church, tickling his sister, running off with buddies to drink beer in a secret wooded place, and falling in love for the first time. His soft, melodious voice transported me, enveloped me in the scent of magnolia blossoms, laid me down in a field of tall, sweet grass somewhere in heaven on the other side of the world. His words were lazy cloud images promenading across the sky, the kiss of summer sweat rolling down my cheek, the taste of ice cubes floating in a tall glass of lemonade, the creak of a swinging chair in front of a stately white house ...

My own childhood—a bookish schoolgirl growing up in the suburbs of Chicago, the offspring of divorced middle-class parents—had nothing very idyllic, and I seldom thought of it. Some of the biggest things in my life didn't even begin until I came to California to attend Caltech. Outstanding among all the beginnings that came that year was my first day of karate practice, back when I was a college freshman—

"Mike, are you sure you want to hear this?"

"It's important to you, isn't it?"

"Yes, I guess it is."

"Then of *course* I want to hear it."

"As long as you're sure. I remember walking into the gym and seeing all the Caltech karate club seniors standing around stretching and talking to one another. It was casual but then again it wasn't. There was a kind of tension in the air, as though something big was about to happen. Then the instructor came in, and suddenly all conversation stopped. Everyone ran to make a line, with us beginners at the far end.

"It was a tradition at the Caltech club to start practice with a set of killer leg exercises. A lot of people show up to karate on the first day thinking that they're just going to dance around a little, hear a little philosophy, and then go home. The calisthenics give them a shock—a *big* shock. All the seniors shout at the first-timers to encourage them so they don't give up. It's a shock to be yelled at, but it's so hard that there's no way you'll get through it without someone pushing you.

"Maybe you can imagine what Caltech students are like— a bunch of klutzy, out-of-shape science nerds. That kind of person has an incredibly hard time when they jump into a really demanding sport like karate. But for that very reason, sometimes it turns out to be a kind of revelation for them. Even if you're already in good shape, though, that first day is still a shock. It's a little bit like special training—that four-day marathon I told you about, remember? They both change your whole outlook. There's an energy in the room that says, 'you don't give up here.

You *must* push yourself.' Even the most pigheaded people can feel it, and they finish the exercises. But after that first day, half of them don't ever come back.

"I was one of the clumsiest and most out-of-shape beginners Caltech ever had. At that first practice I thought I was going to pass out. Going home afterward I could hardly walk, my legs hurt so much. But I also remember, after it was over, listening to the instructor talk, and thinking: this is it. I'm home now. That was thirteen years ago."

"You know," Mike said, "I've always wanted to come to Asia. And I've always been curious about martial arts. Now I've come to Asia and I've met you. It must be fate."

GOLMUD TURNED OUT to be a rambling, pancake-flat town composed mainly of dust and concrete. Its streets were wide, its blocks were long, and its buildings were drab rectangles completely devoid of grace. Beyond the city limits buildings petered out into a sea of bone-dry sand and gravel broken only by sparse, scrubby plants clinging precariously to life. However, for Mike and me, there was one feature of Golmud's landscape that compensated for a lot of adversity: the Kunlun Shan to the south. We often gazed at the row of beckoning, snow-covered peaks imagining what lay beyond, for it was through these mountains that the road to Lhasa led.

Despite Golmud's grim appearance, there were a few good things about the city. Street markets abounded in fresh fruit, bread, and yogurt. The people, largely Muslim Chinese, were friendly and easygoing. Many foreigners had passed through Golmud when Tibet was wide open, so the locals were used to us. Golmud had none of the annoying murmurs of *lao wai* ("ol' foreigner") that had accompanied me as I walked down the streets of places like Litang. No wiseacres yelled "hel-lo!" or "oh-kay!" at my back. It was a good thing, because we would be here for a while.

Like the Ghost of Christmas Past, everywhere around Golmud were relics of the heyday of Tibet travel. About five years previously Lhasa visitors were not only unfettered by groups and guides, they were also trekking into the hills, even bringing in mountain bikes and kayaks. The hotel was full of signs in English meant for tourists on their way to the Holy City. Advice was scrawled on the bus-station wall: "Don't buy your ticket here; the other station is cheaper!" All were poignant reminders of the protests and violence that in 1987 had closed Tibet's doors.

Our first move in Golmud was to Public Security to ask about permits. I showed my photocopied announcement from *China Daily* saying that individual travelers were now permitted to go to Lhasa, but the lady in green was not in the least swayed. She knew her orders: that everyone going to Lhasa had to be part of a tour. Next we went to Golmud's tourist office, but their trips were absurdly expensive—two or three times the going rate in Chengdu; moreover, the minimum group size was four.

Having exhausted all means of getting to Lhasa legally, Mike and I got busy looking for trucks and drivers. There was no shortage of them, since Golmud's chief reason for being was as a transfer point for Lhasa-bound goods. Every morning and evening Golmud thundered with the sound of steel dinosaurs charging up and down the city streets.

There was one truck depot that looked especially promising, belonging to the Lhasa Transport Company. On the afternoon of the third day I targeted this place for my first foray. Mike had not come along on the theory that two foreigners were twice as conspicuous as one, and since I alone could speak Chinese, I had to be the one. Not confident of finding the right words in the heat of negotiation, I had a prospectus folded up small in my pocket that said where we wanted to go, how we wanted to get there, and how much we would pay. Now I had to find someone to show it to.

I went into a noodle shop opposite the depot, sat down,

and asked for a bowl of tea. While it was being brewed I scru-
tinized the restaurant proprietor. Maybe he could act as a
go-between. Was he trustworthy, or would he turn us in?
Rumor was that there was a bounty on foreigners trying to get
to Lhasa. He seemed like an amiable old man, but how could I
be sure? My palms were sweaty and I hardly tasted the tea. I
wished that Mike were here to help me decide what to do.

Just then a skinny Chinese man in a dust-streaked suit
jacket appeared at the doorway. Catching sight of me, he called
"Hello!" and walked over. "Can I sit here?" he asked in thickly
accented English. When I nodded he took the chair next to me
and said, "You are from what country?"

"America," I answered, preparing for the usual round of
questions. We chatted for a while. He seems nice enough, I
thought; perhaps he can help us. "What kind of work do you
do?" I asked him. "Are you a driver?"

"No, I build roads."

This was disappointing, but maybe he knew some drivers. I
looked around to see who was watching—nobody except the
old Muslim couple who owned the restaurant. I dug the note
out of my pocket and showed it to him. He snatched it from my
hand and spread it out on the table to study. In a flash the old
couple were behind him to read over his shoulder. Uh-oh, I
thought, but it was too late to stop now.

The man studied the paper carefully, frowning and mum-
bling to himself as his index finger moved over the characters. I
waited anxiously. At last he looked up and said, "I think I can
help you."

HALF AN HOUR later I was pedaling madly back to the hotel.
Once there, I turned in the rental bike and dashed upstairs to
our room. No Mike. Where could he be? The market! I ran
downstairs again, through the lobby, out the door, and down the
street to an alley where we bought our fruit and bread. Anx-

iously, I hunted through the crowds milling around the stalls. *Where is he?*

"Mike! MIKE!" He didn't hear me, so I pushed through the crowds to where he stood. "Mike! I got us a ride!"

"What? A ride?" Instantly he was alert. "Not so loud; someone might hear! You got us a ride already? Great work, Pam!"

"Yes, and we're leaving in one hour. Never mind the shopping, we've got to get our stuff together and get back to the depot."

We tore back to our room and began jamming things into our backpacks. "What kind of truck is it?" Mike asked as he scooped up hanging laundry.

"I haven't seen the truck yet, but we'll be riding in the back with a bunch of road workers. Twenty of them. And the leader—he's a really nice guy—even knows some English."

"Sounds perfect. He understands that he's got to hide us?"

"Yes, he says it'll be no problem."

When we arrived at the depot I led Mike to a place in the back where the twenty workers and their leader sat waiting in a large barn. There was some hay piled in the corner, and a scattering of small bags that held the workers' meager belongings. The men sprawled over the floor, leaning on one another like kittens in a litter. They stared at us with friendly curiosity but, like people who have spent their whole lives coping with circumstances beyond their control, they asked no questions.

For an hour or more Mike and I sat uncomfortably on the floor, contemplating with a mixture of exhilaration and dread the upcoming twenty-six-hour marathon of being bounced around in the back of a truck with twenty Chinese over 5,000-meter passes. We made small talk with the leader. The minutes dragged on. I got out the Lhasa guidebook and began reading it for the ump-teenth time. Finally the leader got up and went outside. When he returned he said, "Sorry, there is delay. Truck is broken. They are fixing now. We wait, okay?"

We waited another two hours, but still no truck. Mike and I stopped feeling excited; we were simply tired and wanted to be on the road. Finally the leader told us to return to our hotel. He would come in the morning.

The next morning we waited for our friend to come, but he did not. Our bags were packed; we were ready to go at a moment's notice, but there was no sign of him or his truck. We took turns going for meals so that one of us would always be at the hotel. The afternoon slowly passed.

Finally, at around six, our erstwhile Lhasa ticket came. So sorry, he said, the truck was still broken; he had decided to move his people in a bus instead. There was no way to hide us in a bus, he told us with genuine regret.

We thanked him for trying, and he left. Then we conferred. This was a setback to be sure, but we would not give up easily. The search would begin again from scratch. The first offer had come so readily, surely we would find another.

The next morning we hit the streets, both of us this time. Before long we found a group of driverish-looking men loitering by the roadside. One of them said, sure, he'd pick us up at five in the morning, day after tomorrow.

Another day and a half went by. We shopped for supplies and packed our bags. Tension built up anew. At four A.M. when my alarm went off, adrenaline surged through me. This was it! We were finally going to Lhasa! We went downstairs where, according to plan, Mike sat inside the lobby with our luggage, while I waited at the hotel gate.

The street was pitch dark and deadly still. I paced nervously up and down, humming songs to myself. Presently a truck appeared in the distance. My heart raced. Is this it? Headlights come toward me, blinding me; no way to see the driver's face. As the engine's roar grows louder my heart pounds faster, and I station myself prominently at the curb. But the truck doesn't stop. It roars onward, leaving me to stare sadly after it as it rounds the corner and disappears.

Trucks passed by again and again, but none of them ever stopped. At seven-thirty it was getting light. I heaved one last sigh and went inside. Mike was sitting in the lobby, looking utterly forlorn as hotel girls mopped the floor around him.

There was nothing to say.

UPSTAIRS IN OUR room Mike went to sleep. Overcome by melancholy, I got out my map and started looking at possible avenues of retreat. Some other travelers had told me about recently opened Tibetan towns in Qinghai province. The first of these places lay about two days east, on a little-used road that led to western Sichuan—and Kham. So much of Kham still unexplored! My mind flew back to the glory days of Tagong and Litang: nomads, tents, yaks, monasteries . . . Imaginary warriors on horseback came galloping into view, sweeping me off my feet and bearing me away into a fantasy world a million miles removed from horrible Golmud.

A few hours later Mike revived, and we considered our options. "It's obvious now what our big mistake was," he said. "We were idiots to wait here for that guy to pick us up. We should have gone to where his truck was and waited for *him*."

"You want to try again?"

"Do you?"

I thought about it. So many times I had heard it—from books, from fellow travelers, from Tibetans, even from a few Chinese: go to Lhasa, go to Lhasa, go to Lhasa. Mike and I had such magnificent plans for all the things we would do. To give up was simply intolerable.

"Yeah. Let's try one more time. I just can't stand the thought of failing."

"Neither can I," he agreed. "You know what that means, though. You've got to go out and find us another ride."

"I'm sorry, Mike, but I just loathe the thought of going back to that depot."

"I tell you, babe, I would do it if I could. It's just not fair that you're having to do all the dirty work. But that's the way it is. I can't speak Chinese. You've got to do it, Pam. And you can do it. You'll find us a ride. I believe in you."

After Mike's pep talk I felt a little better. That dog-eared piece of paper covered in my twisted, childish characters went back into my pocket. I hit the street once more. This time I found a van. The man whose vehicle it was said we would leave early the next morning.

Twelve hours later Mike and I were again arising in inky predawn blackness. We both knew that this was our last chance. It was now or never.

Outside it was raining lightly. Our boots went *snick-snick-snick* as we walked down Golmud's long, silent streets. The ordeal had gone on so long that both excitement and worry seemed pointless now. Besides, my mind was elsewhere. Back in Hong Kong I had gotten news from home that mentioned summer special training, giving the dates. As the month of June passed, a small portion of my consciousness had been devoted to ticking off the days, counting down until special training would start. Here I was, far, far away, sitting on this dusty heel of the world, entangled in a thicket of unfulfilled desire, far from California, far from karate practice, and far from special training— but still I couldn't get it out of my mind. For the first time since I had begun karate, I would miss it.

As Mike and I walked in silence, I looked at my watch and calculated back to California time. And with a pang that was neither homesickness nor longing but just a kind of mystical awareness, I realized that the wait was over.

Soon they would begin.

14

RELEASE

"MIKE, I'VE GOT something on my mind. Can I tell you about it?"

"Of course. What are friends for? Is it about this ride?"

"No, it's got nothing to do with going to Lhasa. It's something completely different. Remember how I told you about special training?"

"That's where you go off with your karate friends and go crazy for a few days, isn't it?"

"Right. It's happening right now. I found out the date when I called home from Hong Kong. I know the schedule—they do things the same way every year—so I know exactly what they're doing right now, this very second. It's on the other side of the world, but it's so real I can *feel* it."

"What are they doing?"

"Well, the practices haven't started yet, but people are starting to arrive. They're at a small private school in the foothills near L.A., overlooking the ocean. It's a beautiful place, and isolated from the rest of the world—good for a special training. You can keep your mind focused, and there's less temptation to run away in the middle of it. That's one of the rules: you can't leave. The other rules are: no sex, no drugs, no alcohol—nothing to distract your mind or weaken your practice.

"Anyway, right now people are walking into an old-fashioned dining room to register. It's like a big old family reunion, with all the seniors doing a lot of handshaking and backslapping and catching up. But underneath the bonhomie there's an edge, because everyone is keyed up over what's coming."

WE HAD ARRIVED at the depot. Everything was quiet. It was so early that the gates were still closed and locked. Rain continued to fall lightly. Mike found a sheltered place under the overhang of a nearby building and we settled down to wait.

A few trucks came down the road, invisible but for their headlights probing timidly through the drizzle. They rumbled past us, heading south. From my endless pouring over maps I knew exactly where they were going: the mountain ranges, the towns, the passes. Depending on road and vehicle condition, it would be a two-day journey over some of the most desolate terrain in the world. We watched the lights recede into the distance.

"Maybe we should forget about that van and try flagging down one of these trucks," said Mike.

"Maybe we should," I answered. Neither of us moved. After a minute or so another truck went by. "Let's wait a bit longer and see if our driver turns up. It's almost time."

"Okay."

So we waited. After a time an old man came to open the front gate. We went inside and walked to the back of the compound where the van was parked. There was no sign of the driver. We put down our packs and waited. An hour or two passed. The rain ceased and the sky lightened, revealing a sodden yard paved with soupy mud and a little gravel. A few mud-spattered trucks were parked here and there. Mike and I stayed in the back, trying to conceal ourselves in case any "enemy agents" were about.

Around midmorning a Chinese man came to join us. He said that he, too, was going to Lhasa and had arranged to ride in this same van. Here was tangible evidence that the van was really going. Mike and I began to feel more optimistic. The three of us waited together for another hour. Someone came to tell us that the driver was still sleeping, but that soon he would join us.

In between pacing back and forth and looking at our watches, Mike and I fumed about the inconsiderate habits of Chinese. Why did they always give wildly inaccurate answers when asked what time something was going to happen? We should have been on the road hours ago. It was exasperating, but there was nothing we could do. By now most of the other trucks had left.

The morning wore on. At last the man with whom I had made the arrangements appeared. He was not nearly so friendly as he had been yesterday. He said that there had been a change of plans. The van would not be leaving today after all, and anyway, he was not the driver, so he couldn't promise that we would ride with them tomorrow when they did leave. *That* decision was still under discussion, not yet settled. We should come again tomorrow to ask.

Mike and I looked at each other in despair: Screwed again!

There were still a few trucks parked around the compound. As a last-ditch effort we made the rounds of all the drivers, but they all shook their heads no.

Slowly, we walked the long way back to the hotel.

MIKE THREW HIS pack down on his bed in disgust. "That's it," he said, with finality. "The handwriting's on the wall. The *Gonganju* must be on to us. I'll bet they've been on to us for days, and they've been warning off all the drivers. It's hopeless."

We sat glumly for a while in silence. I pulled out the article from *China Daily*—the one saying that Lhasa was now open to individual tourists—and morosely scanned the lines. They seemed nothing more than a monstrous joke.

Mike saw the paper in my hand and said, "That article is the most hypocritical thing I ever saw. I can't believe that they would publish such a blatant lie. And that woman at Public Security looked at it and denied it was true—the word of her own government. How can she live with herself?"

"It's not her fault. She's just doing what she's told."

"And that girl at the travel office. We've been in there twice, and every time we ask, the rules for a tour to Lhasa change. She looks you right in the eye and says that the minimum group size is six, when last time she said it was four. It's an insult to our intelligence."

"I guess inconsistency doesn't bother them the way it bothers you."

Mike jumped to his feet. "You're *always* defending them!" he cried. "Whose side are you on, anyway?"

My disappointment welled up uncontrollably, and I fired back, "I'm on our side, of course! But I can see their side, too. You just don't have any compassion. You ought to try to understand their point of view."

"Whaddaya mean I don't have any compassion! That's not true! How can you say that?" Mike was livid now, and stalking angry circles around the room.

"Wait, I take that back!" I said quickly, horrified by what I had done. "I apologize. That was an unfair thing to say. But you really ought to put yourself in their shoes. Maybe then you'd understand why they act the way they do."

"What's there to understand? They're lying. It's as simple as that. How can you forgive them?"

"Maybe if you knew more about China, you wouldn't be so quick to judge. If you had lived through the Cultural Revolution when everyone in the whole damn country had to turn around and spit on the things that were most important to them—like religion and family and education; if you had been put through struggle sessions where you had to condemn your own parents in order to survive; if you had had to live with a government that changed its policies every week—so that if you didn't follow along and mouth the latest slogans, then maybe a bunch of Red Guards would come to your house and take everything you owned; if you had lived through all that, then maybe truth and consistency wouldn't be so important to you. Not as important as survival, anyway."

At these words Mike's anger subsided. We both realized that we weren't upset with each other, just with failing. The argument fizzled to a close, and soon we were back at analyzing what had transpired at the depot and cursing Beijing's devious policies. Mike wanted revenge, to expose Beijing's perfidy to the world. We talked of writing to newspapers, trying to make a stir; but in the end we concluded: what would be the point? Who really cares if foreigners can go to Lhasa or not? Would anybody be really surprised to find out that *China Daily* is riddled with untruths? No, there was nothing to do but lick our wounds and move on. As the Chinese say, we had to *chi ku*—"eat bitter."

This day marked the parting of our ways, for now Mike was determined to get out of China for good. We had expected to spend many more weeks together, putting into action all our plans and dreams, but it was not to be. I felt as though a child of mine had died. Together we went to the bus station to buy our tickets, his to the northwest toward the Pakistan border, and mine to the east, the first leg of the journey back to Kham.

That evening we turned in early. But I was heartsick knowing that after tomorrow I would no longer have Mike to share my confidences, so I kept him up with conversation late into the night. We talked about this and that, his answers gradually growing shorter and fainter as he drifted off to sleep.

On the verge of surrendering to sleep myself, I glanced at my watch, and was suddenly seized with a powerful awareness of the special training now occurring on the other side of the world. It was a peculiar form of mental transportation, to experience another place so completely and precisely. It jolted me awake. "Mike."

"Yes?" came the mumbled voice.

"Right now—at this very *moment*—at special training they're getting up for the first practice. I really need to talk about it. Do you mind?"

He rolled over. "Go ahead."

That was all I needed. A torrent of memories began to pour out—in exactly what words I no longer know, but the substance of the delivery was this:

"It's five o'clock in the morning over there. It's pitch dark outside, but a few black belts are walking down the hallways of the dorms, throwing open doors and switching on lights, waking up everyone for the first practice. A lot of the juniors have been lying awake all night, petrified at what's coming; but no matter how awful they feel, there's no turning back now. They put on their uniforms and go outside.

"Now they're assembling on the driveway: three hundred white-suited figures, lining up in order of seniority from the oldest old-timer at one end to the greenest white belt at the other. It's a little cold, and the grit on the driveway hurts your bare feet, so everyone walks gingerly to their places. At one end of the line are the highest black belts. They are a little bit macho the way they stand around chatting and making wry jokes. The seniors have been comrades-in-arms for decades, so they are bound together by deep affection and mutual respect. It's inspiring to stand shoulder to shoulder with such people, preparing mentally for the battle ahead.

"At the other end of the line are the white belts. They're scared stiff. They stand like pale, wide-eyed zombies, saying nothing. After all the preparation and buildup, they're in shock that special training is actually beginning.

"When everyone is assembled they'll start the warm-up run. The distance is not so far—about two miles—but very steep: first down to the bottom of the road, then all the way back up, over a ridge, and down to the athletic field. It's beginning to get light now, and it's quite a sight to see three hundred white ghosts pouring down the hill as if a dam suddenly burst. The pavement is rough and it chews at your feet; that's why, from time immemorial, we've called that road 'Hamburger Hill.'

"I'm not a very good runner, and at my first special training, I had a really hard time on that hill. My chest constricted and I was wheezing so hard I couldn't get enough oxygen. But all the seniors who were passing me kept telling me not to give up, and somehow I made it. Just getting up Hamburger Hill on the first day was a big victory for me.

"By now they've probably finished the run. Everyone is coming down onto the field. It's soft and grassy and wet with dew—a real pleasure under your feet after that horrible road. Everyone runs in a big circle around the perimeter until the last people come in. Then the leader, who is standing in the center of the great white vortex, shouts *YA-ME!* at the top of his lungs, and the vortex collapses into mixed-up pandemonium as everyone dashes to form lines for meditation.

"By now they're probably in seiza—that's kneeling in traditional Japanese fashion. Far away to the front, sitting in front of this great army, is the lone figure of the leader. He is a beautiful and inspiring sight, his form so clean and white and perfect against a sea of grass.

"After meditation he makes a short speech, something like: *'Now we begin Shotokan Karate of America Summer Special Training. Put everything but special training outside your mind and push yourself from beginning to end!'*

"The first practice is *kihon*—that is, basic blocks, punches, and kicks, more than a thousand of them altogether. Everyone makes an enormous grid across the field, and moves together to a shouted count of one of the black belts.

"Ideally, each technique should be delivered with all your strength, as if your life depends on it. When you have so many people expressing their strongest mentality all at once, the energy that comes out is simply incredible. To be in the middle of it, surrounded by kiais—that's a method of explosive breathing, sort of like a shout—it's exhilarating, sublime. If you can forget the problems you left behind at home, forget the guy next to you, forget your ego, forget your sore feet and how tired you are, and just become one with the technique—well, that's what it's all about. . . ."

But now Mike was sound asleep.

EARLY THE NEXT morning I went with Mike in a taxi to the bus station to see him off. The only sound on the empty streets of Golmud was the loud putt-putt-putt of the taxi's tiny engine as it blazed past shuttered shops and deserted markets. Inside the waiting room a few bleary-eyed Muslims sat on benches. Mike and I sat down among them. I looked at my watch. "You want to know what's happening now?"

If I had stopped to think, I would have marveled that Mike could be so drawn into this world of mine on the other side of the globe, a place he had never been, people he had never known. Perhaps it was the disappointment of not going to Lhasa that made him yearn for escape just as I did; perhaps it was his curiosity about martial arts and his natural intensity that interested him in special training—or maybe he was just humoring me. At any rate, he said simply, "Let's hear it."

"It's afternoon, and hot. The sun is blazing. It's time for *ten no kata* practice. The name means 'kata of heaven,' although we don't really consider it a proper kata; it's a drill where we make block-attack combinations like those used in sparring. Three hundred people is too many for everyone to do this practice together, so they divide everyone into groups according to rank. Each group gets its own senior black belt leader and a team of assistant leaders.

"The white belt group is great because, although they're

not so skillful, they've got a naive, jubilant kind of energy. They stand in a big circle, a fiery crucible in whose center are the leader and his assistants. To the rhythm of a shouted count, the white belts aim attacks at the seniors. The two sides don't ever touch, but the juniors' mentality is amplified and reflected back by the seniors' blazing techniques. People feed on one another's energy, challenging one another to push harder, to *kiai* louder.

"*Ten no kata* is good sweaty exercise and not very complicated, so everyone likes this practice. I remember when I was a white belt how inspiring the seniors were, how whenever I started feeling tired suddenly there would be a black belt in front of me just burning through those combinations like they were nothing—and with fantastic form, too. And no matter how exhausted I was, with that kind of inspiration I was always able to break through to some new level."

There was silence for a minute while each of us dwelt in our own worlds. Then Mike said, "Tell me something, Pam."

"What?"

"When you go back to Kham, are you going to try again for Lhasa? You can do it, you know, on the Sichuan-Tibet highway—the same road that Rob and Pierre and I were traveling on just before we met you in Tagong."

Ever since I had plotted my retreat to Kham, that tempting east-west highway had been very much on my mind. That I would try again for Lhasa was certain. "Yes, Mike, of course I'll try again."

"Promise?"

"Promise."

"Good." Mike looked at me very hard. "You've *got* to make it, Pam. Do it for me."

The bus arrived. We were distracted by the confusion of everyone surging toward the vehicle, hoisting luggage to the roof, then jostling their way on board. Finally Mike was the last one standing on the pavement. The driver started the engine.

This was good-bye at last, but I could hardly stand to let him go. We embraced, unmindful of the staring Chinese around us. Then he turned to climb the dark, narrow steps.

Not wanting to prolong the agony of his departure, I left the station and began plodding back to the hotel. My heart was aching and my head was swimming. It was bad enough that we failed to reach Lhasa, but to lose my best and only friend at the same time made me unutterably sad. The road to Kham was long and full of obstacles—who knew if I would ever get there? And even if I did what if I found no warriors there? What if I failed again to get to Lhasa?

What would I have to show for this long journey then?

Walking down the empty street, in the distance I heard a *hhhrrrmmm* behind me—Mike's bus approaching. A minute later the vehicle caught up and passed me, leaving a stinking cloud of fumes in its wake. As the bus accelerated, I saw a blond-haired figure hanging out the rear window. Hat in hand, he was waving and shouting, "You'll make it, Pam! You'll make it!" as the bus bore him swiftly out of sight.

A FEW HOURS later I was in a different bus, heading in a different direction. It was a splendid ride, a balm for my sorrowing soul. Dramatic crags crouched like great gnarled dinosaurs over the road; at other times we bee-lined across miles of sandy waste. Occasionally we bored through sleepy desert towns of mud-and-wattle houses, wispy barefoot children, and regiments of poplars growing arrow-straight by the roadside. Everything was baked to dust by the relentless summer heat.

The sun set and still the bus rolled on. We were going to continue all night, I realized, not stopping until we were in Xining. Getting into my tiny bus seat had been like climbing into the cockpit of a jet fighter, and now I couldn't move. The chair's back didn't recline, and with so much luggage everywhere my feet barely fit into a little pocket of space below, forcing my knees into a painfully acute angle. So began a long uncomfortable night.

When the light was totally gone, the land became an endless moonscape of rocks and sand reeling past my window. It hadn't been dark long when we passed by a few open-air restaurants lit by hanging lightbulbs. The bus didn't stop, but as the restaurants flashed by, enough of their light shone through the window that for a moment I could see my watch. Automatically, I calculated California time, and the answer snatched me out of China and tossed me on that grassy field at special training. There was no one to talk to now, but a voice in my head began to speak as if Mike sat beside me:

"*It's just before dawn, and time for* kibadachi, *the most dreaded of all practices. By now they've finished Hamburger Hill, and they've finished stretching. The groups are forming circles. A signal comes to get ready; then the command:* Kamae!

"*The air is so tense and the command so ferocious, that you expect the field to suddenly detonate with action. But all that happens is that everyone simply bends their knees to assume a semisquatting posture. This is* kibadachi, *horseriding stance. We'll stay here, motionless, for one and a half hours.*

"*They must have started by now. I can see the faces, rings of them facing inward. People's legs are shaking, sweat dripping, expressions alternately steeled and struggling, torsos drifting higher or lower according to the tide of battle—lower when the mind is strong, higher when in retreat, but never lower than knees' height—the ideal* kibadachi *form.*

"*Today the seniors are devils, pushing me through my pain and my self-imposed limits.* Wake up! *they say, amplifying the inner voice that I so desperately want to ignore.* Bend your knees *they say, forcing me to push my aching legs into a deeper, more powerful stance. What's wrong with you? Don't baby yourself. Stop making excuses; you're not even close to passing out.* Face yourself!

"*Once I saw someone truly fearless, someone who plunged into* kibadachi *practice like a battle to the death. It was unforgettable. In* kibadachi, *ideally you should feel calm, immutably rooted to the earth, yet at the same time coiled to spring like a tiger. Breathing comes slowly, powerfully, from the lower abdomen. The guy was all of that, an oaken Buddha—low, strong, and utterly imperturbable. He stood that way for over an hour before he passed out. . . ."*

PINCHED IN THE SEAT's viselike grip, my legs throbbed. My mind was caught, too: between the surreal reality of the desert moonscape outside and the intoxicating unreality of special training on the other side of the world. The bus rattled on to Xining. When at last we entered the city's outskirts, a blue-gray twilight heralded the coming day. But instead of waking me from my dream, the sight of mud-walled farmhouses stepping out from dusky gloom seemed even more fantastic than the netherworlds in which I had been dwelling all night.

At the Xining bus station I pried my aching bones out of that wretched seat, limped down the bus steps, and a minute later nearly fell from the weight of my backpack when a wiry Muslim handed it down to me from the roof. I felt like the red-haired adventurer in H.G. Wells's *The Time Machine* who, near the end of the story, escapes to his own time, worn and haggard from his just-fought battle with the ogre-ish Morlocks. But instead of returning to a comfortable English parlor full of familiar faces, I would be resetting my machine to another destination. I went straight to a window and bought a ticket for the next bus south.

And as I sat on the steps of the station waiting for my bus, three hundred white figures were churning out furious kicks under an afternoon sun.

The bus to Gonghe was full of Tibetans. In the first hour we left Xining behind and drove up onto endless mounds of grass—an impressionist's canvas of a million green brush strokes under a soft white light. For days I had seen nothing but cutting sun and parched sand. How could this place be so soft, so green?

Truly, my time machine had launched me into a wholly different world.

We climbed higher and higher. At around 3,000 meters
above sea level, yak appeared. If I had been more than
half-awake, I would have rejoiced at the sight of those dumb
beasts, for they meant I had at last returned to the high plateau.

Just after noon we pulled into Gonghe, the first overnight
stop on the road south. It had been a marathon twenty-
four-hour journey. I went straight for the nearest hotel and went
to bed. But before I drifted off to sleep, in my addled head the
voice started once more:

*"It's half an hour before midnight, and outside everything is still.
Inside, the wake-up committee is moving down the dormitory hallways,
rousing everyone from their exhausted sleep. It's time to get up and do
one thousand oizuki. That's a front lunging punch, the first technique
a beginner learns, the last an expert masters—the most subtle and
demanding one of them all. A perfect oizuki is considered by many to be
an unattainable ideal, the Holy Grail of karate. It's something to spend
a lifetime on.*

*"By now everyone's on the field, and they've begun the practice.
Midnight practice is different from the others. For this one the kiai
(explosive breathing) is silent. It's like olden times in Okinawa, when
karate students trained in secret in the dead of night to avoid detection
by their Japanese overlords. Even though there are hundreds of people
around, in the darkness you feel perfectly alone. All you hear is the distant voice of someone counting and the concentrated exhalations of three
hundred people destroying three hundred invisible enemies.*

*"For some reason—perhaps it's the quiet and the solitude—this
practice is wonderfully cleansing. When they finish they will meditate
briefly, sitting in seiza on the cool grass. Then they'll walk silently up the
paths to their rooms, fall into bed, and plunge into a deep, dreamless,
sleep. . . ."*

While I slept, the folks in California rose again to make a
kata practice against the rising sun. Hours later, when the sun
came around to my side of the world and touched my hotel

room window, a battle was being fought on the grassy field. When I awoke I could almost hear their *kiais*.

"*They're in the* kumite *practice now—that's sparring. After* kibadachi, *this session is the one everyone fears. They begin by making two long lines, each person facing someone opposite. The lines stretch so far that you can't even see all the people you're going to spar with before the practice is over. At the leader's signal, they fight. It's a prearranged form of sparring: the attacker is allowed exactly three* oizuki *to the stomach, so the defender's task is manageable. He is allowed one counterpunch, but it must stop just short of touching. The attacker's three punches, on the other hand, are completely real—if you don't block or get out of the way you'll likely be knocked out.*

"*Good* kumite *is beautiful to watch, but it's hard to spot it in the pandemonium that is usual for this practice. More likely what you'll notice is the bloody faces and bruised limbs, the punches that go wild, and the people falling all over one another. It looks utterly savage.*

"*White belts are wild-eyed, snaking their fists in from unpredictable directions. Brown belts stomp across the grass like enraged bulls. Black belts operate with surgical precision—at least in the beginning; but as time goes on the edges are worn off their fancy footwork. After twenty or thirty opponents, a bulletin flashes across my mind: 'God, this is hard,' or 'damn I'm tired,' or 'how much longer?' But then the seniors' voices override: Tight your mind! Now is when practice really starts!*

"*Here comes a big bad brown belt. He is hungry. This is his finest hour. He wants to smack me, and he doesn't care much for the rules. His eyes are intense, burning. He glories in his awakening power.*

"*Here comes a gray-haired man with a paunch. He's not quick. His blocks don't work. His attacks don't work either. He's been fighting in the sun for over an hour, and now he's looking faint. At the end of each engagement I find myself staring down his red throat as he* kiais, *his eyes wide, his hair on end. We all salute this kind of courage. For him I measure out my cleanest, straightest punches.*

"*Here comes a tiny white belt woman. Her head barely comes up to my chin. When it's her turn to attack she steps and punches, but she's so small her knuckles can't possibly reach me. When I attack her I could* almost put my fists through her body up to my elbows. How does she evade my punches? How on earth did she manage with her last opponent, the black belt next to me in line, a monster nearly twice her height? She is crying from the ceaseless horror of it all, but fights on, dancing around my fists, her spirit and power and feeling exploding like a grenade in my face when it's time for her to counter. It would be an insult to show her any mercy.

"All the while I listen for the call: yame! Like a joyfully clanging bell, it marks successful completion of one more unit of survival. Stop. Return to our places. Briefly we all become people again instead of frenzied battle machines. Bow thankfully: you gave me a clean feeling, you didn't cheat, you helped me express my best, and I didn't die—thank you!

"Near the end of the practice black belts face their colleagues, and I meet my senior José. From the beginning, when we bow, there is a crystal clarity that expunges all extraneous thought. Mindfully, he makes a preparing stance. There he waits, watching me for an instant of weakness. Meanwhile I stand ready for his attack; when it comes—no, before it comes—I must preempt with a devastating counter. But if my mind wanders for even an instant, if he catches me unawares—then all is lost.

"Together we wait, possessed by the emptiness of complete expectation, everything fallen away but simply being. Each watches the other for some minuscule break: a flickering eyelash, a fleeting thought, a carelessly taken breath—anything that heralds momentary weakness. This moment is the largest, the most real, the most intimate, the most honest, when everything is stripped away. Together we stand at the brink of a cliff, ready to plunge into nothingness.

"There is no greater mark of respect—and love!—than the best, cleanest, most ferocious attack, utterly free from any taint of ego. A successful defense is like bursting through the gate of heaven—glorious! Then we change roles and I return his favor. There is a link between us, like two atomic particles in mutual orbit, connected by a powerful, polarizing force that pulls us together again and again, avoiding destructive collision by the slenderest of margins. It is a cosmic dance.

"The command comes to stop and suddenly our living umbilical is severed, an abrupt power failure that leaves me still quivering and hungry. Carefully, mindfully, we withdraw to a safe distance. The engagement is completed with a bow.

"I note with relief that I have escaped unscathed—this time. On to the next opponent.

"When kumite *is over, it's like being born again, everyone is so happy."*

15

RETURN TO KHAM

TWO WEEKS LATER, I was in Kham.

I was riding on a crest of euphoria, for the journey had been glorious beyond all expectation. It was summer, and monsoon rains were at last feeding the thirsty soil of the plateau. From Gonghe across the Bayan Har Mountains, all the way to the Sichuan provincial border was one immense velvet carpet of wet grass and wildflowers. Now I understood why the province was called *Qinghai* ("green sea"), for it seemed as if a colossal ocean had been abruptly stilled, then an angel had flown overhead, scattering seed on the frozen waves to detonate into thick, exuberant life.

The road had taken me through Golok territory, an area between Amdo and Kham. Golok Tibetans were notorious in former times as ruthless brigands, rivaling even the Khampas in their reputation for lawlessness. Bandits the Golokpas might once have been, but to me they were gentle as children—like one old man in Serxu who literally jumped up and down for joy as I snapped his picture, though he knew I had no photo nor anything else to give him.

If the land was enchanting for its people, it was doubly so for its wildflowers. Blooms burst out everywhere: carnations, poppies, sandwort, androsace, asters, knotweed, bellflowers, mustard, potentilla, edelweiss and more, some probably unnamed in any language. And these flowers were not the lolling, foppish creatures of lowland meadows; they were tough, rambunctious little soldiers swarming over the plateau, overrunning it. In every direction the alpine flower bed stretched to the horizon and beyond, bearing millions upon millions of blossoms standing faces to the sky. As if every flower was singing, the land echoed with a resounding chorus of wild and limitless beauty.

The bus left me in Maniganggo, a tiny crossroads town where the back road from Qinghai joins the Sichuan-Tibet thoroughfare. At last I was back in Kham, but still I had further to go.

From Maniganggo I went west, riding in the back of a pickup truck beneath a ridge of glacier-laden peaks. The road ascended to where there was neither grass nor dirt, only barren stone. We groaned and bumped over a ridge, then went down, down, down. The road was so perilously crumbly that I stayed poised to leap clear in case the highway should dissolve beneath us. At last we descended into a valley soft with grass and pines—one of the many fertile bowers tucked into the cracks of Kham. Thick pine forests climbed up the slopes, and abundant summer rain had fed a tangle of undergrowth in the valley bottom. With greenery everywhere I looked, the place indeed seemed like a garden of Eden.

THIS WAS THE ancient Derge[20] Kingdom, historically the cultural center of Kham. Inhabitants of Derge's valleys are barley farmers, living in stout two-story houses of logs and rammed earth. With flowerpots set upon the balustrades and windows graced with lacy wooden lattices, Derge seemed a charming, prosperous place.

20. "Derge" is the usual Romanization of the Tibetan name, but local pronounciation has it rhyming with "reggae." The Chinese name is Dege, which rhymes with "sugar" without the "r."

I stayed two days in Derge town, a rough-and-tumble out-post set in a crack between mountains. It is an out-of-the-way place as most people think of places, but still one that draws a share of visitors. The attraction is Derge's famous printing house, one of the last remaining workshops in Tibet where sutras are still produced. Although work ceased during the Cultural Revolution, now it is back in operation, shipping its product all over the Buddhist world.

Derge straddles the fast-flowing Serqu River as it rollicks westward to meet the Yangtze a few dozen kilometers downstream. Now, in the height of the summer trading season, Derge's streets were full of swashbuckling Khampas. But I could not stay here long; the town's *Gonganju* were aware of my presence and I didn't want to test their patience. Besides, I had other plans.

The morning of the third day found me hiking west out of town. I was headed in the direction of Lhasa, some 1,500 kilometers down the road, but Lhasa was not my destination. I had been given vague but intriguing directions to a monastery in the mountains.

It was still dark as I walked for half an hour or so to get clear of the town and official eyes. Parallel to the road, the Serqu River roared west, its mud-laden waters boiling over the banks and flooding adjacent patches of grass. Trees extended their green arms over my head. When I was well out of town, I set my pack down by the highway to wait for passing trucks.

Traffic on this road was infrequent, and though I waited for an hour or so, no one stopped to offer a lift. Then a pair of figures came walking down the road: two Tibetan girls in long black *chubas*. One had a ribbon of magenta yarn studded with turquoise woven in her long black hair. The other girl was smaller and more plainly attired. She was pushing a bicycle.

"Hello!" said the tall one with a giggle—perhaps laughing at the patent absurdity of speaking to a foreigner. They stopped to look me over. "Where are you going?" she said in thickly accented Chinese.

"Babang Gonpa."

"Where?"

I repeated the name.

"Babang? Babang?" The two looked at each other. "Where's that?"

Haltingly I tried to explain where it was. Their Chinese was if anything worse than mine, and my few words of Lhasa Tibetan didn't help much. But at last a light dawned in their faces. "Palpung!" they exclaimed.

Evidently "Babang" was the Chinese pronunciation of the monastery's Tibetan name.[21] "Yes, Palpung Gonpa," I said.

"How are you getting there?"

"I'm waiting for a truck."

"Ah." They nodded. Hitchhiking was a normal if unreliable means of transport in this area. "How much you pay?"

"Umm, I don't know. How about forty yuan—is that enough?"

They conferred together in whispered Tibetan, then one of them turned to speak to me. "Trucks are very few here. There are no more trucks today. Why don't you come with us on a bicycle?"

"Bicycle?"

"Yes. We have two bicycles. One to carry you, one to carry your bag. How about it?"

I looked at the two girls. They had stopped giggling, and now looked quite serious. Could they really mean it? They were rather small: a head shorter than me, and slender. But Tibetans are a tough breed. "You can really take me? Are you sure? I'm very heavy, you know."

One of them looked doubtful, but the other exclaimed, "Oh yes, no problem!"

"How much money do you want?"

---

21. "Palpung" is the standard transliteration, but the way they pronounced it sounded more like "Pepung" with two soft p's.

"You pay forty yuan and we'll take you. It's easy, no problem at all." Now they were both caught up in the joke; their eyes were overflowing with merriment. I suspected that forty yuan was far above the going rate, and that I was being had. Anne had warned me about doing business with Khampas: "They've been trading goods across the plateau for centuries," she had said. "No one can match them when it comes to bargaining."

"Forty? That's far too much! Twenty yuan."

"Twenty is not enough. We have to go all the way out and then come all the way back. It'll take all day. Thirty-five yuan."

"Thirty."

Another consultation. "Okay, thirty," they agreed.

I knew that I was still being taken. But what the heck. To go with these two girls on their bicycles would be fun. Besides, if I didn't go with them, I might have to wait all day for a ride.

The girls seemed ready to explode with amusement. One of them said, "Come with us. We'll go to my house and get the other bicycle."

So off we went, the three of us marching down the road. They laughed and asked me questions and laughed some more and chattered to each other in the Derge dialect. We walked a few hundred meters further down the road, then turned off onto a narrow dirt path that snaked between plots of barley, to where a house stood built against a tree-shaded slope.

It was not one of the Derge's fancy log houses, but a plain adobe structure arranged in two stories, the second floor opening out onto a veranda. The two girls began hallooing, and a woman came out and beckoned us up. Access to the living quarters was by a notched-log ladder leading to the second floor.

Soon we were all sitting on the clay floor of the veranda having tea and *tsampa*. The women all had a good giggle over my *tsampa*-kneading ineptitude, but at least I had no problem swallowing a bowlful of the stuff. When it was time to leave, one of the girls brought another bike out of the house. Cycle slung over her shoulder, she zipped down the log ladder with impressive ease. We picked up the other bike and headed for the highway. It took a few minutes to lash my pack to the rear rack, but at last all was ready.

Many times I had seen Chinese (and Tibetan) cyclists carrying passengers on the rear, and so I knew how the passenger is supposed to mount. She (for it's usually a she) stands by the roadside while the pedaler gets a running start, then jumps on the bike as it flies past. Everyone in China over the age of twelve or thirteen has perfected this skill, and it's taken quite for granted. I tried to act nonchalant, as if we Americans do this all the time, but it was with not a little trepidation that I regarded my tiny chauffeur pedaling toward me. Carefully, I aimed my backside, waited until what seemed like the appropriate instant, crossed my fingers, and jumped.

The girl let out a yelp; the bike dipped and swerved, coming nearly off the road—luckily there was no passing traffic at that moment—before both recovered gamely. Meanwhile I was precariously perched with my rear half on, half off the rack, desperately clawing for something to hang on to. Finally I grabbed the rack itself, and by a series of small, quick adjustments—each one making the bike lurch alarmingly—I slid my posterior into place. We were off and rolling.

It was a perfect summer day, with bright sun trickling down through the leafy branches that overhung the highway. After one or two kilometers it became obvious that the only reason we were making any headway at all was that most of the time the highway slanted downhill. From the top of each hill we'd roll until the road leveled out, then the girl would have to start pedaling like mad; but it wouldn't be long before all our momentum was used up and I had to hop off and walk.

After a while we began switching around; first the girls traded bikes; then I took a turn at the pedals. We saw few people, but they all gaped in amazement at the preposterous sight of one foreigner, two giggling Tibetans, and a lumpy blue bundle piled on top of two bicycles. It was embarrassing—a fully grown woman being carried by a tiny Tibetan girl. But they didn't mind; to them it was all a lark.

After a couple of hours we came to a *chörten* marking the turnoff. There we left the Serqu River and turned onto a rutted path of gravel and mud. It was uphill and riding was impossible, so we began to walk. The valley was narrow and intimate, with a few houses, jewel-like meadows, and an icy brook babbling down from the highlands. After three or four kilometers the path narrowed and turned away from the stream, climbing into thick underbrush.

The girls informed me that they would go no further. There was no more road. We rested a minute, but soon they were up again, eager to get their money and set off for home. I gave it to them, we said our good-byes, and they disappeared.

SO WHAT NOW? It was a pretty place. I considered pitching my tent by the stream, but first I walked up the path to check out the faint outlines of a building I had glimpsed through the trees.

It was indeed a house, and in front of it were half a dozen people standing around three horses loaded with bulky sacks. I approached the nearest man, a young Tibetan with curly hair under a gray felt hat, but before I could open my mouth, they all turned and noticed me.

"How do you do!" cried the man jovially in English, and everyone burst out laughing.

I was dumbfounded. "You speak English?" I asked in Chinese, and they laughed even harder.

"No, no! He's just joking," the others said. "Who are you? Where are you from?"

"I'm American. I'm going to Palpung." There was a general hubbub while they absorbed this information. "Are you people going to Palpung, too?"

"Yes. We're making a pilgrimage."

"Can I put my pack on one of your horses?"

"They're not *our* horses. You'll have to ask *him*," he said, gesturing toward a man in a maroon *chuba* who was adjusting a girth on one of the animals. I approached the man and began to dicker. Before long we agreed on a price of twenty yuan. My pack was quickly lashed on top of one of the loads; then we all set out walking.

The trail was steep, and the elevation—about 3,100 meters at the start—made it no easier. Before long I began to have grave misgivings about this trek. In the last few weeks I'd had no regular exercise beyond walking around Golmud; I'd just had the flu for a week in Golok territory; and now I was woefully out of shape. The others were chattering and laughing while I was panting and heaving. They wandered all over the trail, racing ahead to keep the horses in line, picking flowers, and hurtling stones over precipices while I plodded slowly in the rear. But it was too late to turn back now.

The Tibetans were from Derge. They dressed in city clothes, wore their hair modishly short, and spoke Chinese as easily as Tibetan; but they still observed the precepts of their ancestors. When we passed a *mani* wall—a stone cairn in the middle of the path—they each picked up a pebble to toss onto the pile as they filed past. Occasionally one of them stopped to lift a worm from the trail and lay it safely aside so that it wouldn't get trodden on.[22]

The mischievous fellow in the felt hat who had said "How do you do!" was the tallest of the group, in his late twenties, with a boyish, heart-shaped face and a wisp of a mustache. He was the biggest goofball of the bunch—keeping the others in stitches with his constant jokes—but he was also the kindest. He slowed down his Mandarin so that I could understand and, seeing my difficulty, offered to carry my camera. His name was Shandro.

22. Part of right conduct (one of the Eightfold Path) is to refrain from taking life. Buddhists outside Tibet are often strict vegetarians; but on the plateau the variety of available foodstuffs is so limited that the prohibition is relaxed, and meat is an integral part of the Tibetan diet.

Gradually we were leaving the Serqu River far behind and approaching the high plateau. Across a giant chasm I saw coniferous forests marching up near-vertical slopes, yielding to homesteads on the mountaintops and shoulders. We passed a few houses—ramshackle wood and stone affairs with no sign of paint or any other manufactured luxury. Unlike the people living down by the highway, these farmers were very poor.

The trail continued steeper and steeper, and I began to wonder how I was ever going to keep up. Sure, the others were city Tibetans—not nomads—but they had been born in Derge at about this elevation and were used to it. I was falling behind, but Shandro stayed with me, patiently waiting when I stopped to lean panting on a rock, and urging "slowly, slowly!" when I stumbled in my rush to catch the others.

At length we surmounted a crest and came down to a meadow covered thickly in buttercups—a waving mass of gold. The horses were unloaded and turned loose to graze. I lay down spread-eagled in the flowers and closed my eyes, ready to sink into the earth. If only I could just lie here among these flowers, I thought, and never move again. The cheerful voices of my companions hardly pierced the swimming in my head. After a while I opened my eyes and saw them pulling refreshments out of their bags. Soon they were sharing with me their bottles of beer, cans of cola, and slabs of chewy, fortifying bread.

Much too soon, the time came to pack up and resume walking. Now we were climbing out of Kham's labyrinth of river-sliced gorges and were mounting the high plateau. Trees and farms were far behind us now. My watch altimeter, which tops out at 4,000 meters, had been off-scale for some time, yet the pass still lay ahead.

By now the sprightly steps of my Tibetan companions had been reduced to a trudge, for the thin air was affecting even them. As for me, I was weary beyond anything I could remember. At last the pass was visible, a cleft in a brown ridge ahead. As we slogged up the final slope, each of us snatched a pebble from the trail and tossed it on the crude *chörten* that proclaimed our victory. A pause for photographs, then we turned toward the descent.

The land that swelled before me was huge, treeless, and rolling. The forest-filled valleys were all hidden; I saw nothing but grass- and flower-covered high plateau. I had arrived in the land of nomads.

We marched for fifteen minutes or so until we came to a stream flowing down a crease in the hills. My companions knelt to put their lips to the water. I was parched with thirst, but when I started to follow their example, Shandro touched my arm and said, "No. If you drink that water, you'll get sick." Then he went to one of the horses and drew out a bottle of boiled water. "Drink this," he said, and I drank it until it was empty.

"You know," Shandro went on, "that we won't reach Palpung today. We'll go there tomorrow." Then he said some things I didn't understand, finishing with: "You can go with *him*" (indicating the taciturn fellow in the maroon *chuba*) "or you can come with us."

Wherever these horses are going—that's where I want to go, too, I thought. The walking is hard enough already; I sure don't want to carry a backpack. Besides, I like these people. "Can I come with you?" I asked.

He smiled warmly. "Yes, you can," he said in Chinese, then added in Tibetan: *"ndro!"* Let's go!

16

ON A PILGRIMAGE
WITH TIBETANS

NOW ON THE wide-open spaces of the grasslands, the seven of us marched on for a half hour or so over fairly level terrain. Then the path forked. Straight ahead was a fat, obvious trail sloping steeply downward. To the left was a barely visible track leading uphill toward a ridge. Everyone stopped walking and began to pull off the small bundles that dangled from the horses' loads.

"You should pay him now," Shandro said to me.

"Now?" Palpung was nowhere in sight, so I didn't understand why I was supposed to pay *now*, but I trusted Shandro so I pulled out twenty yuan to give to the man in the *chuba*. He accepted it, then began moving down the main trail, descending toward Palpung, horses in tow. The others were picking up the bundles from the grass. My backpack lay among them, and one of the men, a lanky fellow in a white "Asian Games" sweatshirt, hoisted it and strapped it on. The five of them began to file out along the faint path to our left. I stood there, rooted to the spot. What was going on?

"Come on!" they called, and Shandro added in Tibetan, *"ndro!"* I hurried after them, reducing the gap by half after twenty or so breathless steps. Why was that fellow carrying my pack? Why were the horses going a different way? As I followed them onward, a light slowly dawned in my exhausted, oxygen-starved brain. The horses weren't coming with us; they were going to Palpung with the man in the Tibetan coat. Those big loads on the horses' backs were not tents and equipment for my friends to use during their journey; they belonged to that man and were going with him to Palpung. My friends' belongings were all in the small satchels that they now carried. They were walking a pilgrim's route, a circuitous path that would take us in a gigantic loop around Palpung Gonpa. Who knew where it would lead, what it would be like, or how long it would take. . . .

We were just beginning what would probably be a difficult trek indeed, and already I was a basket case. I only wanted to get to the monastery and rest, not to go walking on some wild-goose chase. But it was too late now. Every second the man and his horses were getting farther away. Could I run after the one in the sweatshirt, retrieve my backpack from him, then chase the man with the horses? It would make me look like a fool, but perhaps there was a chance. I tried to hurry a bit, but it was as much as I could do just to keep the pilgrims in sight, let alone overtake them. And the farther I went along this trail, the farther I was from clearing up this awful misunderstanding. You've made a big mistake, I told myself. You've really blown it this time. I wanted to shout at Shandro to come back, to get me out of this awful mess, but instead I only staggered along behind, quietly stricken with a growing sense of doom.

It wasn't much later when I suddenly remembered those prostrating pilgrims on the road to Lhasa. With a rueful half smile I recalled how much I had admired them, how I had dreamed of making a pilgrimage myself with such people. Now I had gotten my wish, but instead of being happy, I felt only exhaustion, helplessness, and dread. If this was the path to enlightenment, I could live without it. I was disastrously unprepared for this trek. What on earth would become of me?

Now the sun was diving toward the horizon and the sky was getting dark. We had already been walking for about six hours, yet my friends were as frolicsome as children. They skipped across the swampy grass, fairly shouting with joy. The one carrying my backpack hardly seemed to know it was there. I had a terrible feeling of foreboding. How far were we going today? I had a tiny tent and sleeping bag in my pack, but where were the others going to stay? Their insignificant luggage couldn't hold much more than the food we had eaten on the way up.

Gradually the sun dropped and the world began to turn gray. After thirty minutes or so of tromping over squishy marshland, we came to a wooden stele sticking out of the ground, engraved with a paragraph of Tibetan. My friends stopped for prostrations. I was only too happy to cease walking. I tried to join them, but all I could do was to press my hands together in a feeble but heartfelt prayer for deliverance.

When they were done Shandro pointed to the stele and said, "That's the first one. There are eleven more on this trail." As he spoke the others were already walking away. He must have seen how nearly spent I was, for he fixed me with a brief compassionate gaze before saying cheerfully, *"ndro!"* Wearily I followed him as he moved off.

We moved off the ridge and began traversing the side of a slope. Somewhere above us was a spring, and the trail under our feet became a marshy quagmire, forcing us to leap from one peaty mound to the next. My friends were wearing only cheap cloth tennis shoes, but they stayed dry, for they were far nimbler than I was.

Now the sun was gone, smearing orange all over the western horizon. We veered off the ridge and descended to the left to where a nomad tent was pitched below. We were still a hundred meters above the tent when we were stopped by a fearsome chorus of barking dogs. A small black-coated figure whom I could barely make out in the gloom emerged to see who had come.

The men in my party began shouting down to the nomad, asking about shelter for the night. The answer came back negative, and I noticed that now even my invincible Tibetan friends were starting to look a little worn. As for my own weariness, it was beyond description; I longed to get out my little tent and make camp right then and there. But my friends needed shelter, and I needed them, so there was nothing to do but walk on. Far away on a distant slope there was another nomad encampment, and we made straight for it.

When we were about 200 meters away, four of us sat down to wait while Shandro and one of the other men went to reconnoiter. We watched them pause momentarily outside the tent, then disappear inside.

Now all was still. The sun's last glow was fading from orange to blue to black. Overhead, a cloak of monsoon clouds was fast enshrouding the stars. A breeze grazed my face and tugged my hair, but there was no other sound. For a long time we waited: four small, silent creatures clinging to a speck of heaving earth.

At last, from the tent emerged a figure that was fired red by the flickering light within. It called to us from across the empty spaces. My three companions sprang to their feet. "Come on," said the woman happily. "He says we can sleep there tonight."

In the gathering gloom, we hurried across the grasslands toward the promised shelter. Around the tent stood animals— white, motionless, and silent like denizens of a sculpture garden. But I hardly noticed them; I saw only the open tent flap. I dived in, stumbled to a corner in the rear, and sank onto some piled carpets. There I laid back and closed my eyes, caring for nothing but sweet repose. Voices percolated around me, but I didn't hear them. Behind closed eyelids I floated slowly down through layers of gauzy blackness, sinking into nothingness.

After a time someone jogged my knee, and I opened my eyes to see a proffered mug of something steaming. It was tea, made with the rich milk of a yak fed on summer grass. I had never tasted anything so good and so replenishing. After a few sips my spirits began to revive, and I sat up and looked around me.

The tent was not as large as some I had seen, but spacious nonetheless, perhaps four by six meters in area. It was of standard Tibetan design, made of black strips of woven yak hair sewn together into a box. Interior poles and exterior wires held the thing up, while an opening at the top allowed smoke to escape. The tent was lined with heaps of belongings: food sacks, rugs, pelts, an ancient rifle, and many mysterious bundles. At the center was a massive stone-and-clay stove in which wood and dung were burning. The family had a large assortment of kettles and battered aluminum pots.

It was hard to discover how many people belonged to this tent, for everywhere I looked were little dark faces peering from the shadows. In the end I decided that there were four little boys and one older sister who was twelve or thirteen. Mother and daughter wore black Tibetan dresses, and their hair was studded with turquoise. The father, who was perhaps forty years old, had on trousers, a tattered shirt, and an old hand-knitted vest.

While I sat silently drinking my tea, the men fell into a long discussion. They all spoke Tibetan, so I could make little of it, but it seemed to be a rundown on the news from the outside world. The nomad family listened raptly, as though news of this kind did not often reach their home.

The father was all hospitality, pouring tea and distributing *tsampa*. But he was far from servile, and he didn't look innocent or childlike to me like the nomads I had seen in towns, away from their homes on the steppe. In their homeland, nomads are different people; masters, competent in all things. A herdsman understands the meaning of every plant, every animal, and every hoofprint in the dirt just as surely as I can read street signs, or use a telephone, or follow the dictates of a timepiece on my

wrist back home. Now our roles were reversed: I was the innocent one, watching wide-eyed and childlike as the father went
about brewing tea, clumsily kneading my bowl of *tsampa,* and
smiling eagerly but without understanding at anyone who
deigned to throw a word my way.

From my corner of the tent I watched the nomad's strong,
intelligent face; I watched him move deftly and speak with quiet
authority; and I began to think: perhaps they are warriors after
all. . . .

When the evening grew late we were escorted to another
tent, a small one with white canvas sides and a yak-hair roof. The
edges of the cloth were not sealed to the ground, nor was the
floor dug out flat. Inside were assorted quilts and woolen pads
that we quickly arranged into beds. We six just barely fit. The
floor was lumpy with mounds of grass, but it was soft, and I
quickly found a way to nestle the curves of my body into its
nooks and crannies.

Soon we were all settled, our six bodies side by side, with
nothing but thin fabric to fend off the infinity outside. As we lay
down a light rain began to fall. The others spoke quietly for a
while, but then their voices trailed off. Safe in the womb of the
grasslands, I fell into a deep, blissful sleep.

IN THE MORNING I awoke to the steady sound of raindrops on the
tent, some burrowing through the loosely woven yak hair and
plopping on my face. Looking under the edge of the canvas I
saw water-drenched grass outside. Overhead, the sky was an
impenetrable gray blanket. Bad news, I thought. The others have
no proper shoes and no rain gear save for their flimsy jackets.
Surely we can't go on in this weather.

Soon I was rousted out of my warm bed. We all went back
to the main tent for breakfast. The tea, *tsampa,* and dried-up
pieces of bread that months ago I had had to force down now
tasted better than I ever imagined. The Tibetans chatted by the

fire. I sat hoping fervently that we would stay in this warm dry place until the weather cleared; but my hopes were dashed when my friends began getting to their feet and picking up their bags. Then came the dreaded call: *"ndro!"* We were setting off again!

In no time we were marching, sometimes hopping from mound to mound to avoid the water underfoot. The landscape was completely veiled by mist. The others moved swiftly, oblivious to the weather. I was rested now, but still the altitude held me back, and I huffed along in the rear.

We had not gone far when Shandro slowed his pace to mine and said, "Today we have nine hills to climb; then we will reach Palpung Gonpa. Shall I carry your camera?"

"Thank you," I said, handing it to him gratefully. It was only a few pounds, but I needed any advantage I could get. Then I wondered: what did he mean by "hill"?

After a short tromp across the grasslands, we descended into a maze of waist-high shrubs. Rain continued to fall. I was wearing a slicker, but it did a better job of keeping sweat in than keeping rain out. The trail was easily followed as it wended through the brush, but it was full of muddy puddles. In no time I was soaked through.

After a couple of hours we stopped to rest on a grassy promontory where there was a pile of stones and one more of the wooden steles. Another group of pilgrims had stopped there: men and women, some holding umbrellas. The crowd looked utterly miserable in the pelting rain—even the yellow flowers drooped forlornly. The promontory looked out into what must have been a gorgeous panorama of forested valley, but all was enshrouded in mist. Perhaps Palpung was down there, but I could see nothing.

We stopped so long at this place that I began to think that the monastery must lie just around the corner; but in fact the hardest part was just beginning. After leaving the promontory we started a descent, tortuous and tricky, down a steep, slippery slope. It brought us into viny underbrush overhung by trees. I held my breath with each footfall on the sloping mud, for one wrong move could send me careening down the hill and over a precipice. It wasn't long before even the most surefooted of our party had had a misstep that sent him flat on his back in the mud and desperately clawing for a handhold. The walk had devolved into a scramble, and I was grateful at least to have two free hands for the purpose. But the handholds were treacherous: the rocks often gave way and the bushes were full of thorns.

The descent didn't last long, and soon we were climbing again, hand over foot up a chute of mud. Climbing was less fearsome than descending; but now the altitude plagued me. Going down had been a matter of skill and concentration, going up was purely a matter of pain. Four or five meters of gain had me gasping and heaving, my limbs weighing like lead. A few meters further and I was obliged to stop and gulp oxygen. Shandro urged, *"Kale kale ndro!"*—go slowly!—but his sensible words were drowned out by the voice within, recollections of my seniors reproaching me sternly, "Don't baby yourself! You are *much* stronger than you think." Commanded by that inner voice, I straightened up and again started to climb.

From here onward the trail allowed hardly any rest; we were always picking our way down death-defying descents or pulling ourselves up to minor passes. Whenever the terrain allowed a break in concentration, I mused on the irony of my situation. I had wanted so much to go with Tibetans on a pilgrimage, but now that I was doing it, it was hell. My longing had turned around to sting me. I could almost see the huge, round belly of a laughing Buddha jiggling uproariously at my expense.

Back at the promontory we had joined forces with the other group, and now the slower members of both parties had combined to form a rear guard. There was Shandro and his brother Dorje, who had an injured leg, a long-skirted woman from the other group, the lanky fellow who was carrying my backpack, and me. Now at the more dangerous places on the trail Shandro's hand reached out to take mine, helping me up or down, steadying me and keeping me from falling. His silly jokes had abated, and he had become the solid, dependable leader of our small clan.

On and on we went. I was so wet by now that I was oblivious to the rain. Occasionally we stopped to rest, but took no food and drank no water. We passed more of the wooden steles—I had lost count of them now, and the others' prostrations were becoming perfunctory. We had forgotten everything save survival on this treacherous trail.

The terrain became even steeper. At one place we climbed through a chimney of rock, at another we descended through a tunnel. We came to several cliffs that would have been unscaleable but for notched-log ladders someone had left there. We traversed across walls where the path narrowed to merely a slippery ledge. When I stopped to think about it, I was astounded that the fellow carrying my pack was not only keeping up, but even held his shoes in his hand, leaving only one hand free to steady himself. But most of the time I thought of nothing except conquering the endless flow of obstacles.

Noon arrived, and still the sky remained a blanket of smothering gray. Rain fell relentlessly. No one said a word, for each of us was locked in our individual struggles, completely focused on the vital business of placing our hands and feet. We came to a place suitable for resting, and in unspoken agreement we all squatted down on rocks beside the trail. Then I saw Dorje and Shandro gesturing to each other. Dorje had a questioning look, so Shandro held out his palm and began drawing Chinese characters on it with his finger. Then I realized that the silence was deliberate. Was it an impromptu pact made between my companions or yet another of the customs associated with this holy pilgrimage? I didn't know, but now that I knew the silence had a purpose, I felt its significance.

Too soon the rest was over. Shandro looked at me and tilted his head toward the trail in an unspoken *ndro!* We rose and resumed our toil. And now I sensed something here— an atmosphere, a feeling—that it was right to protect from the spoken word. As we went slowly onward through the mighty jungle, the silence seemed to emphasize our puny, fragile human- ity and the sacredness of our journey.

We passed more steles. We came to a tree festooned with small rocks that were tied up by odd bits of string and hung from low branches. While Shandro and the others got busy tying up new rocks, I found one piece of hanging string with an unoccupied loop in it and wedged an oblong rock into the hole. I had no idea what I was doing or why, but in this mystical pil- grim's universe each of these small acts felt intrinsic to the whole.

By now the rain had ceased its steady downpour and was falling in fits and starts. We had been walking for some five or six hours, and I had nearly forgotten about Palpung; the relentless succession of agonizing climbs and terrifying descents occupied the whole of my consciousness. But now Shandro was showing me his watch, pointing at one of the numerals to say that only thirty minutes of walking remained.

There is a saying—often quoted at special training—that ninety-nine miles of a hundred-mile journey is just half way. Palpung might lie just around the corner, but if I let my guard down for an instant I could die here. The last hurdles of a race, the ones vaulted when energy is all but spent, are the highest hurdles of all. *Tight your mind!* goes the command given when concentration starts to flag. Don't think of the end; we are only halfway there!

Sure enough, we now came to a series of steep undula- tions. Thinking that each uphill stretch would be the last, I climbed hand over foot without pausing, trying to ignore the heaviness in my limbs and my lungs' fierce ache. But still the trail snaked on: under branches, up cliffs, down funnels, around boulders, and over flowers. Again: a false summit, a short descent, and then—always!—yet another climb. Soon I was totally spent. I stopped to lean against a tree, but Shandro, who was a little way ahead, wouldn't let me rest. With a curving sweep of his hand he told me that only one final climb remained.

Tight your mind! With energy extracted from the depths of my marrow I followed him up that last slope.

As we mounted the crest, as if by providence the clouds opened and the sun blazed through. Coming over the notch I found myself standing on a steep, treeless slope. Across a huge gully was a spur sticking out of the mountain, and on the spur stood an immense red fortress.

It was Palpung.

The monastery was long, tall, and boxy, like a railroad car that had rolled down the mountain and skidded to a halt on the edge of the cliff. It hung in the center of a natural amphitheater whose walls were covered thickly by pines—the trees seemed to stand at attention, like a cheering multitude. The promontory that held Palpung stretched to join a great slanting wall, and on the saddle was a flock of small houses. Between them and me was a narrow track traversing the near-vertical slope.

Shandro and I walked across a field of yellow flowers to where the whole gang was lounging on the grass. Now that we were within sight of the *gonpa* the spell of silence was broken. My fellow pilgrims lay on the grass talking and laughing under the golden light of the sun. A chorus of welcomes greeted me as I plopped down next to them. But the others would rest here only a moment, for they were not finished yet. The pilgrims' circuit led all the way down to the Baiqu River a hundred meters below. Then they would climb again, at long last to reach the monastery.

One thing was certain: I was *not* going down to the river and back up again. I had already accumulated quite enough merit that day, thank you very much! They left me sitting on the slope, my pack beside me, while they cheerfully tromped down the mountain. I rested for a while, chewing some bread they had given me and relishing the triumph of finally reaching Palpung. Then I hoisted my pack—very heavy!—and began slowly to pick my way across to where the *gonpa* lay waiting.

17

PALPUNG

I APPROACHED PALPUNG Gonpa with only two things on my mind: a change of clothes and a cup of hot tea. It should have been a straightforward matter to procure these life-giving essentials, but as I neared the monastery's entrance, its fortress-like walls loomed unexpectedly aloof and forbidding. I knew no one here and had no invitation. It had been a long journey, one that used up most of my physical and mental resources, and now I was all out of bravado. Even to step through the *gonpa*'s great doors without an escort seemed more than I could manage. Wearily I sat on the steps outside, vaguely hoping that someone would come to my rescue.

A few women villagers were about, but none made a move to help me. Finally one gestured toward the interior of the monastery, an imperious wave that hinted how silly I really was being to sit outside. By the time I had gotten to my feet and shouldered my pack she had gone, so I walked alone through the heavy double doors to the courtyard within.

It was a massive place, three stories high, with a slightly madcap arrangement of different-size windows and mismatched abutting wall sections. The walls were made either of logs or clay, and the carved and decorated window frames were of exquisite workmanship. Palpung looked a great age, for the wood had darkened to bittersweet chocolate, and the clay surfaces were flaking and uneven. What had once been vibrant color on the lintels was peeled and faded. Everywhere were signs of shifting, leaning, and cracking.

I later learned that Palpung is considered to be one of the finest examples of classical Tibetan architecture in Kham. The main building, the Chölhakhang, is 270 years old, and is so large and splendid that it has been called the "little Potala Palace." Palpung belongs to the Karma school of the Kagyu Sect, one of the four major sects of Tibetan Buddhism. Among Kagyu institutions, Palpung is second in influence only to Tsurphu Gonpa near Lhasa, and claims more than 100 submonasteries throughout the plateau. Four incarnate lamas make Palpung their traditional seat, and many notable scholars and artists have also lived there.

In my soaking wet clothes I was rapidly getting chilled to the bone. The men and women working there—sweeping the grounds and carrying things to and fro—stared at me curiously but blankly, as if I was a faux pas that was best ignored. Appealing to the women, I pointed to my wet things and gave an exaggerated shiver, gestured to indicate the act of disrobing, then glanced huntingly all around the courtyard in an attempt to put across the idea that I needed a place to change. But their expressions hardly altered, and they did nothing.

Finally I gave up on them and went looking for a secluded spot on my own. It crossed my mind that undressing in the monastery courtyard might be considered a breach of etiquette, but if I didn't get some dry clothes on soon I might well catch pneumonia. The most private place I could find was a dark, tunnel-like side entrance. It was open on two sides, but at least the onlookers were all female. Perhaps once they saw what I was doing they would protect me from intruding men.

I threw down my pack next to a pile of logs and pulled out

a change of clothes from a waterproof stuff sack. Before the widening eyes of two women, I stripped off my wet things and quickly pulled on dry ones. When I was nearly done—legs just ready to receive a dry pair of pants—a couple of men came cruising through the passageway, walking right past me without a single sideways glance or even batting an eyelash. When they had gone I finished putting on my pants, then looked back at the women. They were staring blankly as before, as if nothing had happened. I could not hold back a phrase of English: "Thanks a lot, girls."

At least now I was warm and dry, and starting to feel much better. Perhaps an alarm had been sounded *(Red alert! A foreigner is stripping in the courtyard!)* for now some monks showed up to take charge. At last: friendly people! I was led to a room where I was invited to sit before a blazing fire. My body ached from top to bottom, but I was subjected to the usual social ritual, including tea and *tsampa* that were enormously restoring.

One of the monks was Han Chinese, about thirty years old. His Mandarin was of course much better than the others', so he acted as my host. On the other side of the fire he sat among the Tibetan monks, and they hung on each other affectionately. I couldn't help noticing that when the Han monk spoke Tibetan he drew out and caressed each word, as if speaking the language itself was an act of devotion. Sometimes the other monks corrected him, and from their fond and gentle manner I could see that teaching him their language was a labor of love.

Presently a call came that my friends the pilgrims had arrived. I went down to see them. They had climbed from the Baiqu River and had just completed the little circuit that wrapped tightly around the Chölhakhang, the final part of their pilgrimage.

After we had exchanged greetings I asked them if they would stay at Palpung that night.

"No, we're going that way—" Shandro gestured toward the high plateau. I knew that somewhere up there was the main trail, which would take them back to the start of the pilgrim's loop. "Tonight we'll stay in that same nomad tent."

"All the way back there?" I exclaimed. "That's so far!"

He shrugged. "Tomorrow we'll come down here the same way we did today, then we'll climb again to where the trail forks. That'll be two complete circles. After that we'll go over the pass and home to Derge."

"I'll wait for you to come tomorrow," I promised.

When they had gone, the Han monk escorted me through a labyrinth of corridors to the place where I was to stay. It was a dark, austere chamber on the third floor, with log walls and a rough plank floor. There was no furniture. The only light came from a single window, about one meter square, fitted with sliding wood-lattice panels covered in white paper.

But I would not stay alone here. Before the window were two thin sleeping pads, and on the pads two shaven-headed Han girls sat cross-legged. They were tiny things, dressed in baggy pants and loose-fitting tunics in somber hues of blue, gray, and brown. Each girl sat before a low worktable set up on blocks, and on the tables were spread pages of sutras. One girl had some writing paper and a pen that she had been using to make notes. Around them were small piles of belongings—little more than a sheet, quilt, and change of clothes for each girl.

My roommates, I realized, were Chinese nuns.

They welcomed me warmly. We introduced ourselves, and I learned that they were from Jiangxi Province in the far east of China. Although they used Mandarin with me, to each other they spoke in an eastern dialect of which I could make nothing. The Han monk, who was from the same part of China, lived in the outer room of this apartment. He was their teacher.

I wanted only to go to bed, but word of my arrival had spread and curious crowds kept coming to stare at me through

the open door. At last the Han monk got up and mercifully
pulled it closed. When I breathed a grateful *"khatro!"* (thank
you) the two girls burst out in understanding laughter; I realized
that they, too, were foreigners in this place.

Later on, at sunset, dinner was served. My adopted family
cooked and ate together. Dinner, which the nuns diligently prepared and served, was *mianpian* (squat little homemade noodles)
stewed with a fibrous, dark-green vegetable and no trace of
flavoring apart from salt. Mealtimes were the only time I ever
heard the nuns indulge in idle conversation.

The three must have enjoyed me as a diversion in their
monotonous lives, for they were tireless hosts, ever ready with
the ladle to administer more noodles to my system. At the end
of the meal each of us got a dose of *kaishui*—boiled water—in
our bowls. Following their example, I drank a bit, then used the
remainder and my fingers to wash the bowl.

As long as I would stay at Palpung, this scene was to be
repeated, identically, every evening.

That night I slept soundly, but in those few moments when
I drifted toward wakefulness, I was aware of rats pattering
around the room. Remembering the pilgrims who picked up
worms from the trail, I smiled and thought: if Buddhists find
merit in saving the lives of worms, perhaps they tolerate rats as
well. If they can do it, then so can I. Then I dropped back into
blissful slumber.

IN THE MORNING I awoke to the sound of an expressive and lyri-
cal tenor voice—the Han monk crooning his daily lesson. His
voice roamed lightly and easily over a half-tone scale, sometimes
slipping into a chant. The scale and meter were non-Western,
there was something about it that put me in mind of gospel
singing. It was clear that he not only knew the sutra by heart,
but that it had become an inseparable part of him.

The girls were already awake. One at a time, they got up to perform the day's prostrations. In a corner of the room stood a smooth board that the shorter girl took down and laid upon the floor. She donned a pair of white gloves, then, with reverent care, she touched her pressed-together palms to her forehead, neck, and heart, then laid them on the board at her feet and slid until she was stretched at full length, chanting as she did so. After about fifteen minutes of this she was finished, and the taller girl took her place. Then they began their lessons.

The short nun began first. She plunked down cross-legged on her bed, arranged the pages of the sutra on the worktable in front of her, cleared her throat, and with vitality and enthusiasm began to recite in a loud, clear voice. I didn't understand the meaning, but I knew right away that she was not reading the Tibetan words but spelling them out loud, letter by letter. I had learned to do the very same thing when I began my study of Tibetan.

The Tibetan alphabet was adapted from Sanskrit and so, like most Indo-European languages, it reads from left to right. But spelling in Tibetan is not the straightforward matter that it is in English because the letters are not always lined up horizontally; many are compounds formed of two or three letters arranged vertically on the page. Consequently a system of oral spelling has evolved that describes all these various arrangements. The nun spelled in the Derge dialect—not quite what I had learned—but there was no mistaking the form: *ma pa yata shia denge shie nago shien.* . . .

Back in Los Angeles, my Tibetan teacher had said that to acquire good reading skills I should spend a great deal of time spelling out loud; but as a sophisticated Westerner I thought myself above such tedious exercise. Now under rigid monastic discipline, these girls were apparently undergoing an apprenticeship during which they were allowed to spell and nothing else. Listening to them, I began to think that maybe there was something to this spelling business after all.

Now the second girl, the taller of the two, joined in. She was less adept than her colleague; sometimes she hesitated and made mistakes. Occasionally her face betrayed impatience at being stuck to such a monotonous task. The two of them carried on in loud, asynchronous voices, spelling the same sutra over and over again. Spelling in Tibetan has a rhythm to it, but it is a far more complex and subtle rhythm than that of English spelling. At first the sound seemed toneless and mechanical, but the more I listened the more I was drawn in. Like the act of making a prostration, it had something that engaged the unconscious mind.

After half an hour of spelling the girls broke for breakfast—*tsampa* porridge. When that was finished they went back to their lessons. That's what they did all day, taking breaks only to fetch water, cook, clean, or wash. While the nuns studied, their teacher in the next room did the same; but he always seemed to have an ear tuned to his pupils' efforts, occasionally calling out corrections. Besides spelling, the girls worked at translating sutras, and studied from the dog-eared pages of a Tibetan grammar book.

Lunch was rice and vegetable stew. As I sat there manipulating a pair of chopsticks I surreptitiously studied the Han monk. He radiated immutable calm, and his sitting form was graceful and harmonious. Yet his gracious manner belied an iron will—at lunch we were at loggerheads over the extra servings of food that he tried to push down my throat. This man's iron will, now bent to the task of hospitality, I would later see in a less benevolent guise.

In the afternoon I was taken to see the sights of Palpung. From the courtyard of the Chölhakhang we climbed to an arcade where I admired the lavish murals: the four Guardian Kings, a Wheel of Life, and a cosmic mandala—map of the path to enlightenment. The main assembly hall had been recently painted, but was comparatively bare of decoration and empty of human life. Beyond, in an adjoining chamber, a twenty-meter statue of Maitreya sat presiding over the silence and falling dust.

In the afternoon I kept a lookout for my pilgrim friends, who would be returning from their second circumambulation. At last I spotted them across the gully—tiny dots against a sea of green. An hour or two later they arrived. I went down to speak to them.

They were not looking chipper at all. Their shoulders sagged and their faces were drawn and haggard. "We had good weather today, so it was much easier than yesterday," the woman told me. "But we are very tired. Dorje hurt his leg, and Shandro is sick."

"What will you do now?"

"We'll go once around the Chölhakhang," said Shandro. "Then we'll climb to the pass again. Tonight we'll be home in Derge."

"I'll walk around with you."

No more words were spoken as we paced the pilgrim's path that encircled the main building. They walked very slowly. Despite their superhuman abilities, this pilgrimage had sucked them dry; it had been for them a Buddhist special training. And now they were at the hardest point, their bodies sore and depleted, yet still with more mountains to climb and the end not quite in sight.

I gave them some mementos of our time together—my spare army knife to the lad who had carried my backpack, small trinkets to the others, and a photo of myself to Shandro. Then they turned toward home. My thoughts went with them. I remembered them often in the coming days, hoping that they were all right.

Although my friends had acquired twice as much merit as I, my body still ached all over. I spent much time sleeping. All around me pulsed the rhythm of monastic life: chanting, study, and prayer. Sometimes I went for short walks to gather wildflowers, and there was always writing or laundry to do; but usually rain and lassitude kept me inside.

EEEEEE! AT A most inauspicious hour of the night I was jerked out of sound sleep by a crash and a scream. When I opened my eyes a surreal scene stood before me. The two nuns were standing at the foot of my bed in a posture of tense readiness. One had an oil lamp in her hand, the other gripped a long stick. What was going on? The answer came in a moment when a small rat jumped out from behind a sack of flour and flew across the room. In perfect unison, all three of us shrieked.

"*Chiti!*" cried one of the nuns, and gave chase. She struck a blow with her stick but missed, and the rat flew like a wraith past my sleeping mat and disappeared into the shadows. Undaunted, the girl with the stick began poking among the sacks of provisions where the rat was last seen.

"*Chiti!*" she yelled, when suddenly it burst out of hiding and bolted past her to a different corner. The other nun took her oil lamp and began probing the spot, trying to see where it had gone. I got out my flashlight and aimed it to where I thought the animal was hiding. Suddenly the rat reappeared, hurtling itself desperately up the log wall as though Yama, the Lord of Death, himself was behind it—as indeed he was.

"*Chiti!*" the nuns cried, and the one with the stick took after it. With more determination than skill she flailed her weapon at the fleeing shadow, but again without success.

The chase was on. I was thoroughly awake by now, and sat up in my sleeping bag pointing my light to wherever I thought the quarry was hiding. The nuns ran back and forth, striking at the elusive flying thing with grim resolve. For minutes at a time the rat would disappear, leaving the huntresses tense and feverish. As soon as it reappeared the alarm would go up again: "*Chiti!*" cried the girls, taking after it with a vengeance and shrieking if it came too close. *Bang! Crash!* went the stick, clattering off the hard wood of the walls, upsetting sacks of grain and pots of butter, and punching holes in our paper-covered window.

The rat was valiant; more than once it ran clear up to the ceiling, then plunged back down again. But it was all in vain, for at last enough blows accumulated to leave it twitching on the floor. Now that the creature was helpless, the nuns' killer instinct quickly ebbed. The door slid open and the Han monk entered holding a towel. He wrapped it around the animal and carried it gingerly outside. When he had gone the girls slid the door closed again, blew out the lamp, and went to bed.

Darkness and quiet restored, I lay in my sleeping bag and thought: so much for my theory about respecting rat life.

THE NEXT MORNING everything was as before. The girls rose and did their prostrations. The man chanted in his room next door. But I began to sense something foreboding in this place. The incessant chanting, the strict discipline, the almost complete lack of ordinary social intercourse—it seemed quite unlike what I had seen among Tibetan inhabitants of this and other monasteries. And what were these women doing here anyway? I had never heard of nuns living among monks, and it seemed an unhealthy situation. Why hadn't they gone to one of the nunneries scattered over the plateau?

The more I thought about it, the less I understood. Why did the girls never talk to each other unless their teacher was present—and then only at mealtimes? The two of them had every reason to be the best of friends, sharing as they did a common background and a common vocation. Living together here in this alien place, they ought to be natural allies, yet they showed no sign of intimacy. Tibetan monks, by contrast, are always talking and laughing together, and are full of physical affection. In the room I shared with the nuns was no laughter, no cheer, and—except for me—no diversions.

Monsoon was beginning in earnest now, and rain fell all day. The chamber that I shared with the nuns seemed gloomy and stifling, but I was held captive by bad weather and by my own inertia. On the third day the only noteworthy event was when one of the women did something—I don't know what—to annoy her teacher. He punished her with a tongue-lashing that stabbed me to the pit of my stomach. I longed to just disappear; I didn't want to see this dark side of monastic life. Are Buddhist teachers supposed to be so harsh? It seemed contrary to the principle of compassion, and the incident left me confused and unsettled.

By now I was ready to move on. I had had quite enough of this dark room, these cheerless people, and their bland, monotonous food. That evening I asked the Han monk to find me a guide, which he did. I would leave in the morning.

When I went to sleep that night, one of the girls was still studying by lamplight. Some time later I was awakened by a clatter, and opened my eyes to another bizarre scene. The Han monk was standing in the doorway, looking grotesque and ridiculous with an orange silk underskirt hanging on his lean but muscular frame. He was not very big, but he loomed over us in the doorway, and seemed all the larger for the huge black shadow that gyrated on the wall behind him. The shorter nun sat cross-legged on her bed, stiff and defiant. Her comrade and I stayed in our beds, afraid to speak or move lest we somehow exacerbate the monk's anger.

Fiercely, the monk rebuked his wayward student. What he was angry about I couldn't guess, for they spoke entirely in their Jiangxi dialect, but the words cut deep into my gut. Nevertheless, the object of his vituperation was unmoved. She listened silently, eyes cast downward, with no sign of emotion or remorse.

Suddenly, in the midst of his speech, she jumped up and tried to run out the door. She was such a tiny thing that she had no hope of getting past him, and he easily pushed her back. But she did not give up; again and again she tried to hurl herself past her adversary, always bouncing back from his restraining arm, pathetic in her helplessness but frightening in her intensity.

After three or four of her futile attempts to escape, he suddenly lost patience, grabbed her arm, and forced her to the floor, making her kneel at his feet. She twisted there for a moment trying to get free, and I thought for a moment he was going to hit her, but he didn't.

Then suddenly the fight went out of her. She went limp, and lay there whimpering in abject misery. The monk didn't move, and looked down at her with an expression that I couldn't make out—was it pity? Or disgust?

Finally she got up and returned to her bed but didn't lie down. She sat before her worktable and blew out the lamp. The monk returned to his room, but continued to watch her through the open doorway, pointing a flashlight into our room so he could see what she was doing. After a few minutes he got up and closed the door, and I heard a scraping sound, as if he was locking us in. I began to breathe more easily, thinking that the horrible scene was over. But it wasn't. Not yet.

After a short time the defiant nun said something to her comrade in the other bed—nothing more than a few syllables, but it sparked a new wave of rage in the monk. He yanked open the door and demanded to know what they were talking about. Then there came another spate of bitter conversation, with him delivering long, angry harangues and her answering in defiant monosyllables. Finally he left our room and returned to his bed.

At last things were settling down, but I was left with a lingering horror for what I had witnessed. It had been so bizarre— the man in his ludicrous orange skirt, the tiny shaven-headed woman, the anger and defiance, and all the words that I couldn't understand. Was this normal monastery practice? I dearly hoped not. Earlier I had thought that monks and nuns shouldn't live together, and now I was certain of it.

All the rest of the night I was tortured by the constant scuttling of rats past my bed. As I tossed and turned, I was only grateful that in the morning I would be moving on.

18

BAIYA

AT DAWN MY guide/porter arrived, a sturdy young fellow carrying a sack of *tsampa* and an umbrella. I said good-bye to my hosts, leaving a donation for the monastery in repayment of their kindness. The guide strapped on my backpack, and we set out, descending the steep trail that led down to the Baiqu River below Palpung.

My destination lay three hours walk downriver, but constant rain over the last four days had swollen the Baiqu and all its tributaries. A short distance down the trail we met some locals on horseback. *"Chö gana ndro?"* they asked in the Khampa dialect.

"Baiya Gonpa."

At this they broke into a babble of advice. "The river ahead is very high," they pantomimed with expressions of great alarm. "You might get trapped in the mud. You might even fall in the water and be swept downstream!"

My guide was looking more doubtful than ever, and I knew that if I let him have his way we'd be going back to Palpung. Alexandra David-Neel, I recalled, never allowed herself to be browbeaten into retreat by fainthearted, mutinous guides. I insisted that we continue, and the lad grudgingly accepted this verdict. The men shrugged and went on their way.

It turned out that the fuss was all about nothing. We made a few short detours, and had to wade through some knee-deep water, but after an hour or two the worst was over and things got gradually better. We made good progress for about two more hours. The route was little traveled, but there were farmhouses on a few flat stretches of riverbank. I was glad to have a companion who could explain my business to local people and ask about conditions down the trail.

Presently he learned that a crucial bridge had been washed out by the floods. We would have to take a major detour away from the river, for the shore on which we stood would so on become impassable. So we turned away and began walking up a huge ravine into a mighty pine forest. It was a dank, silent place; old man's beard draped from the branches like cobwebs in a haunted house. Weighted by gray skies and intermittent rain, even the white blooms of the meadows hung their heads.

After an hour's climb, we emerged from the ravine and began walking along a high ridge. We passed a couple of farmhouses—primitive affairs of roughly hewn wood. Then the mountainside opened up into a staircase of barley fields, and sun started to stab through the clouds. The whole valley seemed caught up in an orgy of wet photosynthesis. At length we met a swift-running stream plummeting down the slope. Following it down to its confluence with the Baiqu, we came at last to the tiny village where Baiya Gonpa stood.

When I saw the place I understood why so many at Palpung did not know of it: Baiya was little more than a single stone building, scarcely larger than the surrounding houses. On the outside were painted vertical stripes of gray, white, and ocher, a sign of the Sakya Sect of Tibetan Buddhism.

Baiya Gonpa was set on a riverbank, walled in by pine-covered slopes. The monastery is small but old—founded over 700 years ago as a Kagyu Sect monastery, later changed to

Sakya.[23] The original main assembly hall was destroyed in the Cultural Revolution, and now its function is fulfilled by a second building, called the Lhakhang Serpa ("New Hall") or Lhaser for short. By the time of my visit the building had decayed, and most of the Baiya's sacred treasures and statues had been lost, leaving little sign of the monastery's former splendor.

In Chengdu, months earlier, a friend had introduced me to the Baiya Rinpoche, the incarnate lama who makes Baiya Gonpa his seat. This saintly scholar, who himself seldom ventures over the mountain passes to his traditional home, had given me a letter of introduction. For months I had been carrying this page of curling Tibetan calligraphy with its flamboyant vowel flourishes. Now the time had come to use it.

With my guide I entered the courtyard. The place was in sad shape. The main monastery building, crudely constructed by the standards of Palpung, was made of rammed earth badly marred by cracks. Surrounding the courtyard was a two-story wooden arcade whose decrepit columns sagged and leaned in every direction. Window frames and eaves bore the ravages of two centuries of Tibetan weather. One good earthquake, I thought, and this place is gone.

There was no one in sight, so we continued through a yawning doorway into the Lhaser. It was dark and gloomy inside, but as I peered down the long room—past a great ritual drum near the entrance, carpeted platforms, and the enormous throne at their head—I could see a light in the far rear. Voices overlaid with the hiss of a kerosene lantern drifted back to where I stood. As I came closer, I saw that the rear chamber contained a great clay Sakyamuni, about five times life size. In front of the statue three Tibetan men—two monks and one lay—sat cross-legged with their backs to me working at something.

23. Wong, et al. *Buddhist Monasteries of Ganzi Tibetan Autonomous Prefecture, Western Sichuan, China.*

Nearby two more monks were busy using a mold to form little conches out of clay.

I walked up to the fellow with the mold and handed him the letter of introduction that the Baiya Rinpoche had given me. Word of my arrival must have spread like lightning, for already half a dozen people had come to see. They all crowded closely to read over the monk's shoulder. He studied the letter carefully, while everyone waited in silence.

Then suddenly the monk jumped to his feet. Letter in hand, he flew out of the room, off to fetch—I presumed—someone in authority.

In no time the happy, jabbering crowd had swelled to what was, for these parts, a considerable mob. The monk who had taken my letter returned, bringing with him two old lamas, leaders of the monastery. They gave me a hearty hello, but when we tried talking to each other we found we had no language in common. Undaunted, they led me through the courtyard, up a steep flight of wooden stairs, to where a heavy wooden door was secured with an ancient padlock. From the bunch that jangled at his waist, one of the old monks drew out a key and opened the lock. Pulling open the door, he motioned me to go in.

The moment I entered my jaw dropped, for this small room was among the plushest Tibetan accommodations I had ever seen—a great surprise after the shabby condition of the rest of the building. The walls and ceiling were lined with glittering silk brocade. The fabric was overhung with *thangkas*: a line of painted Tantric deities frozen into expressions of perpetual kindliness or immortal fury that ringed the room. Two low couches were thickly upholstered in carpets, and more carpets covered the floor. Along one wall was an alcove displaying a collection of ritual objects—offering bowls, a bell, ampulla, ornate cup, a vessel with peacock feathers, and other mysterious things. Every inch was rich and voluptuous.

It was the Rinpoche's quarters, I realized—kept for those

rare occasions when he visits his traditional seat. Standing in this opulent room full of sacred treasures, I felt uncomfortably like an infidel. After a quick look around I started for the door, but the monks pointed to one of the couches, saying *"shu, shu!"* (sit, sit!). As soon as I did so, the others crowded in after me to have a ringside view of the party.

Soon someone came bearing a tray of goodies—crackers, candy, some wizened old apples, and an enormous tin of biscuits. I hated to strain the resources of this humble place, but after the bland food of Palpung these delicacies were hard to resist. In gastronomic heaven, I sat for some time nibbling happily and chatting with my hosts in a mixture of Chinese, Tibetan, and sign language.

Earlier, down in the temple, I had noticed a young man of uncommonly fine appearance. Tall and slender, he had a mop of black ringlets floating about his head, slit-shaped sloe eyes set far apart, and perfectly sculpted features. He was such a thing of astonishing beauty that I could hardly keep from staring. The fellow was certainly not a monk, nor was he a farmer, for he was dressed like a city slicker in a cheap black blazer. Had he been born in the West, I mused, he would have made a perfect teen heartthrob, right down to the kitschy, heart-shaped medallion he worn on a chain around his neck.

This dreamy character, I now learned, was the only one at Baiya Gonpa who had more than a smattering of Mandarin. Now he sat in front of me, running through the usual list of questions and then translating my answers for the crowd. He seemed unaware of his amazing looks, for he spoke with happy, unassuming simplicity.

After an hour or two of inquisition I was ready to get off the stage. Pointing to one of the bundles strapped to my pack I explained, "This is my tent. I'd like to pitch it outside the monastery somewhere. Do you know a good place?"

"Pitch your tent?" replied the heartthrob, whose name I had learned by now was Tashi. "Why?"

"To sleep in. I need a place to stay."

He looked puzzled, and conferred with the two old monks. A burst of uproarious laughter was their answer, and a flood of Khampa Tibetan. Soon everyone in the room but me was chuckling at the joke.

"What do they say?"

"They say that you don't need your tent. You will sleep here," Tashi replied simply.

"Here? Are you sure?"

"Yes, of course. You are our guest. Just tell me what you need and they'll get it for you."

"Well . . ." It all seemed too good to be true. But if they really were serious: "If it's not too much trouble, I could use some washing water. . . ."

Tashi spoke a few words to one of the young monks, who jumped up and disappeared. When the basin appeared, Tashi and the others got up and left me in peace.

Later on one of the old monks brought up my evening meal: rice and a plate of vegetables fried with bacon. Meat! Salt! Grease! Flavor! I fell on it with a vengeance. While I ate, a stream of visitors came to stare at the stranger having her dinner. The monastery was open to all, and no one would think of trying to keep them away. Furthermore, the Tibetan psyche (in common with the Chinese one) is innocent of the Western idea of privacy. The sightseers walked into the monastery, found their way to my room, pushed the open door, and stood there whispering and gaping at my every move.

The villagers were the sweetest people imaginable, and at first I let them look to their hearts' content. But after the first few groups I started to weary of their inquisitive but uncommunicative faces. I tried closing the door but they simply pushed it open again. Investigation revealed that the door had no latch, and there was nothing to wedge behind it. After the tenth group of visitors I was starting to feel like a leopard in a zoo, but to snarl at them would have been unseemly. To my relief, as darkness fell, the flow of visitors gradually ebbed. When it seemed the last of them had gone, I unrolled my sleeping bag on the soft Tibetan carpet and drifted off to sleep.

THE NEXT MORNING I was greeted by a monk bearing breakfast. He was a lighthearted jester with huge ears and a mischievous grin ringed by a shaggy little beard and mustache, and he took the greatest delight in his peculiar guest. From what he brought—rice gruel and *mantou* (steamed buns)—I guiltily realized that someone had risen early to cook my meal.

After a walk up the river, followed by lunch, I was at a loss for something to do. The neighborhood was a perfect island of serenity, with no sound or movement except for birds and tumbling water. The monks had all disappeared. I ambled into the Lhaser thinking to look at the murals, and instead discovered Tashi and a group of monks in the vault in back. They were laboring around the massive clay Sakyamuni that rose ethereally in the gloom. Yesterday I hadn't realized what the men were up to. Now I saw that the statue lacked a few critical appendages, and the clay was still damp. This Buddha was not fully born yet; the workers were bringing him to life.

I sat down on the threshold to watch. It was easy to see who was boss, for one monk alone had the unmistakable aura of a master. I couldn't guess his age, for his skin was unlined and his hair (which hadn't been properly shaved in some time) was glossy black; yet the weight of his authority gave him an older man's presence. He had an amply fleshed, aristocratic face, and under his workman's apron his clothes were precisely arranged. A scaffolding stood in front of the statue, and despite his cumbersome monk's skirts, the master sculptor climbed over it with grace and sureness, swinging his two legs together as one. Up on the scaffold he gave a lofty, godlike impression, but even on the ground he seemed taller than he was. The sculptor spoke quietly, but always with a twinkle in his eye, as if he possessed some marvelous secret.

He was busy overseeing the work of Tashi who, along with a young monk helper, was busy affixing clay hair to Buddha's skull. I recognized the little spiral "conches" that they had been molding yesterday. Tashi smeared a bit of clay onto the statue's head, then carefully applied each twirl of hair, packing them densely all over the bulbous surface.

Meanwhile the master sculptor worked on one of Buddha's gigantic hands, using nothing more than his fingers and a simple tool shaped like a double-ended hairbrush. To my eyes, the clay appendage already looked perfectly complete; nevertheless the sculptor wasn't satisfied. With infinite patience he toiled, pressing more clay onto it, making subtle refinements to its shape, paring imperfections that were invisible to my eyes.

Quickly I was drawn in, for the sculptor's technique revealed a mentality far removed from other craftsmen I had seen. I couldn't explain why, but watching him moved me. Perhaps it was Sakyamuni's face—evolved as it has over centuries to just the form that best engages the unconscious mind. The sight of the sacred shape emerging from clay was wondrous. And standing there in the radiance of his creation gave the man an almost godlike glow.

When the afternoon grew late, the sculptors put away their tools and extinguished the lantern. I was just about to leave when Tashi came to me and said, "I have some Chinese beer. Would you like to share it with me tonight?"

Whenever Tashi spoke to me I had a hard time keeping my wits in order. I couldn't have heard him correctly. In this faraway place, how could he have beer? "Um . . . okay . . ." I stammered.

"All right," he said, "I'll bring it to your room after dinner."

THAT NIGHT, JUST after dinner, there was a knock on my door. Tashi came in, smiling conspiratorially, a bottle of beer in his hand. He set it down on the table before taking a place on the couch beside me. With my army knife I opened the bottle and poured us each a share. Then he noticed my little photo album sitting open on the table. "What's this?" he asked.

"Photographs. My family and friends back home in America." He picked it up and began studying the pictures. I explained in Chinese who the people and places were. We had just finished the last photograph and were about to take a sip of beer when the goofy old monk came in—without knocking—to clear away the dinner plates. The old monk saw the open book on the table and picked it up. Soon I found myself explaining the photos all again—through Tashi, this time—while the old monk's face metamorphosed through expressions of fascination and delight. Then another monk, a quiet young fellow with an angelic face, came in and joined the scene.

As the four of us sat laughing and talking together—the two monks sitting on the floor, Tashi and I sitting side by side on the couch—I unexpectedly felt Tashi's fingers brush against mine. That's odd, I thought, for Asians are invariably meticulous in avoiding contact with unrelated adults of the opposite sex. Was it intentional? In seven months of travel I had met hundreds of men—both Chinese and Tibetan—and although a few would flirt ("Take me home with you to America," was a common theme), none ever came close to touching me. Occasionally a sophisticated urban male might shake my hand, but that was all. A minute later our fingers brushed again, and I was swept by a wave of something electric.

The two monks stayed and stayed, while Tashi and I looked longingly at our beer but did not touch it. It was getting dark, so one of the monks lit the candle that was on the table. Finally the two left. Tashi and I exchanged relieved smiles, lifted our bowls, and drank a silent toast. I wasn't at all sure what was going to happen next, but according to the rules I was accustomed to, this was the time to make small talk. With my lousy Chinese the talk would have to be minuscule indeed. I began trotting out some standard schoolbook phrases.

"Where do you come from?"

"Derge."

"How old are you?"

"Twenty-seven."

"What is your work?"

"I'm a *thangka*-painter."

"A *thangka*-painter! How wonderful! Did you paint these *thangkas*?" I indicated the works of art that adorned the room.

"Oh, no!" he laughed. "I'm just a beginner. I studied *thangka*-painting at Palpung, but now I'm learning sculpture. That monk with the apron is my teacher."

Suddenly the door flew open to reveal two village women. Their eyes sparked when they saw me, but they came no closer. If Tashi was annoyed at the intrusion he gave not the slightest sign; he said something to them in Tibetan and they came in. Soon we were back at the book of photographs, going through the routine of explaining them to a rapt audience.

When they had gone, we two fell back into labored conversation. I learned that Tashi was living with his teacher in a tent somewhere up the hill. They had been here for a month rebuilding the statue. I asked him to write his name for me, which he did with great care in beautiful Tibetan script. It was evident that he'd had a monastic education. But when I tried to clarify something by writing down Chinese characters, I learned that he knew no written Chinese at all. Indeed, even with my paltry command of the language I noticed his mistakes in grammar.

"Have you ever been to Chengdu?" I asked.

"No. But four years ago I went to Lhasa. Have you been to Lhasa?"

"No, not yet."

"Are you going?"

"I'm going to try. It's very difficult for foreigners, you know," I said.

"But four years ago I saw lots of foreigners in Lhasa. Why do you say it is difficult?"

I was saved from answering this prickly question because again the door suddenly flew open. This time it was two of the young Baiya monks. Again we had a photo exhibition, studying my book before the flickering candle. After that I sat back bemused while the three Tibetans fell into a long discussion. Although I couldn't understand Tashi's words, listening to his dusky voice and his homespun way of speaking—liberally sprinkled with Khampa interjections like *oh-ya!* and *ah-re!*—was like tasting something sweet and savory at the same time. Meanwhile his hand rested casually on the couch beside mine. The two just barely touched, and neither of us ever looked down, but I felt a powerful alchemy.

When the two monks had left, we poured the last of the beer into our bowls and drank it. Tashi said, "I have to leave now. My teacher is waiting." He stood up. "Good night!" And with that he disappeared into the night.

I sat motionless for a long while, gazing at the door that had closed behind him as the candlelight leaped and danced over the tapestries in the room. Then I blew out the flame and lay down to sleep.

THE NEXT DAY it was raining, so there was nothing whatsoever to do but sit in the Lhaser and watch Sakyamuni take shape. But I didn't mind. I was gradually understanding more about the work. The master sculptor and Tashi performed the most exacting tasks. The other monks, who belonged to Baiya Gonpa and were not professional sculptors, helped in whatever way they could in between their tasks of study, prayer, and housekeeping.

Inside the vault Tashi was creating Buddha's left hand, the hand that would lie on Sakyamuni's crossed legs, palm upward to cup a monk's begging bowl. Tashi began with nothing more than a crude skeleton of twisted wire wrapped in white raffia. He measured the wire fingers with a strip of cloth that had units marked off on it, making sure that they were all in the correct proportions. Then he began plastering handfuls of clay onto the frame, building it up bit by bit to proper thickness. Every now and then he looked up, saw me watching him, and shot me a radiant smile that warmed me to the tips of my toes.

The master sculptor was busy putting the finishing touches on Sakyamuni's other hand—the one that lay draped over Buddha's right knee, palm inward. The longest finger of that hand just touched the ground on which the Sakyamuni was sitting, a simple but powerful gesture invoking the Earth as a witness to his enlightenment.

Fascinated by the entire procedure, I watched the master sculptor use a measuring tape to check the dimensions and placement of the right arm. He must have carried all the figures in his head, for I never once saw him refer to any notes. Now he picked up his smallest tool and began working over the arm, making changes to its shape far too subtle for me to appreciate. The sculptor's hands were soft from working clay every day, yet also sensitive and intelligent. But there was something in the man's technique that went beyond his hands, although I could not make out what it was.

Flanking Sakyamuni were the remains of two other clay statues. They were so badly mutilated that it looked as if someone had taken a sledgehammer and tried to smash them to dust. Heads, arms, and legs were missing; all that survived were grotesque stumps of cracked clay with bits of wire sticking out. I knew without asking that these images had been victims of the Cultural Revolution; and that the central image, the one now being rebuilt, undoubtedly had been similarly desecrated. The reign of madness and terror that had destroyed these statues must have been far-reaching indeed to have found this faraway spot. But now the horror of those broken, mutilated remains—

and all they implied—was assuaged by the radiant new figure coming to life. I couldn't help being moved by this splendid symbol of Buddhism's resurgence in Tibet.

The day flew by, and before I knew it, it was quitting time. On his way out Tashi said to me, "I haven't got any more beer, but I'll come and visit you tonight anyway, all right?" Hours later, when he appeared in my doorway, it was already dark. "Sorry I'm late," he said, "but my teacher was talking to me."

Again we sat side by side on the couch while visitors came and went. When we were alone we spoke in short sentences about mundane subjects—the numbers of brothers and sisters we each had, the merits of Chinese versus Tibetan food. He teased me about my fancy, high-tech flashlight—whose batteries were nearly dead—comparing it unfavorably with his spunky little Chinese light. Unlike others, Tashi did not ask about wages in America, nor was he interested in the cost of my gear.

When others were there to talk to Tashi I sat back and listened to their earthy Khampa dialect. I understood less than one word in twenty, but instead of being frustrated, I felt deliciously childlike. How pleasant it was to surrender the responsibilities of adulthood! It would be marvelous, I fancied, to stay here and grow up all over again among these enchanting people.

The conversation flowed back and forth while I listened and daydreamed, perfectly content.

THE NEXT DAY I gave up all pretense of having anything to do but watch the sculptors work. Tashi was making slow but steady progress on Buddha's left hand. Sitting on the floor with his legs splayed, work propped up between them, Tashi looked more like a child in kindergarten art class than a trained sculptor—but the care with which he attended his work belied that impression. The shape of Sakyamuni's hand was not up to Tashi's whim, but was mandated by centuries of Buddhist tradition. With a measuring tape he frequently checked the length and circumference of the fingers. Sometimes he paused and held out his own hand, studying the curve of the finger pads and the creases on his palm. Gradually Buddha's hand assumed its proper shape and began to take on a life of its own.

As beautiful as Tashi was to look at, I spent far more time watching his teacher. The martial artist in me was entranced by his every move. I was now beginning to perceive what made him different from the others: while they molded clay merely with their hands; the master sculptor worked it from deep within his lower abdomen. This place, which the Japanese call the *tanden*, is the body's center of gravity; but it is more than that; Japanese believe it is the place where courage and health are generated, for it is the proper center of breathing, and breathing (as I have been told time and time again) is what unites mind and body. Aikido master Kisshomaru Ueshiba wrote, "The power from a stable tanden is inspired by fullness of spirit, and passes through every part of the body flowing outward . . . through the tips of your fingers, your toes, even from the glitter of your eyes . . ."[24]

That power was evident, I now realized, in the sculptor's flowing movements. When he molded the clay, the force began in his tanden, creating a line of power that stretched from his toes to his fingertips, flowing without interruption into the clay itself, as if they were all one being. It had the same dynamic as a well-executed *oizuki* (front punch). It was extraordinary to watch.

Now my conviction was growing that soon I should leave this place. I was a strain on the humble resources of the monastery, and besides, I had unfinished business. Just a few miles away lay the mighty Yangtze River, the dividing line between Sichuan Province and Tibet Autonomous Region. From there

24. Kisshomaru Ueshiba, *Aikido,* Hozansha Publications, 1985, p. 23.

Lhasa was five or six truck-days west, and I had forgotten neither my promise to Mike nor my yearning to reach the Holy
City. But while Lhasa pulled me west, Baiya was starting to feel
more and more like home. It was especially wrenching that
the person I had to ask for help in leaving was Tashi himself.
Yet when I did ask, he bent himself to the task with no sign of
hurt. Arrangements were quickly made; I would depart in the
morning.

That night Tashi came to my room for the last time. Everything was as before, except that now, as he sat beside me, his
warm hand closed around mine. We two had used up all our
stock of common phrases and there was nothing more to say,
but our silent communion was stronger than ever. I yearned to
surmount the barriers of language and culture between us. If we
could really communicate, stay together for more than just a few
days—what might happen then? Perhaps as an advanced Buddhist he had mastered his earthly attachments, for if he shared
any of my frustrated longing he gave no sign. He never even
asked for my address—

But then, I never asked for *his* either. Like butter sculpture
melted down at the end of Mönlam, like a sand mandala swept
away into oblivion, knowing Tashi was a lesson in the impermanence of all things. At the end of the evening when we were
alone I clipped off a lock of my hair to give him as a keepsake.
Then he stood to leave, and I walked with him across the carpets
to the door.

He kissed me—then he was gone.

19

UNEXPECTED MEETING

WELL BEFORE DAWN the two old lamas came to bring my last breakfast at Baiya. Half an hour later the guide arrived. He was a local farmer, and had brought with him an aging but sturdy brown-and-white mare, saddled and loaded. My pack was added to the load and we set off, walking up the Baiqu River along the trail I would have arrived on if the bridge hadn't been washed out. First we would head in the direction of Palpung, then climb to the grasslands, over the pass, and down to the dirt road where I had parted with the two girls and their bicycles just over a week ago.

Thirty minutes of walking brought us to that crucial bridge. Already local farmers had replaced the fallen logs, and we crossed easily. It was a perfect sunny day, a welcome change after so much rain. The Baiqu had receded, so most of the trail was dry. Thick, sweet-smelling grass, phalanxes of wildflowers, and tall straight pine flowing up the mountainside—they all filled me with rapture; but the taste was bittersweet, for now I was leaving this garden of Eden. What triumphs or heartbreaks might lie on the road to Lhasa I didn't want to contemplate.

By the time we had reached the valley below Palpung, we had become a caravan of travelers: myself, my guide and his horse (which I sometimes rode), a bowlegged old man on a fine white stallion, and a Tibetan family on foot. After some initial surprise at finding a foreigner in their midst, the newcomers quietly accepted me. It was a joy to travel without fanfare in local fashion, almost as if I belonged.

After passing Palpung, we left the others behind and began climbing to the pass. This climb was the last leg of the pilgrim's route around Palpung, the circumambulation I had begun a week earlier. Wanting to finish my pilgrimage in proper fashion, I dismounted and continued on foot. A couple of hours climbing brought us above the tree line. Now I was walking on a flying carpet: golden buttercups and purple asters, robust knotweed and delicate mint, exuberant pink primroses and shy edelweiss—a tapestry of color under a fierce blue sky.

We went on for a little way before mounting a rise, then came down into a great meadow. It was just a stretch of pasture like a thousand others, but it carried an unexpected sight. Scattered all over the grass were groups of nomads clustered around cooking fires, and at least half a dozen white canvas traveling tents were pitched. Interspersed among the tents and people, horses grazed contentedly, their bells tinkling as they tore off mouthfuls of grass.

It could only be a temporary settlement, for the people had come without the yaks, sheep, and dogs that are indispensable to nomad life. What had brought them here? My guide spoke no Chinese, so I looked about for someone to ask. A family of nomads sat picnicking just off the trail: men and children lounging on the flowers while the women brewed tea. One of their number—an old man with but one tooth—knew a little Chinese, so I put the question to him.

"*Palpung Huofo lai le! Palpung Huofo lai le!*" he replied in great excitement—the Rinpoche of Palpung is coming!

"The Rinpoche of Palpung! Here? Now?"

"Yes, here! Today! Soon he is coming!"

A chance to see this holy man was not something to be missed. I decided that we would wait here to see the Rinpoche.

Knowing how nomads have an imprecise notion of time, I guessed that it might be hours before the Rinpoche actually arrived. But there was plenty to do in the meantime, for I was rapidly drawing a crowd. The fascination was mutual.

The Tibetans who surrounded me were a handsome, robust race, and only close inspection revealed how difficult their lives really were. The elders had but few teeth left, and even the young people's mouths showed gaps from accidents. Their clothes were blackened with dirt, smelled of yak butter, and had not been washed for weeks or months. Most of them had probably never used toilet paper in their lives. Romanticism aside, life on the plateau is not easy; it takes a toll.

But seeing nomads now, in the happiest of times, it was easy to overlook these unpleasant truths. With their erect carriage, high cheekbones, almond eyes, and dark skin they were exquisite to behold. To my naive eyes they were masters of all they saw, and the grasslands that gave them their livelihood appeared unlimited. They stood straight and tall; they laughed with ease and moved with grace; and their singing filled the skies. Nomads need little in the way of material things: just animals from which to obtain food, clothing, and shelter, and to carry their burdens; a good rifle and a sharp knife; *tsampa* and butter tea to ward off winter's cold; and jewelry to beautify their faces. All else—save devotion to Buddha's teaching—is superfluous. Taken on its own terms, the world of a Tibetan nomad is balanced and complete.

I got out my camera and, by way of breaking the ice, I offered the nomads a look through the viewfinder. The children all came running, their faces exploding in wonder when they squinted through my lens.

Then someone spotted the first of the Rinpoche's escort, and my camera and I were instantly forgotten. All eyes turned to the west. I could see nothing, but by using my camera as a telescope I made out a few distant black dots. For some time nothing happened, then the dots began to move down the trail, approaching us. The crowd's excitement swelled. A minute later, the vanguard began to arrive.

They were Khampa riders, thundering down onto our meadow at a headlong gallop while ever urging their animals faster. The horsemen were dressed in the finest robes, their steeds beautifully caparisoned. Chivalrous knights of King Arthur's Round Table, disciplined and fearless samurai armies of Japanese shoguns, Sioux warriors swooping over the American prairie, Genghis Khan's fierce Mongol hordes . . . all the spine-tingling, bloodcurdling thrills of those days gone by— days that live on only in history books, cinema, and dreams— they were all recalled by Khampas plunging over the crest, by the thunder of hooves on earth, by the sound of whoops and battle cries. The horsemen were not riding but floating on top of the heaving saddles, their limbs loose and free as they streaked across the grass. They flashed by me like purple lightning, but as they passed I caught a glimpse of glittering eyes—eyes charged with the intoxication of fully *being*. The riders were spirits dwelling in *that moment only*, the same transient eternity as when two well-matched opponents jump off the razor's edge of life and death and enter each other fully.

These men, their horses, the endless wild steppe—my fantasy had come to life!

At first the men charged down singly, or in twos and threes. But more riders followed the vanguard, and more after them, and then still more, until it seemed that every second brought another dazzling hero in our midst. When they had reached the tents and waiting nomads, the men pulled up their mounts sharply, looking all the more heroic as the animals reared and snorted and stomped. The men dismounted, and stood for a minute comforting their heaving horses. Then the Khampas collected in twos and threes to exchange a few manly words, no doubt on some topic appropriate to champions.

Dozens of riders arrived—perhaps sixty or seventy altogether—until the air was full of tinkling horse bells and the field was full of striding men. The horses were covered in the finest of blankets: thick carpets of red, black, and gold geometric designs, different for every animal. Their metal-studded leather halters glittered; their manes were dressed with ribbons and tassels, and their tails woven with colored yarn. Despite their small size these Asian ponies—smart, tough, and surefooted—seemed the very essence of equine beauty.

The men were perfectly matched to their mounts: handsome, proud, and dressed in all the finery they could muster: maroon *chubas* set off by rich silk linings; shirts trimmed with gold at the collar; boots lashed with string around their calves. And, as always, each had the Khampa requisites: a long dagger, felt hat, and a red tassel woven into long black hair.

But now there was again stirring on the horizon: more riders approaching. When they drew near I saw that they were not warriors but monks—and what monks! Not the frail, bookish stereotype customarily assigned to religious scholars, but dazzling horsemen who rode with speed and style and flourish no less than their predecessors, on steeds equally magnificent. Each man was swathed in voluminous burgundy robes over which was worn a handsome red-and-black jacket. Each monk had a sort of derby sitting high on his head; but in the tumultuous gallop many hats had slipped back and now hung dashingly by their chin straps.

More and more monks streaked down onto the meadow, some bearing white flags that snapped stirringly in the wind. Then, at a slower pace, elder lamas began to arrive, their robes augmented by princely red brocade. When they reached the meadow each dismounted expertly as if he had spent his life in the saddle. One fellow, about fifty years old with a gray beard, mutton-chop whiskers, and a collection of ancient keys dangling from his belt looked just like a medieval wizard—except that there was nothing of black magic about him, just a steady gaze that hinted of spiritual mastery.

But now everyone was pointing up the trail, for the Rinpoche himself was in view. Nomads, warriors, and monks rushed to the path to welcome the holy man. The Rinpoche was surrounded by a huge entourage, but there was no mistaking the man himself, for he alone was clad in a long silk gown of imperial yellow and a matching wide-brimmed hat crowned with a diamond-shaped spire. The Rinpoche looked perhaps twenty years old,[25] and possessed a beautifully formed, intelligent face that expressed serenity and wisdom far beyond his years. He was preceded by two mounted standard-bearers carrying flags, and his horse, magnificently adorned as befitting his rank, was led at a stately walking pace.

The Rinpoche looked uncomfortable in the saddle; his shoulders were hunched and his balance looked uncertain. But with the crowds that rushed up to greet him he was completely at home, and he smiled at them with boundless affection. However, the monks at his side allowed him precious few minutes to commune with the adoring masses; no sooner had he dismounted than he was hustled into a waiting tent.

I was disappointed, for it appeared that whatever was going to happen would be hidden behind tent walls. But as soon as the Rinpoche entered, crowds surged up to the tent, engulfing it. Within a few minutes the walls of the tent had come down and were trampled underfoot, leaving only the tent canopy. Fortunately there was no stampede, and the nomads were organized into an anxious line three or four bodies wide that slowly oozed into the tent toward the Rinpoche as he sat in a high-backed chair.

As the nomads passed before the Rinpoche they bent low to accept a blessing, their faces aglow with religious rapture as he touched each head with the palm of his hand. *Khata*—gauzy white scarves traditionally used as offerings in Tibet—piled up

25. This man, known as the Jamgon Kongtrul Rinpoche, was thirty-seven at that time. Sadly, he was killed in a road accident in April 1992. As of this writing he has not yet been reincarnated.

before him. Those leaving the tent looked dazed and ecstatic, as if suddenly transported to some higher plane.

All too quickly—and with many nomads still waiting—the audience was concluded. The Rinpoche was brought back out of the tent. He stood before the assembled throng for a minute, speaking to them and probably blessing them en masse. Already the Khampa riders had mounted their horses, and were flying away to the east, heading toward Palpung. Soon the Rinpoche's stately procession was riding away, getting smaller and smaller, climbing over a ridge, then vanishing from sight.

I looked around. The nomads all seemed to be packing up and moving off; streams of people on foot and horseback flowed over the hills in all directions. Then my long-forgotten guide appeared. Compared to all these long-limbed laughing men of the steppes, my plain stubby farmer suddenly looked like a mule among stallions. He motioned to me that he wanted to get moving again. By now it was late afternoon, and we still had a long way to go.

Soon we were loaded up and on our way, pacing a dusty brown trail that cut lazy curves across the swells of green. Many people were heading in our direction, all of them in a good mood. At first there was much laughter and discussion, but as the path grew steeper the conversation gradually faded. My guide, who must have thought me ridiculous for wanting to walk so much of the journey, insisted that I mount his horse. We reached the pass in a large group, but during the descent the others gradually left us.

Down we went, the sun's slanting rays igniting emerald fire in forests and fields below. I dismounted shortly before the pass, for an old Tibetan proverb advises a rider to rest his horse by walking downhill. Hours later, when we reached the place where I had first met Shandro days before, it was dusk. I was taken down the road to a sprawling Tibetan house-inn not far from the highway.

Having delivered me safely, my guide was ready to go on his way. First, however, he wanted to be paid. I pulled out the agreed-upon sum of one hundred yuan and offered it to him; but something was wrong. He was talking rapidly and would not touch the money. The innkeeper, who could speak Chinese, intervened.

"He's saying that because you stopped for so long to see the Rinpoche, you owe him another twenty yuan."

"Another twenty yuan! That's ridiculous! Even if we hadn't stopped, he still couldn't go back to Baiya today."

"He still says you owe him one hundred and twenty, not one hundred."

Tired though I was, I wouldn't be browbeaten out of another twenty yuan. It was a matter of principle. "I won't pay."

We argued back and forth for a while to no avail. Finally I just stopped talking and held the one hundred yuan out in front of him. He hesitated mightily, then snatched the bills and left in a huff. After he had gone the innkeeper said, "That man is no good. He was cheating you. One hundred yuan is already too much; the usual price is about fifty yuan. Next time you need to hire a horse and guide, you come and ask here at my hotel, okay?"

"Yes, I certainly will. Thanks!" Despite my embarrassment over being cheated, I secretly had to smile. This was, of course, just the legendary Khampa business acumen at work. Looking back, I realized that I had drastically overpaid just about every Tibetan I had ever hired. It was not really a matter of money, but of face: because of me these Tibetans must think all foreigners are stupid. I resolved to be tougher in my business dealings in the future.

"Come inside," the innkeeper said. "You must be hungry and tired."

"How much is this going to cost?" I asked warily.

"Don't worry! At my place foreigners stay for free!"

A notched-log ladder led up to the second-floor landing. Upstairs, I followed the man down a hallway and into a dark room. The sun was gone now, and inside just a single candle burned. I was invited to sit on a carpet-covered couch. From out of the gloom someone handed me a bowl of tea, then *tsampa* and butter—the very stuff of life to me by now.

When at last my hosts left me alone, I tried to close my eyes and rest, but the excitement of the day's events and pains zinging from my blistered feet kept me awake for a long time. Then at last my tired body won the battle, and I slipped into sweet unconsciousness.

I needed that rest, for soon I would face the hardest challenge of all.

20

THE KOAN OF
UNFULFILLED LONGING

NOW I WAS smack up against that hurdle that for months had
been my nemesis: Lhasa. Just a short walk from the inn lay the
Sichuan–Tibet Highway, a ribbon of gravel and dirt that rolled
for more than 2,000 kilometers to the Holy City. Before, when I
had been at Derge, Lhasa had seemed tantalizingly close, with
the checkpost at the Yangtze River crossing just a minor bump
in an otherwise smooth road. But now that the time had come
to attack it, I was acutely aware of how easily my hopes could be
dashed by those green uniforms at the bridge, less than an hour's
truck ride away.

In spite of all that had happened in the last week, I still felt
the pilgrim's call to the Holy City. Certainly those Khampa
riders had been dazzling; but really, in the final analysis, they
were just young men riding fast on horseback. They were the
Tibetan equivalent to thrill-seeking hot-rodders back home—
immature warriors at best. I had come to Tibet not to see
testosterone-fueled display, but to see—and to *experience*—
warriorhood of a deeper kind. A true warrior, I was convinced,
is not one who shouts and swaggers and boasts, he (or she) is the
one with absolute self-knowledge and imperturbable strength.
The true warrior seeks strength not for how it looks, but for
what it can do—the difference between someone who merely

collects tournament trophies and someone who uses martial arts to polish his entire being. The true warrior seeks challenge not for admiration; but because blood, sweat, and tears—and sometimes failure!—let him know he is truly alive.

I believed that warriorhood lay not in the Khampa riders swooping over the plateau, but in those pilgrims I had met prostrating on the highway three months previously. The pilgrims' glowing eyes, their grace and balance, their humility and quiet strength—all those extraordinary qualities remained with me still, inspiring and unforgettable. Since then I had made a small pilgrimage of my own, and the self-knowledge I obtained from walking that circuit around Palpung was worth a thousand horsemen. And yet my journey to Lhasa was still incomplete. What more might there be to learn from this, the ultimate pilgrimage in Tibet?

After her first failed attempt to reach the Holy City, Alexandra David-Neel wrote: "It was then that the idea of visiting Lhasa really became implanted in my mind. Before the frontier post to which I had been escorted I took an oath that in spite of all obstacles I would reach Lhasa and show what the will of a woman could achieve! But I did not think only of avenging my own defeats. I wanted the right to exhort others to pull down the antiquated barriers that surround, in the center of Asia, a vast area extending approximately from seventy-nine to ninety-nine degrees longitude."

No, I wasn't finished. Not yet.

I RESTED FOR one day at that inn; then, on the second morning, I rose very early and walked out to the highway to look for a ride. Less than an hour later a truck pulled up carrying a couple of bewhiskered Chinese Muslims. I asked them where they were going and they said Chamdo, about a day and a half away, the only major town between here and Lhasa. In Chamdo I would have to find a ride onward.

"Chamdo is fine," I told them. "I'll give you a hundred yuan to take me there, okay?"

That was way over the usual rate, and they happily accepted. Then I added, "But I want to ride in the back."

"What?"

"In the back. I need to hide," I said, pantomiming by crouching behind my spread palms. That was as much as I wanted to tell them, for if I explained any more they might change their minds. They seemed to understand—at any rate they asked no more questions—but after they had finished lashing my pack to their tarp-covered load, one of them held the cab door open for me to get in.

"But I want to ride in the back—" I protested.

"You should ride up here," the driver's friend replied, making room for me on the seat.

I hesitated. If I argue, they might not want to take me. I might have to wait hours—or even days—for another truck to pick me up. Perhaps the checkpost at the bridge over the Yangtze won't be a serious one. So far I had brazened through any number of checkposts, and no one had stopped me yet. Maybe it would work again this time. I climbed into the cab.

When the engine started up I felt a burst of euphoria. Another hurdle crossed. I was on my way!

We quickly covered the distance to the provincial border, where we emerged into the immense canyon of the Yangtze, here at least a hundred meters wide. The roadway became a mere scratch on the Yangtze's great shoulder and our truck a mere ant crawling along it. The sight of that mighty mass of swirling, mud-laden water hurtling southward took my breath away. We ran parallel to this flowing colossus for a short distance. Then we turned onto the bridge.

At last: The Bridge. This was the moment of truth. I slouched and pulled my broad-brimmed hat down to cover my face. Perhaps if I didn't move and didn't breathe, no one would notice me.

Crossing the Yangtze seemed to take forever. We must be on the other side by now, I thought, my heart pounding. But the truck hasn't stopped. Have we passed the checkpoint?

Cautiously, I took a quick peek out from under my hat. Instead of the bridge railing and a backdrop of water, outside I saw a brush-covered slope. We were on the other side. I had made it! I could hardly believe it. It had been so easy!

But now the truck was slowing down. *Oh no!* Ahead, a red-and-white-striped barrier blocked the road. Next to it was a small brick building and a sign in the crisp characters of Chinese officialdom. Damn! The checkpost isn't on the bridge as I expected; it's here on the Tibet Autonomous Region side.

The truck pulled to a stop. I felt sick to my stomach. I had taken refuge under my hat again, but now, slowly and cautiously, I peeked out from under the brim. Through the windshield I saw a Tibetan man in a green army overcoat and visored hat decorated with army insignia. The army man looked very, very irate. He stalked back and forth across the road in front of the truck, but didn't even glance at me. Had he noticed me? He must have! But still he paid no attention, as if I didn't exist. What was happening? I looked at the driver and his helper. They were sitting silently in their seats, utterly stupefied.

Now the soldier was walking around to the rear of the truck. He called to the driver, who got out of the cab. The two of them looked under the tarp to check the truck's load: no more foreigners back here. When they came around to the front again the soldier was still incensed. He appeared to be taking this all very personally. His face was dark red. He looked apoplectic. His face bore prominent frown lines, as if umbrage was his habitual state. How very un-Tibetan, I thought. But still he ignored me, as if I was just an inanimate lump. His ire had nothing to do with me; it was all directed at my poor, hapless driver.

By now the driver's friend had gotten out of the cab, leaving me sitting by myself. I could hear the soldier shouting at them. His Chinese was completely fluent and full of wrath. He bawled them out for some minutes. There was a pause while my driver was allowed to emit some apologetic squeaks; then the soldier began raging again, and I caught his words of mock incredulity, "You didn't know? You didn't know?"

They all disappeared inside the guard shack. I waited grimly in my seat to see what would happen when they came out.

But I had a pretty good idea already.

When they did come out, the driver had a piece of white paper in his hands. He looked as if he had been condemned to death by firing squad the next morning. He and his friend got back into the truck. Then we turned around and retraced our path to the bridge, crossing it. Disappointment washed over me in waves. As we came over to the Sichuan side, the driver began muttering in a stricken voice, "Five hundred yuan! Five hundred yuan!"

They're taking me back to Derge, I thought. And the driver's been fined five hundred yuan. That's more than two months' wages! No wonder the poor man is in shock. Why do they fine him and not me? It's all so unfair!

I took a deep breath. It would hurt, but it's the right thing to do. I pulled out my money belt and brought out five hundred yuan of crisp, fresh Foreign Exchange Certificates. On the black market this will fetch a bit more than the five hundred yuan of *renminbi* "People's Money" he will have to pay. But I owe it to him. I handed him the money. He took it incredulously, without arguing.

MENCIUS SAID, "WHEN Heaven is about to confer an important office upon a man, it first embitters his heart in its purpose; it causes him to exert his bones and sinews; it makes his body suffer hunger; it inflicts upon him want and poverty and confounds his undertakings. In this way it stimulates his will, steels his nature and thus makes him capable of accomplishing what he would otherwise be incapable of accomplishing."

These words, which appear in Funakoshi's *Karate-do Kyohan,* had helped me through many discouraging moments in my karate practice. So by now, I was not in the habit of giving up. Besides, I knew a way to get around the checkpost— although, out of consideration for those who helped me, I can't say here how I did it. Two days later I was sitting in my tent on the other side of the river, grinning wickedly. I had outsmarted that odious man in the green overcoat. Victory was delicious. But I still had to find a ride to Lhasa. . . .

My machinations were interrupted by the tinkling of a horse's bell and the sound of approaching voices. When they drew closer, I could see that they were a group of Tibetans, no doubt inhabitants of one of the many little hamlets hereabouts. I had run into locals before without any problems, but still it was better if they didn't see me. Perhaps they would pass by and not notice me through the trees.

"Oh! Who's that?" There was a hubbub of excited voices. They were three men, two women, and one loaded horse heading in the direction of Gartog, the first town on the Tibet side of the river. They stopped to look at me, all agog. Then one of them came forward, a young man with a mop of untidy hair. He assumed a stiff, official posture and asked, "What country are you from?"

"America—Los Angeles," I said, preparing for the usual round of questions. But he was not in the usual frame of mind, for he commanded gruffly, "Show me your passport!"

Inspecting him more closely, I saw that among his ragtag garments was an unbuttoned army jacket and a pair of dirty army pants. Many people wear army clothes, but this fellow's jacket carried real insignia. He was a soldier. Suddenly this encounter looked serious. I quickly got out my passport and handed it to him.

He examined the little blue volume, but of course could make nothing of it. When he was done he handed it to his friends, who were greatly enjoying the drama. While they turned over the pages he continued the interrogation. "Where are you going?" he asked in a tone of command.

My mind was racing and my palms were clammy, but I put on my best friendly, cooperative face. "Gartog."

"How did you get here?"

"Walked."

"How did you cross the river?"

I nodded in the direction of the bridge.

"How did you get through the checkpost?"

"Sorry, I don't understand. Excuse me, my Chinese is very bad. What did you say?"

"The checkpost, the checkpost! How did you get through?"

"Sorry, I don't know that word. Just a minute, I have a dictionary." I fished around in my pack, found the little book and offered it to him, but he waved it away impatiently.

"What are you doing here?"

"I'm a tourist."

"A tourist?"

"A tourist."

"I want to search your things."

"What? Sorry, can you please speak more slowly?"

"Show me your things!"

I opened my pack and began pulling out stuff-sacks and emptying them on the ground while he inventoried my effects: sleeping bag, tent, toilet kit, dirty laundry, first-aid kit, camera, film, journal, photo album, and a couple of paperback books. He examined each item while I explained what it was, then he passed it back to his friends so that they could look, too. They all oohed and ahed and made the usual noises of awe and interest.

Did this man have any authority? As the interview went on, he became less and less the gruff arresting officer, and more and more the curious country Tibetan. Maybe he didn't know foreigners weren't supposed to be here. So far, except for that vile soldier at the checkpost by the bridge, I had never met an army man who cared anything about foreigners. But he could still arrest me and take me back to his base, a mile or two up the road, where someone was bound to know the rules. Surely I was going to be sent back to Chengdu. The jig was up. I prepared myself for the worst.

I was running out of things to show him, yet still the soldier didn't seem satisfied. He looked at me and my pack and my things up and down again, but whatever he was looking for he did not see. Finally he asked, "Do you have a gun?"

"A what?"

"A gun, a gun!" He held an imaginary rifle up to his face and fired it.

"Of course I don't have a gun! I'm just a tourist!" I let him inspect the inside of my pack to see that it was empty.

"Oh yes, just a tourist!" he echoed. He seemed convinced now, and the atmosphere was warming up. He handed back the last of my things. "So!" he said, "Do you have anything to sell?"

Despite my anxiety, it was hard to keep from laughing. These Tibetans—no matter what clothes they wear, every one of them is really a *tshongpa* (trader) at heart! "No, sorry, I haven't anything to sell. I need all this stuff. But I have some Foreign Exchange Certificates. Do you want to change money?"

"Let's see 'em."

I brought out a twenty-yuan note. They studied it quizzically, apparently not knowing what it was. No deal. Now the soldier's friends began showing me things that they were carrying, to see if I wanted to buy. This was a scene I had played in countless times. I looked over the items they offered—a flint, a prayer box—but saw nothing I hadn't been offered dozens of times before.

My things were still scattered all over. Hoping to postpone whatever ignominious fate the soldier had in mind, I began to gather them up as slowly as I could. Any minute now he would order me to come along to his base. Arrest would swiftly follow. I was resigned to failure. At least nobody could say I hadn't tried. Perhaps if I stall long enough, an idea will come that will get me out of this mess. . . .

"Well, we'll be going now," said the soldier. "Good-bye!"

"Good-bye!" said his friends.

"Good-bye!" I echoed. And with a parting wave they were gone.

SOON AFTER THAT I was heading west on another truck. My new driver and his friend had a box of Granny Smiths on the floor of the cab. Starved for fresh fruit, I munched happily while we inched up great looping switchbacks that seemed to be taking us straight up to heaven itself. At length we reached a pass; then a quick dive took us into a valley thick with fir and spruce. A few hours later, in midafternoon, we reached the outskirts of Jomda.

I dreaded arriving at another town, for towns had people, some of whom were bound to be police. I could never tell if they would be the friendly kind (like so many in Sichuan where they knew nothing of the rules governing foreigners), or the nasty kind, like that place back at the bridge. Sure enough, at the entrance to Jomda was another of those abominable red-and-white barricades. A uniformed man came out of the guardhouse and greeted my driver as an old friend. I was sitting in my seat quietly cursing my stupidity for not hiding in the back or getting off before the checkpoint, when the man caught sight of me. I waited for him to come and arrest me, but he didn't. His friendly demeanor didn't change, and he invited me inside for tea.

I followed the man into the guardhouse, heaving a sigh of relief. This, apparently, was a friendly town.

After tea, the truck took me the rest of the way into Jomda and dropped me off. This was unexpected. Hadn't they said they were going all the way to Chamdo? Never mind, I went into a restaurant and had the first really square meal I'd eaten in several days. When I came out I began making the rounds of all the trucks parked nearby, looking for a ride onward. No dice; everyone was staying here for the night and moving on the next day. I would have to find a place to stay. Next door to the trucking compound was the *lushe*—traveler's hostel. The lady who ran the place said that to stay in their establishment I would first have to go and register with Public Security.

No problem. This was a friendly town, right? So I went.

And that was, at last, the end. The very end.

I SAT IN the *Gonganju* office for an hour or more, earnestly, patiently, desperately explaining to the man why I needed to continue west. No, he said, you can't. Jomda is closed. If you want to go to Lhasa, you must buy a plane ticket in Chengdu. They won't sell one to me, I argued, and besides, it's too expensive. Then go to Golmud, he said, and take the bus from there. I tried it, I said, and it's impossible. Well, he said, regardless of that, you can't go to Lhasa from here. But I must go to Lhasa, I pleaded, it's very, very important.

Round and round we went. He didn't mind talking to me; he had nothing else to do. The officer, a Tibetan, was pleasant and kind, but his will was set in concrete. Tomorrow, he said, you will return to Derge.

I went back to my room and stared blankly at the wall. Despair covered me like a leaden blanket. And yet I didn't have to give up. I could wait until dark, sneak out of the hotel, walk up the highway a few kilometers, wait until morning, then flag down a truck going to Chamdo. The Jomda policeman might look for me tomorrow, but then again he might not. He might phone the police in Chamdo to be on the watch for me, or then again he might not.

Or there was a safer plan: I could pretend to go obediently back to Derge, then turn around and try again, this time avoiding the obvious mistakes of riding in the front of the truck or trying to stay in a hotel.

The koan stood before me, gazing at me in sardonic amusement, issuing a wordless challenge.

Or I could go back to the Kham I loved, back to the nomads and the high plateau.

It had been so hard getting here. The road ahead to Lhasa was so long. And I was tired now, so very tired. I didn't want to be a fugitive anymore.

Perhaps my pilgrimage was meant to be Kham after all.

21

CHANGING SCENERY

"SO AFTER YOU were arrested, then what happened?"

"The cops put me on a truck headed back to Sichuan. Say, Paul, from where I'm sitting, I could take a great photo of you with all those Tibetan kids. Want me to take one for you?"

"Sure," he said, passing his camera over. "Can you get Dave in the shot, too?"

"No problem. Just lean a bit closer together—"

After everything that had happened, meeting these two American travelers and coming with them to this little Tibetan village was like a sweet dessert. From the highway the village was hard to miss: twenty-four white tents pitched neatly in a circle. They formed a perfect bull's-eye, pulling us like arrows off the bus, down the slope, across a space of watery marsh, and into the lives of the tents' inhabitants.

The tents had been pitched for a weeklong picnic—a summertime tradition all over the plateau. Like Tibetans everywhere when they want a retreat from their workaday lives, the people of this small hamlet had moved out of their houses and into canvas.

I had met the two foreigners in Garze, a few hours up the road. They were both seasoned travelers and both Californians—congenial traveling companions as well as an understanding audience for my pent-up verbal torrent. When we arrived here the villagers had welcomed us, inviting us into the tent of one of the elders. Now we sat on carpeted couches around a table heaped high with twists of greasy bread, hunks of dried meat, dishes of candy, and bowls of fresh yogurt. *"Sama sa, sama sa!"*—eat, eat!—the Tibetans had been imploring ever since we had arrived.

". . . Hold it right there," I said when the tableau of faces was perfect. I squeezed the shutter. "Got it."

"Thanks," said Paul, as I returned his camera. "And you were in Garze how long?"

"Three days."

"Three days! They only let *us* stay there for one night."

"That's because I have so much practice in talking to *Gonganju*—but let's not talk about *that*. How long do you guys think you'll stay in this village?"

"We'll probably leave tomorrow," said Paul.

"Then what?"

"Barkam. We're supposed to rendezvous with some friends there. And you?"

"I'm on my way out. My visa's about to expire, but in Chengdu I think I can get it extended for just long enough to take my bicycle up to Xinjiang in the northwest. Then I'll ride it over the border into Pakistan."

I didn't tell Dave and Paul, but after Pakistan I was bound for the Nepal Himalayas. There I would try to find "real" Khampas—veterans of the guerrilla army of Mustang, those fearsome warriors that Judy had described five years earlier.

IN THE COOL of late afternoon the villagers gathered to make merry on the grass. I watched the men dancing, tracing loops and arcs and S's endlessly across the green. The oldest man, lean and sinewy, with only a string of burnished prayer beads to cover his dark chest, was the best dancer of all; he stepped and hopped and slid sinuously across the grass, arms snakelike, eyes laughing.

When the men began to dwindle, the women rose up to form a second circle. For an hour or more their swaying black dresses gracefully orbited the field while they sang the same simple melody over and over again, their long braids swinging in time to the music.

Meanwhile children tumbled together on the grass and adults worked cheerfully to prepare dinner. Soon the sun retired, chased below the horizon by deepening indigo in the east. Everyone settled down on the grass, for the evening's entertainment was about to begin. An old film projector was brought out and wired up. Two poles stuck in the ground had a sheet pulled taut between them. Then out came the reels of an old Chinese black-and-white movie. After dinner I went out to join the Tibetans sitting in clusters before the screen.

Like the villagers, I understood little of the movie's Mandarin dialogue. But it didn't matter. A midsummer's eve sitting on a soft, cool lawn in Kham was enough fantasy for me. In the life of this village this was just an ordinary time, but its sweet simplicity was eloquent—the stuff of which the happiest childhood memories are made. Perhaps this is how human beings are meant to live, I mused.

The first reel ended, and there was a long intermission while the next reel was put on. A murmur of laughing voices rose gently on the breeze. The sky was a cathedral of soaring pink clouds immersed in deepening purple, now slowly fading to black. Amid the expanding darkness, the circle of tents glowed warmly, like landing lights in a limitless universe, a platform of peace and security that calls the traveler home.

HAZY IMPRESSIONS: TEARS sliding down my face as the last of Kham slips past my window . . . shabby, urine-smelling hostels in truck-stop towns . . . dropping off the plateau into a sweltering Sichuan summer night . . . endless paddy, sweat-glazed faces, the shriek of cicadas . . . abandoning a broken-down truck, boarding a bus and feeling indescribably grimy and barbaric as I squeeze through a crowd of white-shirted urban Chinese. . . .

I arrive in Chengdu. They know me at the hotel and give me my mail. My bicycle is still here, a little rustier than I remember. Before long my visa-extending, banana pancake-eating, fax-sending city *persona* emerges from hibernation——too easily, much too easily.

MY QUEST ISN'T done.

Like a karate kata—which, according to tradition, must begin and end at the same place—this pilgrimage will not be complete until it returns to its beginning: Nepal. It was there that I first heard of Khampas five years ago. In Nepal, while testing myself against the mighty Himalayas, I can ponder the many koans this pilgrimage has given me. And if, against all odds, I meet a battle-scarred Khampa along the way, that will be a fitting climax to this long journey.

But first I'm taking a vacation from Tibet. With my bike I fly to Xinjiang Province in China's extreme northwest, a vast, sparsely populated expanse of mountains and desert once known as Chinese Turkestan. I land in Urumqi, Xinjiang's capital, and it tosses a bucket of culture shock in my face: The locals are round-eyed and fair-skinned; they look like Turks, not Asians. They are Uighur, a race of Muslim farmers and herders who live in oases scattered around the rim of the desert. Uighur women wear print dresses, baggy stockings, and head scarves in clashing colors; Uighur grandmothers are huge and doughy, like Russian babushkas. This is definitely not Tibet anymore; nor does it seem like China.

In Urumqi I load my bike onto a bus for a three-day

journey around the Taklamakan desert. Sitting by the window on the sunny side of the bus, I ride in heat-induced torpor, waking only to buy tea and watermelon at rest stops and to cart my bones into the grimy hotels that signal each day's end.

Then: Kashgar.

Since the earliest Silk Road caravans, Kashgar has been a famous crossroads and market town. Now it is loaded with tourists. Kashgar is a banana-pancake bastion, a popular stopover on a popular backpacker thoroughfare. Kashgar also draws Pakistani traders; they come via the Karakoram Highway, a road constructed in the 1970s by the two countries as a monument to their friendly relations. The highway follows a Silk Road caravan route whose history spans more than two thousand years. Every season, legions of backpackers travel the Karakoram Highway by bus. I am going by bike.

On a cool, cloudless morning I cycle past yogurt and watermelon vendors on the dusty streets of Kashgar, past oasis farms on the outskirts of town, and into a wasteland of sand. September is a temperate month for the Taklamakan—whose name is Uighur for "desert of no return." But the sand throws off a sizzling, white-hot light that sears my brain and makes me want to cringe. As I pedal through the long, desiccated day, my eyes are fixed on the snowcapped Mount Kongur as it balloons out of the haze ahead. At last I come to a wall of mountains: the Pamir, rising from the sand like great stone titans. Through a breach in the rock issues the Ghez River, a torrent of gray silt that flows down from alpine pastures lying two days ahead. A few herdsmen drive sheep along the highway, and the occasional truck blasts me with its horn, but the land is otherwise silent and empty.

The next day I break camp early to begin a slow crawl into the rocky gullet of the Pamir. The Ghez defile is dry, stark, tawny; its walls utterly devoid of life. After three hours of agonizing uphill effort I reach a police checkpost. Here a Uighur officer graciously informs me that riding a bicycle is *"bu-xing."* I am secretly relieved when he puts me on a truck.

After that brutal climb, to be whisked effortlessly up the gorge feels queer and dreamlike. At length we reach the crest of the canyon, where the Ghez River meanders across gravel flats. A wind kicks up, blowing sheets of dust across the plain. Suddenly I taste mountain air, and it cuts with a cold steel blade.

Karakul Lake is the next place where foreigners are permitted to stop, and that's where I get off. For two days I camp beside its cobalt waters, watching the sun's rays slant onto the great white shoulders of Mount Mustaghata. Nearby, yaks and camels munch the withered pasture. Kirgiz tribesmen amble over on horseback to gaze at me with impassive eyes pinched behind folds of leathery skin. Mustaghata's broad, icy dome commands the scene, changing color as the sun sets. With dusk comes an icy gale to claw at my small tent.

There are no police at Karakul Lake, so after two days I pedal off unhindered toward Pakistan. The day is cold, clear, and brilliant. Fueled by mountain euphoria, I fly over pastures of alpine tundra, shooting past felt-covered tents and their dumbfounded inhabitants. Of course I have no topographical map of this area, and no one warned me about the 4,000-meter pass ahead. Once over the top, I fight against a stiff head wind down into a corridor of rocky desolation. The road eventually flattens out and runs into Kekyor, a small oasis. Here a checkpoint is a welcome sight for at least it signifies humanity. I have ridden sixty-one high, cold kilometers today and don't mind very much when they insist on a bus to the next town ahead.

In Tashkurgan, a community of mostly Tajik people, I take a rest day to feast on fresh bread and grapes. Next morning I ride out into a broad valley full of haze. Steel-gray rocks stretch to misty oblivion under an ash-gray sky. For two hours there is no sign of life at all, nor any feature on the landscape—like pedaling a wind trainer before a blank TV screen. I hunch over the handlebars and my stomach starts to cramp; must be those Tashkurgan grapes.

By midmorning the air clears and the valley is unveiled as a long, upward-slanting corridor enclosed by brown mounds. The Pamirs here are lazy, eroded hills, and only my labored breathing hints of this valley's lofty height. I pass a few oases, but the houses are invisible; only treetops burst out over the high walls. Tajiks working in the fields stop to watch me pass, and the women—bless 'em!—cheer me on.

As morning passes into afternoon, a ring of snow-topped crags peeks over the horizon ahead: the Karakoram. The road grows steadily steeper, working itself up for the climactic leap over the Khunjerab Pass, which separates China from Pakistan. By late afternoon I am weary and cannot pedal fast enough to keep the bike erect. I get off and push.

Near the end of the day, after ninety-one grueling kilometers, I trudge into the last inhabited spot in China. It should be a triumphant moment, but I am drained and ill. At a hostel by the immigration post I am given watermelon and some greasy dumplings. My stomach gets worse. The next morning, too weak to ride the final leg, I board a bus to cross the Khunjerab pass and descend into Pakistan.

PAKISTAN IS ANOTHER universe entirely.

The first town, Sust, is a paradise of inns, restaurants, and shops purveying such exotica as soft toilet paper and chocolate cookies—luxuries I haven't seen in months. After one night's rest here I am fit again. I give my passport to a Pakistani official for safekeeping, then put my bike and myself on a van to retrace my steps to the border, from where I will roll back down. At the Khunjerab pass, 4,730 meters in elevation, I disembark next to a stone marker.

Ahead lies five hours and 1,800 meters of harrowing, transcendent descent.

To the hum of wind in my spokes and the pianissimo sound of tires kissing pavement, I fly swiftly downward. The Karakoram are unlike any mountains I've ever seen—so dry and violent and full of movement. As if a gargantuan construction project was left unfinished, edges are raw and chewed: boulders teeter before great falls; gravel rivers lie halted on colossal slopes. Nothing lives here but the mountains themselves, perpetually shrugging themselves into new configurations, threatening to bury this puny highway in *karakoram,* the black, crumbling rock that gives the range its name.

Stopped for a drink of water halfway down, I am startled by the sound of shattering glass and a sharp *thunk* that is not heard but rather transmitted to my feet through the ground like an earthquake. A rock has fallen from the cliff above my head and struck the pavement a few paces behind me, splintering into a hundred shards. I look up: more rocks coming!—and pedal like fury to flee the place. It is two more hours back to Sust, and I ride uneasily now, often glancing up at the stone that hangs ominously above.

After Sust the real vacation begins. Towns are frequent, hostels cheap and friendly, and the scenery stupendous. According to Islamic custom, local women are often sequestered; but in this much-touristed area I may go about freely. At Passu I stop for a few days to walk among charming mountain villages and glaciers that flow down nearly to the road. Farther ahead is Baltit, the capital of Hunza, a fairy-tale kingdom of jaw-dropping verticality, where green terraces comb canyon walls that rise to majestic, snowy heights.

A week later I reach Gilgit, a great metropolis to eyes long accustomed to the aeries of mountain folk. It's a jolly town, full of mountaineers, trekkers, and tourists. My Karakoram Highway cycling is finished, for the road onward passes through areas ruled by tribal law, and foreigners—especially lone females—are discouraged from intruding. After a few days here I'll take the bus to Islamabad from where I'll ship my bicycle home.

RESTED NOW, MY spirit clean and unweighted, in the hotel backyard I practice a kata called *Kwanku*. The name means "to look at the sky." It begins with feet apart, hands together and low, fingers and thumbs extended to shape a small triangular window. I have made this kata thousands of times before, but as I prepare my breathing something feels altogether different. Suddenly the world whirls and transforms: the small square of Pakistani grass under my feet spreads to a limitless carpet; the barren Karakoram melt down into soft green hills. I disappear from Pakistan and reappear on the grasslands of Kham.

I make the first move of *Kwanku*, drawing breath carefully into my *tanden* while my arms slowly rise. As the hand window rises past the horizon my eyes become pinned to that three-cornered space of blue, following it upward.

Now I stand erect, arms stretched to the zenith. The small opening in my hands has become a cosmic view port drawing my spirit heavenward—a conduit for power that pours from the earth, hurtles through my veins, and shoots like a laser beam to heaven. Skewered like a tomato on this cosmic pipeline, I stand for an eternal moment as the pressure builds. Hoofbeats drum in the distance, a rider approaching ...

Suddenly, the window bursts. Hands tear open the sky, then slice down in twin arcs. From here the kata becomes a furious battle, full of deep, lancelike attacks, hand blades slicing lethal circles, and powerful, explosive jumps—all aflame with the eloquence and energy of that initial heavenly connection.

The creator of *Kwanku* is said to be a Chinese military attaché called Ku Shanku who lived about three hundred years ago. We know little about this man—what he looked like, how he regarded the world—but as I make his kata here, surrounded by the electrifying splendor of the grasslands, I feel his presence strongly. The movements—long, sharp, elegant—conjure him on the grass before me. Kwanku is tall; his face is dark and poetic. His lean body moves bladelike, and his fists cut like a knife. Kwanku is a man of few words, unswervingly strict, with a gaze that instantly withers. He is not a young man. He is in his prime.

I make ten *Kwanku,* feeling this warrior's spirit. Then I kneel in *seiza* on the cold, damp earth, half close my eyes, and meditate there, my human form just a quavering, fleshy speck on the infinite divide between the grass and sky of the plateau.

22

FULL CIRCLE

KATHMANDU!

It is the height of the trekking season and Thamel, Kath-mandu's tourist mecca, is luridly alive. Long-limbed Europeans saunter like gods and goddesses with their golden hair and expensive trekking togs. Sherpa mountaineers, consciously elite, swagger along in twos and threes, boasting easy grins and bran-dishing expedition logos. Shopkeepers provoke from the door-ways: "Excusemebuyacarpetmadam? Excuseme! *Excuse me!*" Sharp-eyed Sherpanis preside in cavelike shops beneath tower-ing piles of trekking gear. Beggars dangle deformities under the noses of passersby and jangle their cups of coins. Wiry teenagers turn the cranks of polychromatic pedicabs, weaving willy-nilly through the swirling throngs. Black market moneychangers amble with purposeful slowness as they cast ventriloquial mut-ters at foreigners in the crowd. Storefronts are one continuous Technicolor display of Kathmanduabilia: carpets and *thangkas,* sweaters and bags, jewelry and masks, clothing reminiscent of another age: tie-dyed shirts, rainbow pullovers, and baggy pants sewn with accents of that ubiquitous Kathmandu gold-maroon weave, all hanging in psychedelic profusion.

I'm back! I'm really back!

It has been five years since that Annapurna trek and the

night that I first heard of Khampas. I have been to Kham, and although I saw plenty of dashing young horsemen, I saw no sign of the guerrillas that Judy spoke of. Where have all those fighters gone?

For years Mustang—a bubble of Nepal that projects into the Tibetan plateau—was the Khampa guerrilla stronghold. Mustang was a natural choice, for although Nepal might have nominal sovereignty over this remote and mysterious land, as a practical matter the Kingdom of Lo (as it is known to its inhabitants) is too large, too distant, and too difficult to access for any outside government to effectively rule. It possesses only a handful of settlements, and they are scattered over an immense wasteland of rugged, windy, waterless high plateau.

Mustang flourished in former times because it lay on an important trade route, so Lopas were able to supplement the land's meager bounty with profits on Tibetan salt, which was exchanged for the grain of the lowlands. But in the last 200 years trans-Himalayan trade has declined,[26] and the towns of Lo along with it, turning Mustang into a forgotten dead-end. Surrounded on three sides by Tibet, it was an ideal place from which to wage a guerrilla war against China.

Michel Peissel, the intrepid French anthropologist, visited Mustang during that turbulent period. He described his adventures in *Mustang: The Forbidden Kingdom*. With only the most reluctant permission from Nepalese authorities, he set off for Mustang in 1964 during the peak of the guerrilla war, accompanied by just a few porters and assistants. Only when he arrived did he fully understand how precarious his position as an outsider in Lo really was, for he had come to a "territory partially under control of the Khampas: men who, I knew, were considered a race of warriors, and professional hereditary highway robbers . . . men whose courage was said to be equaled only by

26. Thomas Laird, "In the Shadow of the Himalaya: A Kingdom Unveiled." *Asiaweek*, Oct. 9, 1992, p. 97.

their brutality."[27] But during his two months in Mustang Peissel was so impressed by the Khampas' courage and so moved by their cause that he became an ardent supporter.

Just west of Mustang is another remote mountain region called Dolpo. Writer/philosopher Peter Matthiessen describes a 1973 expedition to Dolpo in his classic of Himalayan adventure, *The Snow Leopard*. For Matthiessen the journey was not just a walk in the mountains, but a spiritual quest symbolized by the rare and elusive cat for which the book is named.[28] Inspired by Zen, Tibetan Buddhism, and Dolpo's ravishing Himalayan backdrop, Matthiessen's insights are sharpened to a lucid point; his book epitomizes everything that romanced me about the Himalayas.

During his trek to Dolpo, Matthiessen saw a few Khampas, well noting the terror that Mustang's guerrilla army inspired in Dolpo's people. Given the danger perceived by government circles of the "Khampa menace," it was not surprising when, soon after Matthiessen's departure, Dolpo was closed again. It stayed closed for years.

During the time Dolpo and Mustang were forbidden to outsiders, the Khampa guerrillas conducted a remarkably complex military operation, openly running loads of supplies and ammunition up the ancient trade route along the Kali Gandaki River. But in 1974 the Nepalese government, under pressure from the beleaguered Chinese, sent in the Gurkha army to halt the guerrilla war and drive the Khampas out of Mustang. The operation was a success, and peace and security were restored to the Nepal–Tibet borderland. But it wasn't until 1989 that Dolpo at last was opened to foreign travelers.

That's where I plan to go: as close as I can to those mountains trod by Khampas, perhaps even to meet one of their scat-

---

27. Peissel, *Mustang: The Forbidden Kingdom*, p. 77.
28. The formal purpose of the trip was to observe the rare Himalayan blue sheep, a project conceived by biologist George Schaller, who led the expedition.

tered remnants. I yearn to go to Mustang, but that area is still off-limits. Unlike the Chinese closures of eastern Kham, the Nepalese laws have teeth in them. So my plan is to arrange a trek to neighboring Dolpo, following in Matthiessen's footsteps.

In a Thamel bookstore I find a thin blue volume titled *Trekking in Hidden Land of Dolpa-Tarap and Shey-Poksumdo*,[29] for the most part a dry account of the route. On page 25 the following catches my eye:

> In the north, at RINGMO, PUNGMO, DHO TARAP and in the upper TARAP valley, population is mixed. TIBETANS and MAGARS; but all speaking TIBETAN of KHAM. All these people have adopted the costumes and language of KHAM, an immense Territory east of LHASA, in Tibet, Dolpa is the land of the mystic SARKAIN (the snow leopard) . . .[30]

Khampa villages here in Nepal? This news is, to say the least, intriguing. Could they be local folk who have adopted the customs of the occupying Khampa forces? I am eager to find out just how these Khampa-speaking people came to be in western Nepal, more than 1,300 kilometers distant from Kham. It is yet another reason to undertake the journey to Dolpo, for even if the guerrillas have disappeared from the Himalayas, in Dolpo I still have a chance to find something related to my quest.

To get to Dolpo, I need a guide. This, in principle, is easy, for there are trekking agencies on every block of Thamel. I chose one at random and go in.

"Hello! Come in! Sit down!" says the oily salesman behind the counter. "How can I help you today? Trekking? Rafting? Or perhaps a jungle safari—"

29. The place is called Dolpa in Nepalese; Dolpo in Tibetan. See John Smart and John Wehrheim, "Dolpo, Nepal," The Tibet Journal, Vol. 2, No. 1, spring 1977, pp. 50-59.

30. Paolo Gondoni, Tiwari's Pilgrims Book House, Kathmandu, p. 25.

"I want to go to Dolpo."

"Dolpo—oh yes! I can certainly help you," he gushes. "We have arranged many treks to Dolpo. Our guides are very experienced. How many persons are you?"

"One."

"One?" His eyes open wide and he leans forward. "Surely not! Just one? Did you come to Nepal by yourself?"

"Yes, I did."

"Why don't you join a group? Your trek will be much more enjoyable if you go with a group. I can help you find one—"

"No, that's all right. I don't mind going alone. I *want* to go alone." Other foreigners could only get in my way, but that's more than this man could possibly understand. "Just tell me about logistics and costs."

"Ah . . . well . . . let me see. Dolpo, eh?" He rifles through a bin to find the map he wants, then spreads it on the counter. "Now the place you are going to is Phoksumdo Lake—"

"But I don't want the standard trek. I want to go as far east in Dolpo as possible. You see, what I'm really interested in is Mustang—"

"Mustang? Mustang?" He looks quizzical for a moment. "You know what? I think that the government has just decided to open Mustang for trekking. I read about it just the other day . . ."

I sit bolt upright in my chair. "Mustang open? *Hot damn!* Then I want to go to Mustang!"

AN HOUR LATER I leave the office. My mind is racing and I'm almost dizzy with excitement. What a fantastic stroke of luck! Not only is Mustang exactly the place I want to go, but I might even be the first foreigner to set foot there in decades. And according to the map, there is a trail leading from western Mustang straight into Dolpo, so I can visit both places in one trek.

For some inexplicable reason, heaven is smiling on me. To be sure, this particular agency doesn't inspire much confidence. I asked the man about a Tibetan-speaking guide and he wouldn't say that he even had one. And when I asked about costs he just hemmed and hawed. But there are plenty of other agencies. The important thing is, Mustang is open!

The next day I make the rounds of Thamel. Of the agencies I visit, none have gotten the news. When I tell them about Mustang's opening they all have the same disappointing reaction: "I don't believe it. It can't be done. And even if it's true, we don't want anything to do with it."

There are plenty of agencies left, but after hours of being battered by Thamel's mayhem I am getting tired. Just one more, and then I'll call it a day. Next to the gate of the Kathmandu Guest House is a shop window displaying the usual trekking ads. I open the door and go in.

"Hi, I want to arrange a trek for one person to Mustang."

"Oh yes, of course! Please sit down. Would you like tea?"

Here at last is an agent who seems to know what's going on. He is a dark-skinned Hindu wearing a shirt and tie. His English is better than average, and he has that merry, winning way that I remember so fondly in the guides I knew five years ago. I sit down in a newly hopeful frame of mind.

"You know no one has ever sent a trekking group to Mustang before," he says matter-of-factly. "But according to the announcement, the rules will be similar to the rules for climbing expeditions. We have much experience in this."

He goes on to explain the rules and the agency's rates—not astronomical. Next we pore over maps and make calculations: so many days going up to Mustang, so many days in the crossing, so many days in Dolpo, so many days to return. I can do it all and get out before winter snows set in, and—no less important—I'll be home in time for Christmas. They have a Tibetan-speaking guide available. There is only one unknown: getting a permit to Mustang. No one has ever done this before.

The man promises he will check it out; I am to return tomorrow.

THE NEXT FEW days follow a pattern. Each morning I stop by the agency to check on the progress of their arrangements. We study various maps and discuss possible routes. The way into Mustang is difficult but straightforward. After that, there are several trails crossing from Mustang into Dolpo, all of which involve walking for days at elevations over 5,000 meters and crossing passes that might be snowbound at this time of year. As for my permit, they keep insisting that it's no problem, that my application will certainly be approved, probably "the day after tomorrow."

One afternoon I meet my prospective guide. A plain, honest fellow with a round face and stubby features, his name is Ang Babu Sherpa. His English is only adequate, but he knows Tibetan well. His businesslike and self-effacing manner inspires me with confidence.

But still no one knows exactly when or how the permit will appear, for although the government has decided to open Mustang, now that they are faced with a real live applicant, officials are dithering. The agent continues to assure me that everything will come through in the end, so I go merrily ahead with my plans, shopping and preparing for the upcoming adventure.

Yet days go by, and the permit doesn't come. Meanwhile the agent is slowly but inexorably talking me out of the high-elevation Mustang-Dolpo crossing. Somehow he remains cheerful and obsequious while slyly insinuating the foolhardiness of my plan. It is too high and too cold this time of year, he implies gravely. The porters would need expensive equipment. After Mustang, he wants a full retreat to the town of Pokhara, from there to proceed to Dolpo. It is virtually two separate expeditions, and I fret at the added cost. Unlike Chinese officials, who seem to take some malicious pleasure from saying no, the Nepalese are eager to please, and will continue to say yes even when it's not the right answer. But I don't understand this yet, and happily believe his assurances: "Oh yes, Dolpo and Mustang have lots of Khampas."

My Dolpo permit is swiftly approved, but about Mustang the officials are stuck. All they can say is that they still need "two or three more days" to "develop a policy." Meanwhile the clock ticks, the season advances, and I grow impatient with waiting.

Mindful of the hard trails ahead, one afternoon I take a training walk out to Kathmandu's eastern suburbs. Away from the clamor of the city, a winding dirt footpath takes me between squares of growing grain, red brick dwellings, and swarms of barefoot children. My destination is Bodinath, the great Buddhist stupa, largest in Nepal. Just at sunset, I pass through a gateway onto a large pavilion. In the center is a huge white dome, and on its summit rises a golden tower. The stupa's tower is painted with four pairs of sinuous eyes—their haunting, mystic gaze emblematic of all the exquisite mystery that is Kathmandu. Around the stupa an inexorable swirl of the faithful paces steady clockwise circles.

Despite the annoying calls of vendors and beggars, and despite the profusion of tacky souvenirs, this place is strangely cleansing. I join the throngs of Sherpas, Tibetans, pilgrims, and monks of all stripes strolling around the perimeter. In the fading light of sunset, the giant dome glows like a golden sun suspended in a boundless blue universe. In its orbit I feel warmed and safe.

23

EH HOK!

"ʟᴀʀᴇɴ'ᴛ ᴡᴇ ɢᴇᴛᴛɪɴɢ off here?"

After a long bumpy day on a dusty road, at last we are in downtown Pokhara. Ang Babu sits on the seat beside me, calm and unmoving. Everyone else on the bus streams toward the door.

"Wait a minute," he replies. "Bus taking us to camping place." Sure enough, after everyone but us has unloaded, the engine starts up again and we rumble down darkened streets to a hotel at the edge of town. Riding on the bus are three other Sherpas[31]; with Ang Babu they form my permanent staff of four for the monthlong trek ahead. I am not sure of their names yet, and I'm even less sure about the extravagance of having such a large staff. I originally wanted a small party consisting of myself, a guide, and perhaps one or two porters, but the agency wouldn't hear of it. Now as I stand watching basket after basket of provisions being handed down from the roof, my backpacker's frugal instinct grieves.

---

31. The proper noun "Sherpa" refers to a race of mountain-dwelling people in central and eastern Nepal. Sherpas from the Everest region have won so much fame as mountaineers that the name "sherpa" (lower case) has come to mean "mountain guide." The word means "Easterner" in Tibetan.

We pitch our tents in the hotel yard. The cookboy spreads a blue tarp for me to sit on, and I dine in regal solitude. Across the yard, the sherpas chatter away as they consume their *daal-bhaat* (lentils and rice) under an awning. I feel very much alone.

The next morning I have even more misgivings when six porters appear. Can these ten people and all these porter-loads really be just for little me? Packing for a journey, I am convinced, is like making a kata—extraneous items should be ruthlessly cut off. This expedition seems dangerously overloaded.

A bus arrives to take us a few winding miles up a country road to the trail head. At the end of the asphalt I get out to survey sleepy plank-and-clay shop fronts. Brown-skinned men lounge in the doorways while women and children crowd around us trying to induce us to buy eggs. As the loads are taken off the bus and piled on the ground, I watch the buzz of activity, feeling like a spectator at a show in which I was supposed be the leading lady. Ang Babu touches my elbow. Motioning to a footpath leading away from the pavement he says, "We go now, Peima?" (He calls me by my Tibetan name, which means "lotus.")

"Oh!" My reverie is broken. "Yes, let's go to Dolpo!"

THAT'S THE PLAN: we go to Dolpo. When we left Kathmandu the Mustang permit still had not been approved, and with a week-long holiday approaching—during which no official business will be conducted—it would be stupid to waste any more time. On our way to Dolpo we will pass through a couple of towns where the government operates radio transmitters; through them we can contact Kathmandu and find out about the progress of the Mustang permit, and, if necessary, hurry back early so that we will have time for a visit to the Kingdom of Lo.

So we begin the trek to Dolpo. The first days are easy trots over gently terraced hills strewn with prosperous villages. The sun is warm, the harvest is coming in, and the local people, all Hindu, are preparing for the festival of *Tihar*. On the trail we meet laughing women returning to their natal homes where they will place a tika on their brothers' foreheads and ceremoniously wish them a long and prosperous life. The women, wrapped in gauzy sheets of patterned cloth, walk with an easy, sensuous gait, their long braids swinging languidly across their backs. "*Namaste!* they say, a Nepalese greeting that means "I salute the god within you." In the countryside such pleasantries are free and plentiful, one of the many charms of this enchanted land.

My Sherpa staff, once an unfamiliar, elephantine appendage, is fast becoming a useful and companionable asset as I adjust to life on the trail. At the helm of our ship is the sirdar, Ang Babu Sherpa, an imperturbable fount of mountain wisdom and managerial skills. He is unglamorously built: Hobbitlike, with short legs and a long, stocky torso. His features are thick, and after a few days hairs are sprouting from unlikely places on his face. Ang Babu's laugh is a simple, peasant's laugh, mostly at other's jokes, or at himself, like when his two feet slid out from under him at a river crossing and he landed square upon his rump. Despite his simple, unassuming nature and his young age (twenty-five), Ang Babu already has eight years' guiding experience. No matter what problems we have, be they god- or human-made, he handles them smoothly, cheerfully, and with quiet authority.

About the same age as Ang Babu and next to him in seniority is Tenzeng Sherpa, our peerless cook, who masterminds with zeal and flare everything related to our daily nourishment. With a magician's neat little beard on a handsome, square-jawed face, he reminds me of a Japanese, especially when he ties a towel samurai-style around his head. Despite his sober bearing, though, Tenzeng is our chief prankster: the origin of most mischief and the focus of most reprisals. He admits to little

English, but I sometimes catch him listening to me with a secret, knowing smile.

After Ang Babu and Tenzeng, the next man down on the totem pole is sweet-faced, curly haired Phurba Sherpa, our hardworking cookboy, an unstoppable whirlwind of energy and mirth. He carries a basket loaded with half the kitchen,[32] yet despite the weight on his back, Phurba races ahead of the rest of us, shouting or singing or whistling as he gallops along the trail. His Nepalese erupts at a furious pace, well spiced with lusty epithets; but he's at his most endearing when a rare English phrase pops out. In a lilting tenor, he'll say "I no am sweemming," or "Shoes outside tent, please," or (a favorite) "Good idea!"

The other half of the kitchen is carried on Karmi Sherpa's back. He is a kitchen porter, the lowliest of the four. Karmi is small and looks frail: spindly arms and legs emerging from a brave, thin body. His tightly drawn flesh and deep-set eyes give his face the poetry of a dancer. At the ripe old age of twenty-seven he is an experienced carrier, yet he is the slowest of us five and usually trails by some distance.

On the third day, our trail is snaking through stair-step terraces, just as it has since we began. This afternoon, however, we have just reached my old friend the Kali Gandaki River, now roaring below. It's huge and fresh and deafening down here, unlike the emaciated upper reaches remembered from my Annapurna trek. The Kali Gandaki River originates in upper Mustang; if my permit is approved I will follow it nearly to its source. Seeing the river now, I say a silent godspeed for my application now being considered in Kathmandu.

The boys are in a good mood; as we march along they sing a rousing tune. It is a simple melody with slow, rhythmic pronouncements ringing up and down a minor key, each stanza

---

32. Two kerosene stoves, three kettles, six pots of various sizes, a pressure cooker, two basins, two colanders, a frying pan, cutting board, rolling pin, two ladles, kitchen knife, spatula, and cheese grater, plus service for four.

building to a crescendo with the shouted words "song la EH HOK!" I don't know what it means, but it's simple enough that I can follow along.

But now our human caravan stretches, Phurba racing ahead and Karmi lagging behind, and the song fades. Buried in my own thoughts, I am startled a short time later by a sound like denting aluminum. I round a corner to see Phurba looking off the edge of a cliff, a broken tump line in his hand. His load has jumped off his back and fallen down a steep, fifteen-meter slope. In a twinkling he is down after it, and brings the basket up again with remarkable ease.

Now back among us, the irrepressible Phurba sets his battered basket down upon the trail, jumps up on a rock, spreads his arms wide to the sky, and with the laughing face of a boy Buddha he lets out a big, roaring "EH HOK!" Then he gets down and repairs his load.

That night we camp in a school yard by the river. Karmi goes out with a flashlight to look for the porters, who are an hour behind. It is pitch dark now, and the kitchen is starting on dinner, working by flashlight as our kerosene lantern is still on a porter's back. I walk away from the others, across the field in the direction of the Kali Gandaki. There is no moon, and although this village has electricity, the lights are too far and dim to be of much use. Their feeble rays ripple on the river's surface, making it glitter like cut black glass. Fireflies trace Himalayan hieroglyphics. In this moment of eerie solitude I begin a kata, stumbling on the rough ground when the town's twinkle suddenly dies, leaving me in total dark.

It was dark, too, the first time I felt something magic in the kata called *Kwanku*. It happened at a twenty-four-hour karate marathon in the high Sierra, an experience I'll never forget. We had been training for sixteen hours straight, and my spirits were by now frozen from cold and dead from exhaustion. An icy mountain breeze was blowing, and the night had reached its darkest hour. Coming away from the scene of an earlier practice, we marched along a dusty road to where it crossed a meadow. There we stopped and formed a long line, each of the fifty-odd brown and black belts occupying his or her own little space of dirt.

We began to do *Kwanku,* each person taking a turn to give the command *hajime!* to begin. It was so dark that I hardly knew who was standing next to me. The line was so long and stretched so far that commands coming from the end were nearly swallowed by the mountains. Conditions were utterly impossible. The ground was rutted and uneven. I was weighted with heavy shoes, winter clothes, and by the indescribable weariness of training without pause since dawn. After the first few kata I was already choking from the dust kicked up by my own feet.

The *Kwanku* I did—over and over again, more than fifty times—was not the elegant sequence of razor-sharp moves I had learned in the dojo back home; it was a clumsy, desperate, scrabbling thing, like a fight to the death. Despite the elevation, we never paused for rest, but did one kata after another. A dozen or so repetitions into the series I was completely breathless, and falling behind the others.

But then I noticed something magical. If, at the kata's beginning, I turned my body to the left ever so slightly, I could catch the moon in the triangle of my hands as they rose to meet the sky. And somehow that silver circle trapped between my fingers flowed like an infusion of electricity in my nerves, oxygen to my lungs, energy to every cell. It awakened power I hadn't known I possessed. From that moment on, the kata burst out of me like water from a fire hose. *Kwanku*—"to look at the sky"— contained sorcery that bewitched me there on the mountain.

Now, as I execute the kata's high kicks and deep cuts, the cries of Khampa horsemen come back to me. *Kwanku* is a sharp, startling kata; it is powerful, poised, and precise. *Kwanku* is a tall man's kata; it is ruthless and proud—even arrogant. And *Kwanku* is a celebration of the open sky.

It is a Khampa's kata!

A FEW CAMPS later Ang Babu announces, "Today we very climbing." This is good news. I am weary of rice-paddy villages and sweat and ants and begging kids. It is high time for some cool air and mountain views.

The climb is difficult but rejuvenating. As we labor up a series of steep switchbacks, boisterous Phurba spurts gleefully up a shortcut and bounds out of sight. At the top we stand in a forest of pines, at last out of the stink of paddy and jungle. The air and sun are altogether different here: fresher and cleaner and more direct. Dhaulagiri's peaks, a jumbled pile of icy pyramids, have jumped up on the horizon. I feel as if I have arrived.

At lunch we catch up to a large party of Dhaulagiri circuiters. They are climbers, French, and are flashing long hairy legs under their minuscule walking shorts. Their enormous crew of heavily laden staff dwarfs my own small party. We will follow the same itinerary through tonight, but tomorrow they will turn north while my party continues west.

The afternoon walk takes us through a series of high-altitude settlements plastered onto the side of a slope of stupendous proportions, a whole world map of fields, trails, and houses turned up on its edge. At evening we reach the village of Sibang atop a commanding bluff. In a school yard we make our tidy camp, while the French crew throws up a tent metropolis. The sky has grown gray, and as the light fades, rain begins to fall. Rain in Sibang means snow on the high passes—where we are all bound—and this is very bad news.

My kitchen takes refuge in the schoolhouse. I follow them inside the dark stone building, find a comfortable perch atop some dusty furniture, and spend an hour exulting in the atmosphere of the place: howling wind outside, flickering candles within; porters bustling in and out; Tenzeng and his helpers slicing vegetables, rolling out chapatis, and boiling potatoes by lamplight. Gusts knock at the window shutters like evil spirits. After dinner, under the influence of a cup of warm arak I start to nod, but am roused by sounds coming from outside.

When I step through the door the sky is black, the rain has stopped, and the grass is cold and wet and glistening. Three school benches are set into an open rectangle; the fourth side is closed by a line of musicians and singers. They have a couple of drums and a little accordion. Already the party is under way: the band is playing, the chorus is singing, and two girls are dancing in the center.

The Frenchmen (and one Frenchwoman), guests of honor, sit before the show. Room is quickly made for me and Ang Babu to sit among them. Villagers bring around cups of *arak*—a clear, potent, whiskeylike liquor—for each of us. I give mine to Ang Babu. It is not his first tonight.

After four or five rounds of dancing the show is getting tedious, but the sherpas in the crowd—mine and those belonging to the French group—are just getting into the party mood. Ang Babu springs up from his seat and jumps into the fray, flailing and twitching in a vague semblance of some traditional Sherpa folk dance. Not very coordinated even in the best of times, now that he is drunk he is a wild and uncontrolled dervish. I'm embarrassed for him, but nobody seems to mind in the least—except perhaps my fellow foreigners, who look a little restless. Suddenly, with a parting *"bon soir!"* the French go into retreat. Flashlight beams recede and now they are no more.

But the party has only just begun. Now Sherpas from the other group jump up to join my gyrating *sirdar*. The villagers keep on playing while they gawk at the awesome spectacle of Sherpa climbing jocks cavorting by lantern light. On the sidelines a gallery of nondancing Sherpas heckles the others, shouting their own bawdy lyrics over the music.

THE NEXT MORNING dawns clean and beautiful, and I feel as though some powerful joy-drug must have been slipped into my *arak* the night before. Despite his hangover, Ang Babu is chanting a Buddhist sutra in his tent, as is his custom. He pauses to greet me in Tibetan, the official auxiliary language of this expedition: *"Tashi delek, Acha-la!"* (good fortune, honored sister!) he says warmly. Phurba follows with an emphatic chorus: *"Yakpo du re, yakpo du re, yakpo du re!"* (It's good, it's good, it's good!)

We climb a bit, and I find myself walking behind our kitchen porter Karmi, lulled by his practiced gait. His steps are slow and steady, metronomic, hypnotizing. A porter can't look up—the weight on his back and the tump line's pull aim his face dirtward. To follow a porter's walk is to commune intimately with the stones and dust of the trail. The inexorable rhythm of Karmi's feet gradually merges me with the totality of walking.

Yagyu Munenori, famous seventeenth-century swordsman, writes, "When you walk, it's bad to be fast or to be slow. Walking in a natural way, gliding, unthinking, is good. To be excessive or inadequate is bad; take the middle ground. You are fast because you are alarmed, rattled. You are slow because you are daunted, afraid of your opponent. The ideal is the state where you are not upset by anything . . . The point is not to lose your natural state of mind."[33]

While I walk my thought gears grind slowly, like a great glacier, or the wheel of karma itself. I consider, organize, and occasionally even solve koans great and small. Upper consciousness rests solely on the mundane business of choosing footfalls on the trail; middle consciousness dwells in another place—back

33. Yagyu Munenori, *The Sword & the Mind,* p. 86.

home in the karate dojo perhaps, or with the nomads on the grasslands of Kham. Meanwhile, for its part in the fugue, unconscious mind plays a rumbling bass, a sound more felt than heard that moves under its own irresistible power. If I chance to look up, the scenery is no more than an annoying intrusion. Dirt and rocks gliding beneath my feet, this is my best thinking time, when many things come clear.

Houses become steadily shabbier as we continue west. The night's camp is at Lalung, a village of low-caste people hanging on a forty-five-degree slope of poor soil. Two dark little girls come to squat by our camp in a huddle of blankets, regarding us with silent, feral eyes.

After dinner I recline on a sleeping mat and share a cup of hot arak with Ang Babu. Phurba and Karmi wash dishes with great industry and enthusiasm, Phurba's furious scrubbing just another expression of his unquenchably joyous self. They talk, and I feel pleasantly irresponsible daydreaming to the music of a language I don't understand. Nepalese is a tongue of rapidly burbled syllables, each sentence ending in a little skyrocket of a final sound: an *eh!* or an *oh!* or a *ni!* Without really trying I pick up a few odd words: *chya* for tea, *dudh* for milk, *pani* for water. But then there's a phrase they constantly use whose meaning I can't quite make out.

"Ang Babu, what does *ma jigne* mean? You guys use it all the time."

"Ah—er—" Ang Babu stammers and turns pink. The others know what I'm asking and their faces are bright with merriment. "I don't know English meaning," he goes on lamely. "It is bad word. Better not to say."

The next day we are "very climbing" again, this time to Jalja La, the first real pass on the route to Dolpo. By the standards of Kham it is a piddling sort of pass, only 3,400 meters above sea level. At the last house—only a rude stone hut—we stop for a breather. The old woman who lives here invites us to come inside and sit before her smoky fire, over which she fries some blood in a long-handled pan for us to eat. The salty black lumps taste nourishing and wild, just like this mountain place.

Now the real work begins, for the trail leads upward ever more steeply. In moments of fatigue I strain forward at every step, my head bobbing like a mule's. Catching myself in such poor form, I resolve to keep my back erect, to lift my knees, to put my hips up the mountain. In walking, as in *oizuki,* hips are the key to powerful, effective movement. Here in the Himalayas walking is my daily practice, so I endeavor to do it well.

The machine is warmed and working now: I feel drawn upward by some peculiar levitating force that comes not from my muscles, but from some inexplicable natural buoyancy. Limbs of alder, oak, and pine knot over my head in a leafy canopy; their twisted roots embrace stairsteps of moist black earth. As we climb higher I spot snow huddling shyly inside nooks and crannies—the first snow we've seen up-close on this trip. A little higher the fluff gains confidence, lying forthrightly all about.

The Dolpo guidebook warns of "tigers, leopards, bears, and also DACOITS (Bandits)" here, but my sherpas are unafraid, and assault the silence with gusto. Cries of *"Eh hok! Etti lamu ke hok!"* and *"Yakpo du re!"* echo up and down the mountain. Caught up in the moment, I toss in a lusty "Two-four-six-eight, who do we appreciate!" It seems to fit the occasion.

We reach the Jalja La at last, and stop to savor the moment of triumph—but not for long; the wind has teeth here. That night we camp in a pretty little valley buried in forest and steadily accumulating snow. By the light of a roaring campfire I bandage porter limbs: one has twisted his knee; another has an open blister. After I clean, disinfect, and bandage his wound, the man regards me with beatific awe.

The next day we arrive in Dhorpatan—at long last, a Tibetan place! I survey with joy the long mani-wall that marks the approach to town. Heaps of stones engraved with the mantra *Om mani padme hum* awaken cherished memories of

Kham. Alas, it has been raining all day and our gear is wet through. We will take a rest day here to dry out, hire fresh porters, and radio Kathmandu to check on my permit for Mustang.

On our way into town we met a group of fifteen foreign trekkers plus a proportionate number of staff. They had been heading to Dolpo but were stopped by deep snow on Jang La, which lies just one more day ahead. Wet and dispirited, they were a gloomy group. If there are no more storms then Jang La might clear in a few days, but these large-scale treks are tightly scheduled and they couldn't wait. Too much of a hurry to go home to their suits and ties, I think smugly to myself, hoping that with my small and flexible party we will succeed where they failed.

Dhorpatan is spread around the perimeter of a huge pasture. A few grazing horses and their tinkling bells remind me of Kham. The town is quiet, as many of the residents have left to winter in warmer climes. One man has a spare room in his house into which our kitchen moves, sherpas arrayed at one end, porters grouped around a smoky fire at the other.

In the morning there is a heavy frost, but yesterday's clouds and rain are replaced by brilliant sunshine. I rise early and pay a visit to the kitchen, where I find Phurba and Karmi hard at work making tea while the head cook Tenzeng is still abed, snoring regally. Tenzeng is their superior so that is his right, but still his laziness annoys me. I kneel down to where he is huddled under a blanket, grab his feet, and commence a furious tickling, meanwhile shouting "GOOD MORNING TENZENG!" at full voice. Tenzeng shrieks, tries to struggle out of my grip, and the room explodes with laughter. Once the victim is thoroughly awake, I quickly withdraw lest the prank devolve into a wrestling match, but the laughter continues to bubble unabated; Phurba and Karmi are nearly rolling on the floor. Phurba wipes his eyes; *"Asta, asta!"* he cries appreciatively as soon as he can find his voice. "Very good idea!"

Soon the frost is melted, and the day grows into a fragile warmth. We spend a morning drying out equipment and sending a message to Kathmandu. Then Ang Babu and I go exploring. We visit the town's monastery, and a carpet factory where brisk Tibetan girls work before giant vertical looms.

In late afternoon a chance encounter breaks my mindless tourist complacency. Ang Babu and I are walking across the valley when, far away, we spot two lonesome, bedraggled figures trudging along the river. Each is bent beneath a large misshapen load, and they look ragged and hungry. From a distance I snap a photo of them walking along the stone bank. They ford the river and begin coming toward us, and I realize with a shock:

They are wearing the red tassels of Khampas!

24

THE NINETY-NINTH MILE

THE TWO TASSELED men approach us. I wait, heart thumping in my chest, to see what will happen next. Do they belong to the routed forces of Mustang? If so, then they are the ones I came all this way to find. . . .

When they draw close I see that they are young—probably in their early twenties. Not imposing figures, the two are small and thin and weathered, but with beautifully carved Tibetan faces. Their loads consist of various odd-size bundles lashed together, with empty plastic drums hanging ungracefully off the top. They look tired, as though they have been walking all day. One has bare legs and carries his shoes in his hands.

Ang Babu speaks with them at length in a mixture of Nepalese and Tibetan, and I catch a few words. They have come from Pokhara with goods for trade. Like us, they are headed for Dolpo and are anxious about conditions on Jang La. Ang Babu apprises them of the latest reports: *"Kha mangpo du,"* he says—there is much snow. So many things I would like to ask them! But suddenly my mind is a blank; I do nothing but stare. Irritatingly, Ang Babu has stepped between me and them, a protective reflex that is certainly misplaced. Anyway, these two can't be veterans of the Khampa guerrilla war—they're far too young. But who are they?

Ang Babu's conversation with them is done. We turn to head back toward camp. "Ang Babu, who were those guys?" I ask, as soon as I can find my voice.

"Traders."

"Do they come from Kham?"

"They coming from Pokhara."

I look back to the spot where they stood, but now the valley is empty again. Did I dream them?

TO CELEBRATE OUR rest day, Tenzeng has baked a beautiful chocolate cake. After dinner we sit around the fire listening to Baktapur, a porter of about thirty-five who looks more like fifty. He is evidently a man of wide knowledge and experience. Now his low, measured storyteller's voice seems to pulse with the glowing embers; his tale—whatever it is—holds them all rapt. At the end of each paragraph comes a punch line and everyone laughs. How I wish I could understand!

Tomorrow will come an eleven o'clock radio contact with Kathmandu, when we will find out about my Mustang permit. I am nervous and excited, wondering if, after so much buildup, my dream of visiting the old Khampa stronghold is to be realized. Whether or not it is, at least the weather looks promising for a try at Jang La, so we have a chance to get to Dolpo. And those two tasseled men we saw earlier make me optimistic that in Dolpo there is something worth finding.

Ang Babu has scoured Dhorpatan for the new porters that we so desperately need, but no one wants the job. Fortunately, Baktapur and two others of the men we brought here have agreed to carry for us to the next town. They will bear extra-heavy loads, which will slow us down; but without porters we could go nowhere at all, so we gladly accept their assistance. These men are a long way from their homes now, and doubtless are wanting to return.

IN THE MORNING we again have sunshine, and Jang La is said to be open. I hanker to be on the trail, but first we must go to the radio transmitting station to receive our reply. Well ahead of the scheduled contact time, Ang Babu, Phurba, and I walk over to the tidy building of cemented stone. The official there knows our business; he was the one who sent our message to Kathmandu yesterday. At the appointed time he sets his radio on the windowsill so he can sit in the sun as he works. I stand nervously nearby, listening to traffic crackle back and forth.

At last it is Dhorpatan's turn, and the operator comes to life. He speaks slow emphatic Nepalese into the microphone. My two sherpas and I stand close, listening intently. Beneath the static comes an answering voice from Kathmandu, but of course I can't understand the words.

Now Ang Babu speaks to the radio operator, who pronounces a question into the microphone. *"Chaaina"* comes the answer. The transmission is finished now, and the operator signs off.

"Well? Did we get the permit?"

Ang Babu looks perplexed. "They not send answer."

"What? What do you mean they didn't send an answer? Didn't they get our message?"

"He says they got message, but still they not send answer."

We stare at each other in consternation and dismay. It just doesn't make sense. The agency wants the Mustang permit as much as I do; how can they not reply? After a pause I say, "Maybe the officials haven't decided yet. They're probably still going round and round with their silly meetings and can't make up their minds. I'll bet that's it."

WE WALK BACK to camp for lunch. All the while I am puzzling over the agency's odd behavior. I can think of no reasonable explanation. It is maddening that the suspense, which I have endured for weeks already, will continue even longer.

While the kitchen is packing up, I pull out my trekking map and try to calculate how many more days to Dunhai, the next town with a radio transmitter. Estimating distance on the map is straightforward enough, but the terrain will be more difficult, and that will slow us down. "Ang Babu, how many days from here to Dunhai? Three or four days?"

"Three-four days," he affirms solemnly.

"Four-five days?"

"Four-five days," he answers again.

"Five-six days?"

"Five-six days," he says, and laughs, for now he perceives that I am making fun of him. In truth, he doesn't know how many days it will take, for he has never walked this route before. In the face of uncertainty Ang Babu simply says whatever he thinks will make me happy—just another instance of the perpetually shifting nature of Asian reality. A year ago it would have made me angry, but now I only smile.

"Never mind," I tell him. "It doesn't matter. We get there when we get there."

WITH THE DAY half gone already, we can climb only a short way up Phegune Gorge, saving the rest for tomorrow. This gorge leads to Phegune pass, the first of three widely spaced high passes on the road to Dolpo. The trail is muddy from newly melted snow, and in the mud are impressions of bare human feet. I call to my sirdar, "Look, Ang Babu—here are the foot-prints of those two Khampas going to Dolpo."

They are not Khampas, but Ang Babu does not disillusion me; he merely nods.

Next morning, with still 900 meters to climb, we resume our long ascent. It isn't long before we are clambering up an endless slanting chute of boulders. We climb steadily, silently, each separately intent. Phegune Khola, a slender, merry stream, winds picturesquely among the dry stones, tittering at our efforts as it plunges to a happier residence in the valley below.

Though my breathing is labored, I hardly notice, for I am totally absorbed in finding my way over the rocks. Route-finding like this is intensely tactile, linking senses and limbs directly, combining them into a machine that seeks handholds and foot-falls in a continuous flow, bypassing conscious thought. The sensation is not unlike free sparring in slow motion, a karate training method that has more to do with cultivating breathing and eliminating ego than perfecting fighting techniques. In free sparring as in this climb, mind and body are forged into a single fluid entity that automatically flows into openings, unbidden by ego and unhampered by intellect. As I ascend, I try to relax into a state of harmony with the rocks under my hands and feet—to forget the distant summit and simply be one with the mountain.

At last I sight the *chörten* on the pass and struggle to it through ankle-deep powder. Sun-blazed images of snow, rocks, and sky razor my eyes. On the eastern horizon is a gathering of great white kings: Gurza, Phutha Hiunchuli, Churen Himal, and Dhaulagiri II, with its big brother Dhaulagiri I behind, almost out of sight. The sun on my skin is warm, but a breeze kisses my neck with ice. This is not a place to linger. We pause just long enough for photographs, then begin the descent.

For half an hour we walk a gentle downslope that hugs the left wall of a gorge. At lunchtime Phurba spreads the blue tarp on the snow, and I eat in airy white brilliance. We wait here hoping the porters will come, but they do not. At length we move on, following a threadlike path that cuts the valley wall. Gradually the snow disappears, revealing angular rocks and wind-burned tundra. Further ahead is a T-intersection where this gorge empties into a deep perpendicular fissure, the bottom of which is a comparatively habitable place with trees, shepherd's huts, and unfrozen streams. It is to this valley that we are headed.

At length we round the corner to begin our descent into the canyon below. But now the trail traverses a sun-shaded wall where the path is treacherously icy. One wrong step could mean disaster, so we advance slowly and carefully, inch by perilous inch.

Humble Karmi Sherpa, who usually lags behind, now exhibits his years of experience as he calmly negotiates the ice; when I have a chance to glance up I see his basket getting rapidly smaller as he pulls ahead. Now Phurba is the slow one, looking like a terrified child as he minces delicately down the slope. Apprehensively I watch his bobbing basket. He has always carried it so well, but now it could easily tear him off the path and send him plummeting.

"Do we have a rope?" I ask Ang Babu as I watch them go ahead.

"No," he replies, as painfully aware as I am that this omission in our kit might now have dire consequences. But we do have an ice ax—usually devoted to the mundane task of clearing our campsites of stones. Tenzeng pulls it out of Phurba's basket and begins hacking crude steps in the trail ahead, making a safe path for the frightened cookboy and the rest of us behind him.

At the end of this icy patch we heave a sigh of relief. The path ahead crosses a spur, and at the saddle is a little meadow where we stop to rest. We five have made it safely, but our minds are on the porters, still far behind. With their huge, awkward loads the ice will be doubly dangerous. It's getting late, too, and soon the light will be gone. We sit for a moment surveying the way we came, clearly visible across the gully. A moment later Ang Babu jumps up, picks up the ax, and without a word stumps back toward the ice. By the time he reaches the dangerous stretch he is just a dot, but through my telephoto lens I can make out his stooping figure. He has not been gone long when Phurba suddenly grabs the walking sticks that Ang Babu and I have been using and gallops after him up the trail.

An hour later Ang Babu comes back looking anxious.

"Any sign of the porters?"

He shakes his head grimly as he sits down beside me.

"Where is Phurba?"

"Phurba going back, looking for porters." Ang Babu is silent for a moment, arranging his thoughts. Then he begins gravely: "Peima, I am very worry. Maybe it impossible to go to Dolpo with such a small party. This trail very dangerous. Three porters not enough." He takes a long breath, then continues: "Pokhara men have walked very far, we should send them home. Tomorrow, when we arrive Pelma, we look for new porters. If no find, then we must go back to Dhorpatan."

This is a sobering pronouncement. But there is nothing I can say. Ang Babu is right.

We continue to wait. The sun drops behind a ridge and the air suddenly freezes. We all glance up frequently to scan the path, straining our eyes for a glimpse of our long-lost porters. At last a minuscule dot appears on the turning, poised against the white. "It's Baktapur," the others say. The figure keeps moving, marching steadily down the trail. Then two more figures appear, one without a load. I hear a whistle, followed by some boisterous Nepalese. Ang Babu shouts back to Phurba, and the two converse briefly over that amazing distance. Ang Babu says to me, "They all coming."

"Hooray!" I answer, greatly relieved. Before long Baktapur is among us, walking calmly and steadily under his huge load. He looks scarcely even winded. The group is all accounted for, but we can't camp here: this bluff is too exposed and there is no water.

"We go down there," says Ang Babu, pointing to the lovely valley bottom that lies hundreds of meters below. With its small pasture and meandering river, it looks like paradise compared to the cold and windy perch where we now sit. Karmi has already started down with his load. In quickly fading twilight I follow the surefooted Baktapur as he steps nimbly down the trail. Ang Babu follows, ice ax in hand to chop more steps for the remaining porters. Tenzeng stays behind to guide the others home.

The descent is nearly as harrowing as the stretch we covered earlier, but at least this slope is peopled with trees, so there is some chance to arrest a fall. Without my stick I am a maladroit walker; several times my feet slip out from under me and I fall into an ungainly glissade down the bumpy slope. But trees, outcroppings of snow, and panicked scrabbling always stop my fall before I slide very far.

At last we come down to the flat bucket bottom whose walls are a ring of mountains. By now it is pitch dark. In a shepherd's hut Karmi has built a blazing fire, a welcome sight. An hour later I hear Phurba's hearty *"EH HOK!"* which we answer with shouts and whistles. A dot of light moves slowly across the valley, gradually growing into four familiar figures emerging ghostlike from the night.

For me, trekking on that icy trail in the dark was perfectly ghastly, but the porters seem in good humor. I'm glad, because without them we'd be sunk. But still they will go no further than Pelma, the place we will reach tomorrow and the only village of any size before the next high pass. If we can't find new porters in Pelma, then all this struggle will be in vain: we will have to turn around and go back the way we have come.

AT DAWN A flaming orange ring spreads slowly down the circle of cliffs. I roust our sleepy cook out of his bed in the now-traditional manner: by tickling his feet and giving a hearty "GOOD MORNING TENZENG!" to launch him on his way. *"Ehhh oi oi oi oi!"* applauds Phurba, who always loves the sport.

The morning's walk begins easily, with a descent through ancient forest to the Ghustung Khola. We follow this rampaging torrent—more waterfall than river—for a couple of hours; then cross it and begin to climb. After a long up-and-down march, in late afternoon we descend into the vast canyon of the Pelma Khola.

Pelma is a photogenic but impoverished village of Magar people. Their faces are broad and plain, with mottled brown skin, and they wear medieval garments of draped cloth. Pelma's houses are built like stair-steps, one nearly on top of the next, on the valley's steep flank. Few manufactured goods find their way here, and in any event there is little money to buy them, so Pelma is made entirely of stone, clay, wood, wool, and straw. My camera loves Pelma's rich earth browns, but they betray a way of life that permits no luxury.

Across the Pelma Khola are the neat terraces of Yamakhar, Pelma's sister village. Stacked on an almost vertical slope, Yamakhar's terraces look as if a Brobdingnagian witch might have scratched them into the wall with her long, sharp talons. Yamakhar looks close enough to touch—as if residents of Pelma and Yamakhar might, with a stretch, reach across the river to shake each other's hands; but it takes an hour to walk between the two.

Harvest is just in and the citizens of Pelma—for now, at least—are well fed. Maize and winter squash are piled on the roofs of the houses; children are feasting on walnuts; grain lies spread out on woven mats drying in the sun. Alas, their bounty is our misfortune, for we learn that a harvest festival is about to begin. None of Pelma's men will leave the village during this, the highlight of their calendar, regardless of the useful goods that might be bought in Dunhai with our generous wages. Although it is fatal to our hopes of getting to Dolpo, I rather admire their spirit.

Ang Babu scours the village, and turns up one man who says he *might* porter for us. If he decides to come, he'll show up when we depart tomorrow morning at eight o'clock. Perhaps word will get around, I suggest hopefully, and the man will bring some friends. It is only a thread of hope, but I cling mightily to it.

THAT NIGHT, AFTER we have gone to bed, a great clamor rises from a house up the hill. Shouting voices, horns, and a mesmerizing drumbeat spread over the valley: BADUM-BADUM-BADUM-badum,   BADUM-BADUM-BADUM-badum, BADUM-BADUM-BADUM-badum. . . . The noise is strangely compelling, a primitive animal sound. The village dogs are affected, too; and their barking is ceaseless. We have a broken and uneasy night's rest. Even after sunrise, the sound continues relentlessly. "Pucking music, pucking dogs," says Ang Babu in disgust, "Pelma is very unlucky place!"

Slowly, we eat breakfast and pack up our camp, hoping against hope that new porters will magically turn up to save us. The sun rises higher and higher, but still no men. The noise and drumming continue unabated. Even our one potential new porter has failed to appear.

At last Ang Babu deems it best not to wait any longer. Our faithful three are dispatched, with their loads, back in the direction of Dhorpatan. The thought of an ignominious twelve-day retreat along the trail by which we have come fills me with melancholy, but at least there is still a chance that I can go to Mustang. Perhaps it is heaven's will.

We sit by our broken campsite for a while, the better to appreciate this, the farthest point of our trek. Half an hour later a local man straggles in. He wants to porter for us! But one carrier is not enough; we need three. Charged with new hope, Tenzeng leaves for a quick run across the river to Yamakhar where he will look for more men. Phurba runs off in the other direction to stop our faithful three from continuing.

While we wait, someone tells us that the drumming is not Pelma's harvest festival as I assumed: it is a funeral dirge. A young woman of the village, one of just marriageable age, died last night, and the whole village is mourning. As we sit waiting for Tenzeng to return, a procession comes marching down the hill. Somber-faced men carry a white canopy aloft on sticks; others play horns or drums. Then comes a group of women, many of them sobbing and wailing. Among them is one old woman with a ghastly upturned face. Her outstretched arms supported by companions beside her, she floats down the path with giddy, tremulous steps. Last comes the young woman's body, a narrow bundle wrapped in a reed mat, borne on the shoulders of four grim-faced men. The procession winds down between the terraces and disappears over a swell.

At length Phurba returns, accompanied by our faithful three and their loads. Tenzeng is not back yet. The suspense continues. Ang Babu goes off in a different direction, to look for more porters at the local travelers' inn. Karmi has disappeared. Phurba and I wait at our deserted camp, porter-loads standing reproachfully around us like tombstones.

Some time later Ang Babu returns with a smile on his face. "I just find three porters at teahouse," he says happily. I burst out laughing: so we will go to Dolpo after all! It is truly funny—the consummate skill with which heaven has kept us dangling for so long. But the joke gets even better, for now Tenzeng comes striding up the hill, three strapping Magar lads in tow. When the day began we didn't have a single porter; now we have six!

After a quick conference, it is decided that Tenzeng's men are much the better of the two groups. I like the looks of these boys. Two of them are brothers, and are dressed in scarecrow coats made from odd-shaped pieces of woolen felt sewn together with bright-colored thread. One carries an enormous khukri—the traditional knife of the Gurkha—stuck in his belt. They smile broadly, as if they are glad to be a part of this enterprise.

The three have been to Dunhai many times, and know the way. We are lucky to have them aboard.

Ang Babu pays off our faithful three. They all shake my hand and wish me a successful journey, then set out for home. We camp that night in a forest a few hours past Yamakhar, then make a hard morning climb over an unnamed pass into the valley of the Seng Khola. There is no living vegetation in this place, just short bare sticks poking up from the ground. Rocks, snow, and mountains are in no short supply, however. Our Magar porters arrive at camp in very good time. With no wood for a fire, everyone retires early.

The next day we turn away from the stream to climb straight up the valley wall. After hours of breathless scrambling we reach the top where a *chörten* marks a pass. This is not the highest point of today's walk, however—*that* comes an hour later at an unmarked ridge. It is the second of the three high passes on the road to Dolpo.

During an afternoon rest Phurba's cheerful but incessant cursing—he spouts at least one *ma jigne* every minute—compels me to lob a handful of snow in his direction. A minute later the snowballs are flying thick and fast in a prolonged, anarchic battle with no fixed loyalties. Though my aim is terrible, I alone have gloves, so I paw fearlessly through the crusty snow and keep up a steady bombardment. The battle's climax finds Tenzeng and me hurtling a continuous barrage at each other from point-blank range, while the porters stand grinning on the sidelines.

Camp that night is our highest at 4,200 meters. At sundown the cold swoops in like a hungry specter set on munching our bones. We have room for no thought save barricading ourselves inside tightly zippered tents, sleeping bags, and clothes that muffle every orifice.

In the morning we have a gradual but breathless climb across ice and snow to Jang La at 4,500 meters. This pass is not so terribly high (the Annapurna circuit trail crosses a much higher one, and so do many highways in Tibet) but still my body seems frozen into torpid slowness, while the airy-white light squeezes my head so that it feels like it wants to pop off into space. We cross Jang La without difficulty, and spend the rest of the day making the long descent to Tarakot.

Tarakot is a warm and pleasing town, suddenly and wonderfully homelike. The next day we hightail it the rest of the way down the valley wall to the Barbung Khola, then make a quick four-hour trot west. In early afternoon we reach Dunhai, a regional administrative center and an oddly civilized place. With its chaparral-covered hills rising behind a wide blue river and neat low houses stacked on the waterfront, Dunhai reminds me of Malibu, California. Dunhai's population is a colorful mix of sophisticated Kathmandu officials, Gurung farmers, and a few really wild Tibetan characters come down from the mountains.

Soon after we arrive, the leading edge of a big trekking group appears to claim a space in the yard beside us. Before long the full complement of six Swiss trekkers, their sherpas, porters, and gear is spread all over the grass. The group has just come from the airstrip in Juphal, half a day's walk west. They have seven tents, which, like them, are clean and new and perfect. By comparison, we are dirty, sunburned, and tired; our camp seems ragged and puny. To have spent seventeen days walking here when we could have arrived in an hour by plane seems absurd, but the agency for logistical reasons preferred the longer route.

Our would-be triumphant arrival to this place is shadowed by exhaustion and by these shiny Swiss. Yet in three days we will be at Ringmo, and Ringmo is—I have to keep reminding myself—the point of this long journey.

In Dunhai we take a much-needed rest day. Next morning, perhaps as a rebellion against our stiff, ordered neighbors, I lead our camp in an outbreak of silliness. It begins at dawn with an imperious "Chocolate *chitala-hoi, ma jigne!*" shouted at the kitchen from my tent. After they bring my hot chocolate, Tenzeng and I have a water fight, chasing each other in circles with a pitcher while the others cheer.

Soon the Swiss push off for Tarakot and we have the place to ourselves. Still suffering from an excess of energy, and even though there's no private space, I make a few kata in the yard. Slowly, not forcefully, the long gliding attacks are a balm on my weary soul. Ang Babu applauds, but it's facetious. "Nice exercise!" he calls out. He hasn't the slightest idea of what he's looking at or how much it owns me. But I need it so much, and it feels so good, that I can't stop just because of the foolishness of my audience or their ignorance.

We radio Kathmandu, and I learn that my Mustang permit has been denied. I take this news philosophically, for somewhere on those high passes my longing was loosened. Detached and irreverent now, I see that Mustang (and all it represents) is just another gaudy Christmas tree of desire. Perhaps some places are better left unseen. By not going there, the dream remains.

The news about Mustang brings a sudden mental shift. Now I know just how much more I must do, and just when I'm going home.

25

THE LAST PRACTICE

THE FINAL PRACTICE of special training.

We've run that horrid Hamburger Hill, we've made thousands of basics and combinations, kibadachi stance for ninety minutes, and midnight oizuki. We've done kicks and kata, and we survived sparring. Nevertheless, we're only halfway home.

The last practice of this special training is one hundred repetitions of a kata called Tekki Shodan. *"Tekki" refers to the kibadachi, or horse-riding stance—the stance used throughout the kata.* Tekki Shodan *is short; one hundred of them, if done at a sprightly pace, should take less than an hour. It's not much time at all really, nor many repetitions. But to make even one really good, really realistic kata is a colossal undertaking.*

FROM DUNHAI THE trail climbs steeply, up to a high bluff. Opening onto the canyon of the Barbung Khola is a great aperture cut by the Suli Gad River, which will lead us to Dolpo. Far below our feet the two rivers entwine, the solemn crash of their waters muted by the mighty distance we have climbed. We will follow the Suli Gad upstream for two and a half days to reach Phoksumdo Lake, which will be the farthest point of our journey.

Phoksumdo Lake and its nearby town of Ringmo are really just the edge of Dolpo—Matthiessen and his party went much farther. But Ringmo is the farthest point for which permits are issued; so, no matter what happens there, Phoksumdo will be the end of the line.

Those charming boys from Yamakhar have gone home; our new porters are three canny Pokhara lads. Cast off by a British group going to Jumla, they are happy to find extra work. The loads are light now, for we have eaten nearly everything we brought with us, and burned most of our kerosene.

The Suli Gad River leads us into an enchanted piney canyon—steep-walled, dark, sweet-smelling, with almost no people. The trail wanders up and down, sometimes scaling the gorge's immense flanks, at other times treading close beside the river. Although our net elevation gain is not great, the path vexes us with its constant rising and falling as it darts around cyclopean protuberances in the valley wall.

Our progress is often interrupted by caravans coming the other way: trains of yak, goats, and sheep shepherded by families of mountain-dwelling folk. Each time we meet them we must get off the trail; otherwise we'll spook the flighty animals, wreak havoc with the train and incur the owners' wrath. For this reason I spend an hour or more each day squatting on the slope beside the trail, watching clouds of dust rise behind the animals' hooves, and listening to the whistling and hawing and shooshing that keeps the creatures moving.

Ang Babu tells me that these families are migrating from their mountain fastnesses to winter homes along the Barbung Khola. In this great autumn exodus, pack animals carry food and household goods that will supply the families until spring. The caravan women dress in dark Tibetan dresses and lash striped blankets around their waists. The men braid their hair with Khampa red tassels; but the tassels are the only things about them characteristic of Kham—otherwise they appear to be of mingled Magar and Tibetan blood, adhering to Tibetan ways.

Judging by their prayer beads, these people are Buddhist. Their language is the Lhasa dialect—not Khampa speech as asserted in the Dolpo guidebook. This fact should disappoint me, but in my present equable state it is noted without emotion.

Tawny mountains, shaggy animals, dark dresses, homespun blankets—they are all colors from the earth. But one morning we meet a shocking interruption: peacock blue, chlorine green, and lollipop purple—a troop of Western trekkers is marching in the middle of a caravan line. The foreigners' preposterous clothes are topped by equally preposterous faces: pallid and hirsute, with jutting, angular noses and eye sockets of jarringly simian dimensions. They look singularly uncomfortable as they pant and wheeze their way uphill. Can these ill-favored creatures really be my own kind? Through Asian eyes I see them: utterly fantastic.

Two days of walking bring us to a small village just short of Ringmo. On the way here we passed some hair-raising stretches of trail, places where logs were hammered into a sheer cliff and then covered with a catwalk of stones, planks, and dirt. In one place a man had just lost six yaks; they spooked on a narrow ramp, fell down into the ravine below and were killed. When we passed, one of the owners was below salvaging what he could from the remains. Such an accident is a severe economic loss to these people, whose wealth is measured in livestock.

Next morning we climb hard, for it's the last leg to Ringmo. Caught up in the flurry of the final push, I can't be bothered to remove extra clothes, and quickly overheat. Climbing blindly—for sweat is running down my glasses. He doesn't stop, and I'm not inclined to make him stop, so we climb straight to the top. There we pause to admire a horizon studded with snow-covered summits. I take off my sweater and am instantly clothed in ice.

We go down: through pines, over fields, and cross a substantial bridge festooned with prayer flags, arriving at last in Ringmo. It is a cluster of a dozen Tibetan-style houses of red clay and stone growing like lichen out of a red rock wall. At the local police we register our arrival, and a large crowd of cheerful, friendly farmers gathers to watch the proceedings.

No sign of Khampa guerrillas here.

Later on we make camp by Phoksumdo Lake, a short walk from town. The lake is five kilometers long, astoundingly clear, the color of porcelain sapphire—a hue so pure and deep that it surpasses every earthly blue I've ever seen, second only to the vault over our heads. The lake is hemmed in by a ring of stark red mountains growing straight up from its edge. We are now at the northernmost point of our journey, and deep into the rain shadow of the Himalayas. Evergreens grow near our camp, but the other end is devoid of life, as if we stand on the doorstep of purgatory. Seeing it, I can imagine the hell that lies in Mustang, and suddenly feel a rush of pain for those courageous Khampas, so far from the lush grass and forests of their home.

We take a rest day, during which I go to visit Ringmo Gonpa. The monastery, which commands a corner of the lake, stands like a fairy castle over an enchanted turquoise ocean. We skirt the lake's southern shore to reach eleven decaying *chörten* that line the path to the entrance. The gonpa is small and old, built of many layers of whitewashed stone.

We stoop through a low door into the dark interior. The place is kept by a seventy-year-old lama dressed in layers of grimy maroon, with weathered skin so shrunken that his great knobbish cheekbones seem to have taken over his face. The place is in an appalling state of disrepair: wall and ceiling murals are besmirched with dirt; litter lies on the floor; scarves draped over the altar are grimy with accumulated smoke and dust. Together Ang Babu and I make prostrations and set gifts of cash alongside the offerings of water, incense, and snuff, and instant photos left by previous trekkers.

So many miles, so many temples, so many sacred circumambulations. Is this tiny, decaying place to be the last monastery of my journey?

Outside, a few villagers loiter in the sun. A woman sits sorting recently harvested buckwheat. Buckwheat is the staple here, normally pounded with a pestle into flour and then boiled into mash. I've been asking for *tsampa,* but buckwheat is all that Tenzeng and Karmi can find when they go shopping for victuals in Ringmo. That night, when cooking up the Sherpas' dinner, Karmi has to seize the spoon with both hands to stir the thick, bubbling mixture. At least as the privileged Memsahib, I may forego the buckwheat and dine on our dwindling supply of potatoes.

After dinner the staff retires, leaving me alone with the mountains and the lake and the night. Since we left Pokhara the moon has gone through all of its phases; tonight, a little past full, it is not quite risen. Already sunset's rose-colored alpenglow is replaced by silvery moonlight. It spreads slowly down mountain spires, a hyacinthine echo of this morning's sunrise. Phoksumdo Lake, still in moon shadow, is just a black whisper now, invisible but for the reflected glow of millions of Himalayan stars.

In the morning I will start the journey home.

We form our huge rectangle for opening meditation: black belts left, white belts right, brown belts center, leader in front. Now, as we have on every morning, everyone counts off, to ensure that no one has slipped away. Far to my right I hear the senior-most black belt begin: "One!" It is swiftly picked up by those standing next to him. "Two!" "Three!" "Four!"—and so on, down the line. Quick, clear, and inevitable, like stones dropped into a pond, numbers march swiftly down the line, a role call that passes from senior to junior in a microcosm of the knowledge and feeling and tradition transmitted from teacher to student, beginning centuries ago with the ancient masters.

IN THE MORNING we turn our backs on Phoksumdo Lake, walking on the bank opposite the side on which we came. This path drops precipitously, then edges around the upper decks of a great amphitheater, a huge drainhole into which Phoksumdo Lake empties. Far away now and cupped in the palm of the mountains, the lake is a gleaming sapphire lifted like an offering to the Kanjirobas. Ringmo Lake battles its way out of its stone offering bowl through an underground tunnel, emerging halfway down the amphitheater's northern wall where half a dozen foaming threads plummet in stages to the ravine below. We stop to gawk at this amazing sight. I take photos. We move on.

White-suited figures form a grid across the summer grass. There are a few preliminaries; then we begin. The black belts will take turns calling the commands that start and end each kata. From far behind me, a voice pulled from deep inside the gut rings across the field:

"Tekki Shodan!" *We answer with a silent* kiai, *a sound that tightens the air and the mind.*

"Yo-i" *The string is pulled even tauter as we all move into the ready posture. Air is drawn in in preparation for the coming explosion. Knees and hips coil slightly . . .*

"Hajime!"

Pronounced as one explosive syllable, the command detonates violent movement, a hurricane suddenly unleashed. Three hundred figures tear into half-seen opponents: stomping, elbowing, ripping, cutting, drilling as if with a laser beam. Eventually each person reaches the kata's final technique: when hips resolve, both fists explode simultaneously rightward, and a final kiai *rips out.*

As more and more people reach the kata's end, the kiais become fewer and fewer, and then none. Silence falls upon the field.

"Yame!" *calls the voice, signaling the engagement's end. In one coordinated movement, everyone resumes the ready posture: legs straighten; faces turn back toward the front. But as the body straightens, eyes linger a moment, mindful of that defeated opponent who just might rise up again. . . .*

"Yasume!" *This kata is finished. But there is no time for thought—*

"Tekki Shodan!" *commands the next black belt in line, beginning the whole sequence again.*

THE NEXT DAY we continue south. Like horses who can smell the oats of home, our steps are hurried now, and we go farther between rests. The Sherpas have been patient with me for almost a month, but today they throw patience to the wind. The kitchen runs far ahead and is quickly out of sight. I follow Ang Babu, who scarcely pauses. We walk and walk and walk.

It is past noon when we come to a camping place we used on the way in. It would make a perfect lunch spot, I think, and scan the clearing expecting to see that happy blue tarp spread on the ground and Phurba brewing tea. But they are not here. They have gone on.

We climb to a high cliff and traverse for a while above the immense space of the canyon. The Suli Gad is far away now, just a distant voice foaming beyond the trees. Then we turn onto a tricky downhill shortcut where the path is just a penciled indentation in a slanting wall of earth. Then up again, hand over hand in places, and I struggle not to be left behind while Ang Babu bounds easily like a goat.

We rejoin the main trail for a steep, dusty descent. Caravans here have churned the earth to silken powder that jumps into the air at the slightest touch. Beneath the dust are loose rocks, so at every footfall the ground shifts unpredictably. I lurch unsteadily down the mountain, heart racing, knees protesting.

Finally we reach the bottom again, and march for thirty minutes over the flats. It's a peaceful, shady stretch by the river, but I am so tired that I walk like a zombie. We pass a hundred suitable lunch spots, yet our kitchen is not at any of them. They have gone on.

All the while, as my weary body stumbles down the trail, my mind is working, working, working. This journey is almost

over; soon I'll be going home. But so much is still undone:
Lhasa, Mustang!—all the warriors I have not seen, symbols of
unfulfilled longing.

The exuberance of the first few kata is gone, and now the practice is get-
ting difficult. One hundred kata is not so easy—especially when you are
in the middle of them. Some people's spirit is falling off: their stance
wobbles, their kiai falters, their fists droop. But for each lost heart there is
someone standing nearby to pull him on. Explosive feeling, low stance,
powerful kiai—they whip like a wildfire from person to person, reviving
the exhausted and inspiring the spiritless. The field is a matrix of mov-
ing energy, all driving toward a ferocious culmination.

ONCE, DURING THIS year of wandering, my mother in one of her
many letters offered the following familiar parable. A pilgrim
leaves home looking for something: knowledge, peace, freedom,
enlightenment. He spends years—perhaps even a lifetime—
searching the ends of the earth only to realize, in the end, that
the thing he seeks is not to be found in the external world;
it was within himself all along.

   But how do you discover the power, if not through searching?

   Peter Matthiessen walked the very path on which I now
tread. He stayed in Dolpo for weeks, waiting and watching and
hoping to glimpse a snow leopard. One of these exquisite creatures—or is it two?—lurks near his camp, toying with him,
intensifying his yearning. Resolution of Matthiessen's koan
comes with the realization that happiness grows not from
achieving or obtaining, but from "wholehearted acceptance of
what is." He writes: "Butter tea and wind pictures, the Crystal
Mountain, and blue sheep dancing on the snow—it's quite
enough!"

   Have you seen the snow leopard?
   No! Isn't that wonderful?

And did you find the warriors?
I think perhaps I did.

I found the challenge of cycling alone in Asia, a taste of Tibetan special training, the generosity of so many Chinese and Tibetans who helped me when I was in need, Shandro's gallantry, Tashi's parting kiss, lessons on Buddhism and the meaning of compassion, Ahtsong's shy smile, kata on the high plateau, Mike's eternal friendship, the artistry of the sculptor at Baiya, Khampa riders swooping over the grasslands, and the boundless joy of these four Sherpas leading me over the Himalayas. And then, most of all, there were those unforgettable prostrating pilgrims—

It's enough; it's quite enough!

WE REACH SEPKA, a place with only a solitary stone house beside the river. Here is my long-lost kitchen, a truly wonderful sight. Here is the blue tarp. Here is Phurba brewing tea. I sink down and close my eyes against the sun. Almost home.

Hours later the day grows late, and still we are walking. We round a corner and plunge into an immense tributary canyon of the Suli Gad River. Soon we will reach a campsite that we used on our way out. It's an uncomfortable place, composed of two horizontal terraces just big enough for our three tents on an otherwise highly canted hillside. It was cold there, too, for little sunshine slips past these high rock walls. But now that I have walked so hard and far and long, even that wretched campsite will be sweet reward.

The final thirty minutes to camp ought to be a last-gasp effort; but suddenly a fit of mischief breaks out. That prankster Tenzeng is poking sticks into Ang Babu's backpack as the latter stumps innocently down the trail. As I laugh at Tenzeng's antics, Phurba is doing the same thing to me, while silent Karmi as usual watches from the sidelines. I soon catch on, and now

Phurba and I jockey to see which of us must walk in front, for the one following can play no end of tricks upon the other. As usual I am the loser, for Phurba is an expert at these games. I bide my time and walk ahead, getting safely around a corner where I stop, water bottle uncorked and ready in my hand. When Phurba comes around I throw a great slosh into his face, and everyone—Phurba included—breaks into uproarious laughter. We laugh all the way to camp.

The next day is our last trekking day. We will spend the morning hightailing it to Dunhai, then turn west for another three hours to Juphal where an airplane will take us back to Pokhara. Despite the length of the journey, and despite my ever-increasing dreams of home, as we pace the final miles nostalgia covers me like rain. How wonderful, how classic it is, to be walking with Sherpas in the Himalayas! Soon they will go back to their homes, as I will return to mine. Life is full of impermanence: beginnings and endings, meetings and partings. As necessary and inevitable as they are, they still discomfit the spirit.

Dunhai arrives too quickly. We have lunch, then cross the river and begin the final walk. The trail is a wide, gravel-covered path beside the Barbung Khola—easy walking, and I expect it to stay that way all the way to the airstrip. But I am wrong. Now the trail is turning away and snaking up into the mountains. The airstrip is not on an alluvial flat by the water as I thought, but high up on a ridge. We begin to climb, and soon nostalgia is replaced by vexation, for this unexpected ascent goes on and on, seemingly past all reason. As I plod uphill, back bent and eyes to the dirt, a relentless wind batters my head, drowning out all other sounds. Ang Babu walks by my side; the others have gone ahead.

Up and up we trudge. Then suddenly we round a corner and the wind stops, the unexpected quiet a vacuum that sucks up all thoughts and emotions. I look up, and my eyes fall on Tenzeng and Phurba and Karmi resting beside the trail in the bright Himalayan sunshine. For once they are not talking, but sit in an unnatural state of silence. For a moment we all look at one another, as if each is suddenly aware of the end of our journey.

"Last kata!"

It's the last kata of special training. I am not tired. Cool, sweet summer air flows like a charge of fire-ice directly to my blood.

"Tekki Shodan!"

The sound is far away, but electrifying. When I start that last— that very last—kata, the movements stretch into eternity; they occupy all time and space, are a universe of their own. Around me, others rip through the moves at lightning speed, sprinting pell-mell toward the fin- ish line. But I take mine slowly, felling opponents one by one in bursts of exultant frenzy, savoring each technique—not a thing to be tossed off and forgotten, but a whole chapter unto itself. As the final moves pour out, I float suspended over the track; like a dream, but too big, too tangi- ble, too real. . . .

THE MOMENT PASSES, and the sherpas burst back into their usual boisterous selves. We resume walking, this time all five together. As we trudge upward, backs bent over the dusty trail, Tenzeng stealthily reaches out to a strap hanging from Ang Babu's pack and loosens the knot in it. A dozen paces later he slips an elon- gated rock into the loop and tightens the knot again, amid an exchange of grins all around between those of us behind the sir- dar. The victim is oblivious to the stone dangling from his back- side, so I give the rock a whack with my stick so he'll know something's amiss. He discovers Tenzeng's mischief, and, true to the nature of his people, he laughs heartily along with the rest of us. Now the game is on: me against Phurba, Tenzeng against everyone, and even Karmi joins in. The trail is a scene of madcap foolishness—all the way home.

REFERENCES AND BIBLIOGRAPHY

Stephen Batchelor (ed.). *The Jewel in the Lotus: A Guide to the Buddhist Traditions of Tibet*. London: Wisdom Publications, 1987.

Stephen Batchelor. *The Tibet Guide*. London: Wisdom Publications, 1987.

Alexandra David-Neel. *Magic and Mystery in Tibet*. New York: Dover Publications, Inc., 1971.

Keith Dowman. *The Power-Places of Central Tibet: The Pilgrim's Guide*. London & New York: Routledge & Kegan Paul, 1988.

Marion Duncan. *The Yangtze and the Yak*. Ann Arbor, MI: Edwards Brothers, Inc., 1952.

Robert Easton. *China Caravans: An American Adventurer in Old China*. Santa Barbara, CA: Capra Press, 1982.

Shigeru Egami. *The Way of Karate Beyond Technique*. Tokyo, New York, & San Francisco: Kodansha International Ltd., 1976.

——— "Megatraining: The 24-Hour Karate Practice." *Fighting Stars*. April 1985, pp. 38-43.

Gichin Funakoshi (Tsutomu Ohshima, trans.). *Karate-do Kyohan: The Master Text*. Tokyo, New York, & San Francisco: Kodansha International Ltd., 1974.

Paolo Gondoni. *Trekking in Hidden Land of Dolpa-Tarap and Shey-Poksumdo*. Kathmandu: Tiwari's Pilgrims Book House, 1989.

A. Tom Grunfeld. *The Making of Modern Tibet*. Zed Books Ltd., 1987.

Heinrich Harrer. *Seven Years In Tibet*. New York: E.P. Dutton and Co., Inc., 1954.

Peter Hopkirk. *Trespassers on the Roof of the World: The Secret Exploration of Tibet*. Los Angeles: J.P. Tarcher, Inc., 1982.

Thomas Laird. "In The Shadows of the Himalaya: A Kingdom Unveiled." *Asiaweek*. Oct. 9, 1992.

Peter Matthiessen. *The Snow Leopard*. New York: Bantam Books, 1981.

Gary McCue. *Trekking in Tibet: A Traveler's Guide*. Seattle: The Mountaineers, 1991.

Luree Miller. *On Top of the World: Five Women Explorers in Tibet*. Seattle: The Mountaineers, 1984.

Jamyang Norbu. *Horseman in the Snow: The Story of Aten, an Old Khampa Warrior.* Dharamsala, India: Information Office, Central Tibetan Secretariat, 1979; also published as *Warriors of Tibet: The Story of Aten and the Khampas Fight for the Freedom of Their Country.* London: Wisdom Publications, 1986.

Tsutomu Ohshima. (Thomas M. Blaschko, ed.). *Notes on Training.* Ravensdale, WA: Idyll Arbor, Inc., 1996.

Michael Peissel. *Mustang: The Forbidden Kingdom.* Toronto & Vancouver: E. P. Dutton and Co., Inc., 1967.

————. *Cavaliers of Kham: The Secret War in Tibet.* London: William Heinemann Ltd., 1972.

Geshe Rabten. *The Preliminary Practices of Tibetan Buddhism.* Dharamsala, India: Library of Works & Archives, 1986.

John Smart and John Wehrheim. "Dolpo, Nepal." *The Tibet Journal.* Vol. 2, No. 1, spring 1977, pp. 50–59.

John Snelling. *The Buddhist Handbook.* Rochester, VT: Inner Traditions International Ltd., 1991.

Eliot Sperling. "The Chinese Venture in K'am, 1904–1911, and the Role of Chao Erh-feng." *The Tibet Journal.* Vol. 1, No. 2, pp. 10–36.

Chögyam Trungpa. *Cutting through Spiritual Materialism.* Boston & London: Shambhala, 1987.

————. *Shambhala: the Sacred Path of the Warrior.* Boston & London: Shambhala, 1985.

Kisshomaru Ueshiba. *Aikido.* Tokyo: Hozansha Publications, 1985.

L. Austine Waddell. *Lhasa and Its Mysteries, with a Record of the British Tibetan Expedition of 1903-1904* (first edition). New York: E. P. Dutton and Co., Inc., 1905; also New York: Dover Publications, 1988.

Wong, et al. *Buddhist Monasteries in Ganzi Tibetan Autonomous Prefecture, Western Sichuan, China.* China Exploration & Research Society, 1992.

Munenori Yagyu. *The Sword & the Mind* (Hiroaki Sato, trans.). Woodstock, NY: The Overlook Press, 1986.

GUIDE TO
PRONOUNCING FOREIGN TERMS

THIS BOOK EMPLOYS a plethora of terms in several languages: Chinese, Tibetan, Japanese, Nepalese, and Sanskrit. Each of these languages uses a different set of sounds, and these are rendered by our Latin alphabet using different systems of transliteration. It all makes for a mixed-up linguistic soup that is beyond the scope of this book to sort out completely; therefore I provide only a *rough* pronounciation guide. The transliteration systems used here can be divided into two categories: Pinyin (the most common method for writing Mandarin Chinese), and everything else. In Pinyin, the following are most likely to trip up the reader:

letter	*is pronounced like*
x	sh
q	ch
c	ts
z	dz
zh	j
a	a in *father*
e	e in *her*
i	i in *petite*
o	o in *gong*
u	u in *crude*
ui	the English word *way*

For languages other than Chinese, I have adopted the following system: e is like the ei in heir, with the remaining individual vowels pronounced as in Pinyin. Diphthongs are pronounced with their component individuals sounded in order quickly but separately (e.g. *oizuki* is "OH-EE-ZU-KEE"). Consonants are pronounced as in English, except that the combinations th, kh, and ph are the aspirated versions of the consonants t, k, and p respectively.

GLOSSARY

aikido (Jap.) A martial art developed by Morihei Ueshiba that emphasizes using the attacker's own power to defeat him, usually through joint manipulation and unbalancing techniques.

Amdo (Tib.) One of Tibet's three ancient provinces, covering an area spread across several provinces of China: Qinghai, western Gansu, and northwest Sichuan.

bodhichitta (Sans.) Commitment to practice Buddhism not for self-gain, but for the enlightenment of others.

Bön (Tib.) Tibet's indigenous animist faith. It is now largely displaced by Buddhism, although the two have adopted many of each other's iconography and rituals. The term "Black Hat Sect" is sometimes applied to Bön.

bu-xing (Chin.) Literally, "doesn't go," or not okay.

chörten (Tib.) A pagoda built to house sacred relics or to mark holy sites and mountain passes. The simplest kind is nothing more than a pile of stones. More elaborate ones may be finished on the outside, painted, and decorated.

chuba (Tib.) A Tibetan coat, with long sleeves and overlapping front, fastened with a sash around the waist. Men's are knee-length; women's are ankle-length. Those worn in winter are often lined with sheepskin.

Dharma (Sans.) The teachings of Buddha; the Truth.

dojo (Jap.) "Way-place." A training room or yard for karate or other martial arts.

F.E.C. Foreign Exchange Certificates. Given by Chinese banks in exchange for foreign (hard) currency, these notes were supposed to be used by tourists for purchase of accommodations, transportation, meals, etc. while in China. Once issued in the same denominations as renminbi, since 1994 they are no longer used.

hajime (Jap.) The command given to start a kata: attack!

Gelug (Tib.) "Virtuous" Sect, also called the Yellow Hat School, the youngest and most widespread sect of Buddhism in Tibet.

gonpa (Tib.) Monastery. Sometimes spelled "gompa."

Gonganju (Chin.) Public Security (i.e. the police).

kaishui (Chin.) Boiled water, for drinking, making tea, washing, etc.

kang (Chin.) A brick platform, heated underneath by coal or wood, for sitting or sleeping in northern China.

karate (Jap.) Literally "empty hand." A Japanese martial art that emphasizes kicking and striking techniques.

karate-ka (Jap.) A student of karate.

Kagyu (Tib.) "Transmitted Command" School, one of the so-called "Red Hat" sects of Tibetan Buddhism.

karma (Sans.) The cumulative effect of one's actions during this and previous lifetimes that determines one's future and the quality of one's future rebirth.

Karma Kagyu (Tib.) The most powerful subsect of the Kagyu School.

kata (Jap.) A karate exercise consisting of a sequence of predetermined movements, performed by one person against imaginary opponents.

Kham (Tib.) One of Tibet's three ancient provinces, encompassing the western half of modern-day Sichuan Province, the eastern portion of Tibet Autonomous Region, and a little bit of northwest Yunnan.

Khampa (Tib.) A native of Kham. Sometimes spelled "Khamba."

khata (Tib.) A white silk scarf, given in religious offering, or as a token of friendship.

khola (Nep.) River.

kibadachi (Jap.) "Horse-riding stance"—a symmetric, bent-knee stance.

koan (Jap.) A riddle or paradox given to students of Zen to contemplate during meditation. The solution is said to bring insight into the nature of existence.

korra (Tib.) Circumambulation about a sacred place.

la (Tib.) Mountain pass.

la-mian (Chin.) A noodle dish commonly eaten in northern China.

Losar (Tib.) New Year.

Mahayana (Sans.) The "Great Vehicle" of Buddhism, in which one is called upon to pursue enlightenment for the benefit of others. Contrast this with the older Hinayana, or "Lesser Vehicle" (also called Theravada) in which one pursues enlightenment for oneself alone. In the world today, Hinayana is prevalent in Sri Lanka, Thailand, and Burma.

Maitreya (Sans.) The Buddha to Come.

mantra (Sans.) A short verbal formula of religiously inspired words meant to be recited, visualized, or written down as a part of Buddhist practice.

momo (Tib.) In Amdo and Kham, refers to bread. In Nepal and India, refers to meat- or vegetable-filled dumplings.

Mönlam (Tib.) A prayer festival held in the first month of the Tibetan year.

nihao (Chin.) Hello.

Nyingma (Tib.) The "Old Ones" School, the oldest of the four major sects of Tibetan Buddhism.

oizuki (Jap.) A karate punching technique in which one steps forward and punches simultaneously.

om mani padme hum (Tib.) "Oh hail the jewel in the lotus!" is one way to translate this mantra, which is characteristic of Tibetan Buddhism. These few words are said to be a concentrated expression of the path to enlightenment.

renminbi (Chin.) "People's money." The currency used by ordinary people in China for domestic transactions.

Rinpoche (Tib.) A Buddhist holy man in Tibet, considered to be either the human emanation of a tantric deity or the reincarnation of a noted teacher. Such an individual is "discovered" as a child, usually several years after his predecessor has died, and then educated in a monastery. The Dalai Lama and the Panchen Lama are the most well-known examples. Also (and erroneously) called "Living Buddha."

Sakya (Tib.) One of the four major sects of Tibetan Buddhism, named for its principal monastery near Shigatse. Confusingly, like Kagyupa, Sakya is also called a "Red Hat" sect.

Sakyamuni The historical Buddha, who originated Buddhist teachings in India around 500 B.C.

samsara (Sans.) The illusionary world of earthly suffering and attachment.

seiza (Jap.) A formal sitting form in which one kneels with a vertical backbone, and the body's weight rests on the calves.

sensei (Jap.) Teacher.

sherpa Mountain guide (colloquial use by foreigners in Nepal).

Sherpa An ethnic group of Nepal whose traditional home is the Everest region.

Sherpani A female Sherpa.

Shotokan (Jap.) The school of Japanese karate that was founded by Gichin Funakoshi.

sirdar (Nep.) Head sherpa.

sutra (Sans.) The teachings attributed to the historical Buddha, which in Tibet are contained in a set of texts called the Kangyur.

tanden (Jap.) A place in the center of the lower abdomen, the center of energy, breathing, and balance.

tantra A class of Buddhist scriptures describing a path to enlightenment that uses visualization of deities and mandalas, recitation of mantras, and yogic practices to channel the body's energy.

thangka (Tib.) A scroll painting depicting religious subjects such as Buddhist figures, mandalas, and the Wheel of Life.

torma (Tib.) Dough sculpture, made from tsampa and butter.

tsampa (Tib.) Flour from parched barley. It is usually mixed with tea and butter and eaten as a dough or porridge. Sometimes called "tsamba."

yame (Jap.) A command given at the end of a kata: return to ready posture.

yasume (Jap.) The command given after a kata is finished: relax.

yoi (Jap.) A command given at the start of a kata: get ready.

zen (Tib.) The long shawl traditionally worn by Buddhist monks in Tibet.

Zen (Jap.) An austere school of Japanese Buddhism, originating in the Ch'an sect of China, that emphasizes sitting meditation and koan as the path to enlightenment. It was particularly popular among the samurai (warrior) class.